Social Problems

Social Work and Social Problems

Working towards Social Inclusion and Social Change

Gerald Smale
Graham Tuson
and
Daphne Statham

Consultant Editor: Jo Campling

MACMILLAN

First published 2000 by
MACMILLAN PRESS LTD
Houndmills, Basingstoke, Hampshire RG21 6XS
and London
Companies and representatives throughout the world

ISBN 0–333–62564–1

A catalogue record for this book is available from the British Library.

This book is printed on paper suitable for recycling and made from fully managed and sustained forest sources.

10   9   8   7   6   5   4   3   2   1
09 08 07 06 05 04 03 02 01 00

Typeset in Great Britain by
Aarontype Limited, Easton, Bristol

Printed in Hong Kong

Contents

List of Figures   xi
Acknowledgements   xii
Prologue   xiii

1 Introduction   1
    What do we mean by 'a social problem'?   2
    Defining social work   4
    Social work, causation and change   5
    Reinvention and the wider context   7
    Overview of the book   9

2 Reinventing Social Work: Key Themes and Tasks   13
    Development and not aid alone   18
    Social work: beyond the individualisation of social
    problems   21
    Social work, social care and change   21
    The UK: our history and the present context for
    practice   22
    The USA   23
    A practice response to fragmentation: a holistic
    approach   25
    Reinvention and knowledge-based practice   25
    Skills for practice: a synthesis of knowledge,
    behaviour and values   27
    The whole enterprise: promoting dependable
    social networks   29

3 Formulating the Task: Aid or Development?   31
    Introduction   31
    Aid and development   32
    Aid downstream or development upstream?   32
    River rescues or upstream work?   33
    Balancing aid and development   34
    Social control   36
    Power and powerlessness   37

Empowerment   38
Managing conflicts   39
Gary and Carol's story as an example of identifying
and managing conflict   39
Conflict resolution   43
Negotiations, shared perceptions and conflicts   44
The marginal worker   44
A mediating role   45
Polarisations: beyond illusions of opposites   54
Unintended consequences: beyond the good
intentions of aid, development and social control   47
Does the provision of aid, development and social
control need expertise or can it just be left to
commonsense and good will?   49
Conclusion   50

4 **Mapping the Task and Processes**   **52**
Introduction   52
A map of the content of social work   53
Change agent activity   55
Service delivery   55
The importance of process and time   57
The content of the task using the map   58
Mapping the process of social work over time   65
Introduction: the spiral of negotiations   65
The spiral of negotiations: the process map   67
Stages in the spiral of negotiations   69
Conclusion: implications for practice   80

5 **Social Problems, Social Control and Patterns
of Interaction**   **82**
Introduction   82
Identifying all the key people   83
The nature of social problems   86
Beyond the individualisation of social problems   88
The community: problem and solution   88
The idea of community   90
People who use services are citizens   91
Deviance and social control   92

Norms and their impact on practice 93
The pivotal position of social work 94
Authority and personal style 95
Six premises for understanding patterns of
interaction 95
Peter and the punctuation of events 100
Punctuation and the organisation 102

6 **Managing and Mapping Change** **106**
Introduction 106
The theory of change and practice 107
Social workers move in an environment of
different definitions and perceptions of the
reality of social situations 108
The formulation of a problem is always a joint
enterprise between workers and other people 109
Assessment, intervention and service delivery are
essentially the same enterprise 109
To achieve change, it is often necessary to reframe
the problem 110
Alternative behaviour has to be demonstrated 110
Resources often have to be reallocated 111
First- and second-order change 111
Mapping change 113
The foundations of change: what changes and
what stays the same? 114
Planning through the Innovation Trinity 117
Negotiations between key people: individual,
family, social network, community and/or
inter-organisation development 125
Feedback and monitoring the consequences
of change 128
Conclusion 129

7 **Assessment and Intervention** **131**
The task 131
Alternative models 132
The Questioning and Procedural Models 133
The Exchange Model 135

The Questioning and Exchange Models of
assessment compared   138
The Procedural Model of assessment   141
The contribution and limits of the Procedural
Model   144
Which model to choose?   145
Models of assessment and conflicts of interest   146
Assessment of individual need or the social
situation?   146
The dependability of social networks   147
Beyond the purchasing of care   147
The Exchange Model of assessment and practice   148
The Exchange Model and professional expertise   151
Summary and implications for practice   152

8 Overcoming Blocks to Change   **154**
Introduction   154
Self-fulfilling prophecies   156
Definitions   156
Self-defeating strategies   157
Conflict and self-defeating strategies   159
Self-defeating strategies and teams   160
Solutions as problems   161
Mutually defeating interactions: the unambiguously
helpful worker   163
The consequences of the mechanism of the panel   164
Dominant actors, dominant perceivers and the role
of perception   167
Deviancy   168
Behaving *as if* predictions are true: contingency
planning, openness and trust   169
Contingency plans and the impact of negative
'as if' behaviour   170
Practice implications   171
Managing multiple perspectives to avoid self-
defeating strategies   171
The behaviour of workers and change: eight
principles   172
Conclusion: towards the positively marginal worker   176

9   Independence and Marginality   **178**
    Marginality   178
    Marginality and marginalisation   178
    Marginality and the Jones family   179
    Balancing expectations, needs and responsibilities   180
    The key elements of marginality   182
    The worker's behaviour   182
    What the worker needs to demonstrate   182
    The capacity to ask key questions   183
    Identifying perspectives on social problems   184
    The capacity to ask the question, 'who is the
    service user'?   186
    Marginality, partnership and deviance   186
    Competence in practising marginality   187
    What knowledge contributes to marginality   188
    Marginality and respect   188
    Marginality, worker stress and independence of mind   190
    Creative use of expertise   190
    Knowing from within   191
    Conclusion   192

10   Core Skills: The Joining Skills   **194**
    Skills and tasks   194
    Core skills as the foundation   195
    The joining skills   196
    Empathy   196
    Empathy and the Jones family   198
    Empathy and negotiation   198
    Empathy and Patrick's family   199
    Empathy and the worker's desire for information:
    the Questioning Model   199
    Empathy and questioning   201
    Consistent empathy: an 'unsocial' behaviour   201
    Empathy and socio-cultural difference   203
    Authenticity and genuineness   204
    Authenticity and trust   205
    Authenticity and the Jones family   206
    Authenticity, marginality and change   206
    Authenticity and modelling   207

Authenticity and Patrick's family   208
Authenticity and difference   208
Authenticity and partnership   209
Authenticity and respect   210
Authenticity and self-awareness   210

11 Core Skills: The Intervention Skills   **212**
Social entrepreneurship   212
The individual worker, the team and the whole task   213
Creating partnerships   214
Social entrepreneurship and the Jones family   215
Social entrepreneurship and Patrick's family:
entrepreneurial flexibility in the division of labour   216
Entrepreneurial problem solving   217
Entrepreneurial reframing of the problem   217
Social entrepreneurship and the enabling manager   218
Competition and collaboration   219
Three-way partnerships   219
Reflection   220
Commonsense and practice   223
Accountability of practice   223
Reflection and partnership   224
How reflection was used in Patrick's family   225
Challenging   226
Elements of challenging   227
Reframing   229
Reframing and the nature of social problems   230
Elements of reframing   231
Reframing and patterns of problem definition   232
Conclusion   233

12 Epilogue   **234**
Overview   234
The social work task: key assumptions   235

Bibliography   239
Index of Names   250
Index of Subjects   253

List of Figures

4.1   The content map of social work tasks   58
4.2   Mapping the specific tasks   58
4.3   The spiral of negotiations   66
6.1   Mapping the key players   118
6.2   Mapping the key roles   120
6.3   Mapping the impact on relationships   121
6.4   Managing Change Through Innovation   129
7.1   The Questioning Model   134
7.2   The Exchange Model   135
7.3   The Procedural Model   141

Acknowledgements

We would like to thank all the colleagues, friends and family that we have worked with, be they service users, carers, workers or managers. They have helped us by sharing ideas and through their determination to confront the social problems they are involved with.

Crown copyright material is reproduced with the permission of the Controller of the Stationery Office.

Prologue

In this book we describe the scope of social work practice and how it can be undertaken. Our definition of social work in Chapter 1 is broad, following the Scottish approach, and covers social work and social care. The aim is to describe the nature of the whole enterprise and core issues. It is not a textbook of comparative approaches to individual and family problems. In Chapters 1 and 5 we describe how we use the term 'social problem' in a particular way, in recognition of the fact that the problems of the wider society are the aggregate of individual concerns and crises.

Social work is about development, not just providing aid in response to crisis. This is neither an over-ambitious claim nor an attempt to expand the domain of social work. We do not see social workers as leading change in the community and society, let alone leading some kind of social revolution. Social workers have no special claim to be the people who decide how individuals, families, communities or societies *should* behave. These issues are rightly the province of society as a whole and there are many other organisations working with the people caught up in social problems: the health service, voluntary and community groups, education, housing, income support, economic development, transport providers and employers. All have a crucial role to play in the resolution – or perpetuation – of social problems.

Serious problems arise for users and carers, practitioners, their managers and organisations, when the relationship between social work and social change is underplayed. To act as an aid or crisis agency, without working with others attempting to bring about change in the circumstances that require aid, runs the risk of the solution itself becoming part of the problem. Focusing exclusively on working with people at the point of crisis can perpetuate dependency rather than independence: maintaining people in their 'client' status, rather than working towards sustainable solutions and their social inclusion.

These issues and other main themes are introduced in the first three chapters. We also describe how workers need to reinvent their practice with the people involved to meet the particular circumstances found in each situation: social work is about problem solving, not applying predetermined solutions. In Chapter 4 we outline ways of mapping the different dimensions of social work and social problems to identify who should tackle the different dimensions of the task. This approach stresses teamwork and collaboration between organisations: social work is a team, not an individual, activity. This is followed in Chapter 5 with a discussion of ideas about deviance and social control and how central they are to understanding key dimensions of the social work task. Chapter 6 provides a framework for understanding and planning changes in social situations: for managing change.

Service users and carers can either be treated as objects of concern or joined with as genuine partners in the process of solving problems. In Chapter 7 we discuss three models of assessment, which inform much current practice, arguing that the full involvement of all concerned requires a particular approach.

Expectations and maintaining stereotypes of people can play a crucial role in perpetuating the position of individuals and groups within social problems. Chapter 8 explores how change is blocked or promoted through self-fulfilling prophecies, self-defeating strategies and mutually defeating interactions. Effective agents of change retain a degree of neutrality when they join with people, acting as honest broker. This marginality is necessary to negotiate a way through the conflicts of interest found in many situations where people's needs go unmet, or certain behaviour causes a problem. This potentially powerful position is discussed in Chapter 9, followed by an analysis of the core skills involved in social work and social problem solving in Chapters 10 and 11.

Social work is a development activity – designed not only to meet the needs of those requiring immediate support, but also to make the social situation, the families and communities that we live in, more dependable. Social workers and their managers should work through teamwork with service users, carers, staff in other organisations and local people to achieve more dependable communities. They can clarify their own positions within the team by regularly mapping out how all the dimensions of the task are being tackled, or blocked, by the different people involved. Unless people work together, the action of one organisation feeds referrals to another, and social problems will be perpetuated rather than resolved.

1

Introduction

Carol and Gary's story: an illustration

Gary and his mother sit nervously on the sofa. The worker opposite them has been in this kind of situation before. A health visitor has referred 'the case', suspecting that the child is being physically abused. The worker has to sort out with the mother, the child and other significant people how the child can be protected, but her role has many other dimensions and includes working with and for the mother and the child to help them and others meet their needs.

The variables in such situations are infinite. There may be different cultures, languages, religions, and the many different attitudes, assumptions and beliefs held by people within them. While recognising the significance of these groupings, it would be unwise to assume too much: any category used by outsiders, be they sociologists or the tabloid press, is likely to be wrong as a predictor of how this particular little boy or this particular woman will see the world. How they feel about what happens in the family, in their community, in their subgroup, what they see as a problem or an appropriate solution will be as individual as their fingerprints, as idiosyncratic as any other person's would be.

The worker brings her knowledge of the law and social policy. These set the frameworks within which decisions are made about the way that children should be cared for. There are 'grey areas' where there is both lack of clarity and conflicting opinions about what is acceptable. She will be aware of, if not experienced in, operating in these areas. If she considers that behaviour within this family at this point in time transgresses these boundaries, she has a clear responsibility to act in the best interests of the child and will play her part in implementing

1

the law. If she judges that the family is eligible for family support she will act to make sure that it is delivered. Often things are less clear cut, and the worker, with the support of her manager, will make judgements on the balance of probabilities of risk and the priorities and demands on the organisation's resources. The worker will inevitably be balancing different people's perceptions, choices, demands and expectations. She will have to strike a balance between helping people retain responsibility and control over their own lives by making good enough decisions and acting upon them, and discharging her responsibility and that of her organisation to take action to protect vulnerable individuals on behalf of society. Often she will do all this as a relative newcomer and outsider to the families and individuals she works with, knowing that their relationships with each other are always likely to be of primary significance to them, even long after they have physically separated.

Clear messages about how statute and organisation policy affect the worker's role must be given to the family. But she will also engage in the more complex processes of finding a better long-term way of solving the problems of the family as well as addressing the current behaviours that are causing concern. This is as true of a referral to consider residential care for an elderly person, where service users or carers no longer feel able to cope, as it is for a child in need. No matter how many 'situations like this' the worker has been in before, she will be seeking a unique set of solutions to the social problems represented by Gary and his mother. And these solutions will be decided upon and implemented by a unique group of people. The worker will be constantly **reinventing practice**: discovering a unique set of solutions in each idiosyncratic situation.

What do we mean by 'a social problem'?

We can see in the story of Gary and his mother a fairly typical referral of an individual child care problem. Or we can see this as a community development problem indicating the need to strengthen the social networks in a neighbourhood, community or town, that leave people socially isolated. Or we can see this as an example of the social problems associated with changes in family, changing employment patterns and child care. It is of course all of these things. Our position is that social work is interwoven into the way that the community at local and wider levels addresses these issues, just as much as it is a response to the individuals and families that turn to social care organisations, or are referred to them for help. This is not just putting social work in its social context. It is to say that the way that we, as social workers, address these problems is part of the way that the community or society that we are part of addresses them. In other societies and at other times in our own history, the response to problems typically referred to social workers will be different.

In writing this book we use the term 'social problem' to refer to situations such as that of Carol and Gary. Here the social problem is an individual mother not sufficiently supported by others and who is in danger of failing to look after her child. We also use the term to describe the problems of a couple providing support to a parent whose physical impairments are increasingly severe, or of the parent herself, referred for residential care. Likewise we refer to individuals caught up in deviant or delinquent behaviour as a social problem.

The term is more often used in sociology and social policy to refer to a set of problems that operate at a societal rather than an individual level. We have used it also to apply to the problems people bring to social care organisations for several reasons:

1   The support needs of individuals and families are often shared by others in the community or the wider society. Social policies, for example, on support for carers or for people with mental health difficulties address issues at the collective level which we also encounter at the individual and family level.
2   A person's need for support only becomes a problem for workers when these needs cannot be met within the family or local community. It is at this point that social care organisations become involved.
3   An effective approach to practice must include an awareness of the essential interconnections between what happens in different parts of an individual's close relationships, their local and other social networks and the wider social and political institutions in which individuals are embedded.
4   As the women's and black liberation movements, the disability movement and those combating ageism have shown, the personal has its political, social and economic dimensions.

Individual and family problems are an essential dimension of a larger issue: *the dependability of the social situation in relation to the needs it is expected to meet.* These individual, family, neighbourhood and community situations are the building blocks of what are conventionally called social problems

Macro problems and micro problems are directly related: they are different aspects of the same phenomena. When there is severe inflation in the economy, individual savings become worthless and prices go up. If enough people are involved it becomes a social disaster – ownership is somehow shared – as opposed to an individual disaster, which is 'theirs' not 'ours'. In some cultures an individual will automatically see that a cousin's problem is also theirs. As soon as social workers are introduced, especially social workers paid directly or indirectly by the state, then we are *all* involved. Our involvement may stop at grudgingly paying our taxes and it may be an infinitesimal amount, but we are as involved as our political representatives. One of the first principles of systems theory is that it is impossible for us not to be involved (Pincus and Minahan, 1973; Goldstein, 1973; Specht and Vickery, 1977).

To summarise, we have used the term social problem for two reasons:

1 Many individual problems are resolved or accommodated without a 'social worker' becoming involved. Social work from the perspective of this book is '**social**'.
2 To draw attention to the need for consistent action at different levels. It is pointless having a social policy aimed at providing one thing for a whole population or cohort of people when at the same time individual work with families operates in the opposite direction. The terms 'joined-up thinking' and 'joined-up solutions' are as relevant to social work practice as they are to current discussions of economic and social policy.

Defining social work

In Scotland all the functions of the English and Welsh social services departments and the probation service are carried out by social work departments. We are aware that within social care organisations, including social services departments in England and Wales, the term 'social work' is often synonymous with the activity of Diploma of Social Work qualified field social workers. Throughout this book we have used the term 'social work' in a wider sense, the way that we might refer to health. For many, talking about health will immediately conjure up the image of a doctor. But most of us will quickly recognise the essential contribution of the other workers involved such as nurses, occupational therapists, physiotherapists, psychologists, medical scientists, pharmacists and many other staff vital to the enterprise of medicine or promotion of health. A discussion of 'health' will include all of these people and the wider mass of people involved, the rest of the population. Such a view of social work is taken throughout this book.

Social work is about the interventions made to change social situations so that people who need support or are at risk can have their needs met more appropriately than if no intervention were made. This involves many people other than field social workers. These include all the people working in residential, day care and domiciliary care who are sometimes called social care or care workers.

This book is not about how to run residential, day or domiciliary services. These are ways in which we as a community respond to, for example, supporting older people in the community. This is a community response, not something 'outside' the community. At individual levels, residential, day and domiciliary services for a child or older person is a way of responding which is part of a change process or way of handling the needs. For support at difficult points and events in a person's life this needs to be a part of a whole: the community response to supplement, or as an alternative to, family and wider social networks.

Social work, causation and change

In emphasising the location of social work in the community we draw on a systems approach: an ecological perspective. Throughout we talk about 'social problems' and not just the needs of individuals, because intervention always involves a web of other people as well as social workers. This is so whether we are concerned with personal support for adults and children, the resolution of the conflicting needs of service users and carers, child abuse or neglect, or young people on the edge or in the midst of a full-blown delinquent career. An ecological perspective on our world and our actions within it helps us understand the knock-on effects of many of our actions upon the environment, both physical and social. We need an ecological perspective to grapple with complex social problems at all levels, from individual work to national and international policy.

Many people's problems are relatively easily managed, if not solved, by the addition of a straightforward service, such as home care support, to their existing social resources. We do not assume that all more intransigent problems are 'caused' by social factors. The jury is still out on the causes of many individual, family, community and social problems. But social work is always involved in social situations, where the impact of the problem, its management, perpetuation or resolution is social. Problems such as those of Gary and his mother are 'social' in the sense that even if their causes are proved to be individually based, they impact on other people, the community and society. For example human immunodeficiency virus (HIV) is a social as well as an individual or family problem, as is tuberculosis (TB) or hunger. If social workers and other staff become involved in tackling these problems they are, by definition, social. This is not a new analysis. Many years ago Helen Harris Perlman saw social work in this way (Perlman, 1957).

The key question in social work and in the delivery of social services is not 'what does this person need?' It is 'who can do what for whom to improve or maintain this situation or slow down the pace of deterioration?' Where children or others are at risk, the question is not just 'is this person being abused?' but 'who can do what to change the situation, to make the person safe?' Where children or adults are referred because their behaviour is causing problems for others, intervention will always involve several, if not many, key people. Social exclusion involves the behaviour of those excluding, as well as those excluded. You can no more change the height of one end of a seesaw without lowering the other than you can change some of the notes without changing the music. These issues recur throughout the book and specifically in Chapter 5, where we discuss social control and social change as an integral dimension of most social work activity.

We do not see social workers as leading change in the community and society, let alone leading some kind of social revolution. Social workers have no special claim to be the people who decide how individuals, families, communities or societies should behave. These issues are rightly the province of society as a whole through its elected representatives. There are also many other organisations working with the people caught up in social problems: the health service, education, housing, income support, economic development, transport and employers, all have a crucial role to play in the resolution or perpetuation of social problems. But serious problems arise for practitioners, their managers and organisations when the relationship between social work and social change is underplayed.

In our view the notion of social work as 'maintenance' is too static. Others (Davies, 1994) have indeed suggested that the role of social work is one of maintaining the status quo, maintaining people in society as it is. However, the community is not a machine that is more or less carrying out its functions, requiring 'maintenance' to keep it running smoothly. Communities, however defined, are ever-changing living entities or human systems. They inevitably change as individual members grow to adulthood, pass through maturity into old age and die. The families, the ethnic and age composition change as do groups that make up the community and link it to others. Major events, both local, national and increasingly international, will cause major change in the way that they, 'communities', and society operate. These range from the closing of a major local factory, natural disasters, to great political and economic changes in countries geographically distant but tied into our own economy and personal lives.

Within this broad context social work operates as one of the ways certain problems are addressed. The community, or at least its political representatives and many others, will want something to be done about a whole range of problems such as child abuse, isolated older people living at risk, or young people in trouble. Social workers however cannot, and should not, do all this work on their own. Faced with an older family member or neighbour needing increasing support for everyday tasks we can either try to resolve problems of their care within the family or immediate social network, refer the problem to social care organisations, or seek to combine the two sources of support. The division of labour has long been a feature of modern societies, and increasingly we rely on this for all kinds of services, from plumbing to policing.

Reinvention and the wider context

The world in which we work and live our personal lives is changing rapidly. The implications for the practice of social work and its management are twofold. First, change and innovation is integral and has to be understood and managed like any other part of the work; and second, social work has a fundamental contribution to make in creating the context in which wider social care and control activities are valued and supported.

This is not a simple how-to-do-it book, and those who expect simple answers to social problems will find both this book and the practice of social work frustrating. Instead our aim is to help workers and front-line managers determine the most appropriate courses of action, in partnership with the key people in the social situations in which they work. Neither is this a book of ready-made maps or blueprints from which solutions to particular social problems can be 'read off', nor is it an anthology of new methodological inventions which can just be taken off the shelf and applied.

We hope this book will assist social workers to work with others and solve or manage social problems. There is much emphasis now on evidence-based practice but social problems are not like physics and engineering, and the knowledge on which we base our practice must include the experience and expertise of users and carers as well as research. Social workers work with many different people who see problems in their own ways and have their own views of how they should be solved. Some aspects of these problems are more accessible to scientific methods than others. For example, we have some clear indications of what a child like Gary needs for his emotional and social development and how Carol's parenting skills or lack of them could help or harm him. But in other situations, such as the resolution of conflicting interests between family members or between carers and those receiving care, the knowledge base is different. Here there can be no scientifically predetermined balance between people's conflicting and changing interests.

This, then, is a book for **mapmakers** -- people who are going to map new social terrain, and for **innovators** – people who are going to reinvent unique sets of solutions to each idiosyncratic social situation they encounter. Unlike the physical landscape which remains very similar over long periods of time, the social terrain, at individual, family and community levels, is constantly changing and needs continuous remapping. Just as in our personal lives we have to reinvent the way we handle our relationships as they change over time, so workers have continuously to change, or reinvent, the way social problems are confronted.

A framework for practice is needed which makes sense of the context in which we are now living and working. We propose a community-based approach consistent with social policies emphasis-ing the central role of the family and the community in providing and supporting social care activities. This book presents a holistic approach to practice which draws on systems and ecological theories to help workers and their managers synthesise the direct and indirect work, service delivery and change activities at all the different levels of family and community characteristic of our increasingly complex modern world.

Overview of the book

Chapter 2: Reinventing Social Work: Key Themes and Tasks

This chapter provides an introductory overview of the main issues and themes. Grounded in a single case study, the chapter introduces several thematic issues including: the question of the balance to be struck between aid and development activities; the nature of social problems; the relationship of social work, social care and change; the problem of fragmentation of services both in the UK and USA; the need for knowledge-based services.

Chapter 3: Formulating the Task: Aid or Development?

Here we draw an analogy between worker responses to social problems in the community and the responses of 'developed' countries to problems in other parts of the world. We argue that while emergency aid may sometimes be necessary, it is insufficient and may even sometimes undermine the longer-term development work necessary to help both countries and communities become more dependable sources of care and control for their members. It is argued that such 'upstream' development work needs to be seen as a crucial part of the whole response to social problems in the community, and brought into a more effective balance with the necessary 'downstream' aid and emergency work.

Chapter 4: Mapping the Task and Processes

A systematic way of mapping the different aid and development dimensions of social work is outlined. Firstly we present a framework for identifying the main elements of the *content* of the social work task: direct work, indirect work, change agent activity and service delivery. Secondly we present a framework for identifying the main stages in the *process* of social work and social problem solving over time. This includes clarification of basic assumptions and values, negotiation of problem definition, forming specific aims, monitoring achievements and other outcomes, identifying development needs and identifying organisational policy goals.

Chapter 5: Social Problems, Social Control and Patterns of Interaction

A particular view of the nature of social problems has been introduced in this chapter. Here we further develop this view by arguing for the need to go beyond the individualisation of social problems. We suggest that ideas about deviance and social control are central to understanding the social work task, and present a framework for understanding patterns of interaction which typically help create and perpetuate social problems. The position of the worker as a relatively independent 'third party' to the network of people involved in particular social problems is introduced.

Chapter 6: Managing and Mapping Change

Previous chapters have developed the argument that bringing about change in social situations through introducing innovations in problem solving by the people involved is central to the social work task. In this chapter we describe a framework for understanding the nature of interpersonal and social change. This recognises that practitioners and managers need to have an explicit approach to guide them in the process of managing deliberate and planned change. Central to this framework is the distinction between first- and second-order change in relationships.

Chapter 7: Assessment and Intervention

Here we discuss the implications of our approach for the way workers tackle the tasks of assessment and intervention. We describe three models of assessment which inform much current practice, and discuss the advantages and disadvantages of each in relation to different assumptions about the overall task of involvement in social problem solving. The three models or approaches to assessment are the Questioning Model, the Exchange Model and the Procedural

Model. We argue that the Exchange Model is most appropriate for an approach to problem solving in partnership with others which facilitates empowerment.

Chapter 8: Overcoming Blocks to Change

We focus now on a theoretical framework relevant to the change agent dimensions of the whole social work task. This helps analyse how attributes of individuals, including those of the worker, and the policy and practice of the organisation, influence interactions and thus the perpetuation of, or change in, social problems. We identify patterns which are common in everyday interactions within families, groups, organisations and communities.

Chapter 9: Independence and Marginality

Social workers are employed to 'do something', in partnership with others, about particular social problems in the community, that is to act as agents of change. Change may be achieved in a range of ways including the delivery or commissioning of services, but whatever the mode of work, in order to be effective the worker needs to retain a certain neutrality in the face of the many pushes and pulls from others in the networks of people involved. The worker needs to be able to be both participant and observer in often complex social situations, and maintenance of this position, discussed in this chapter, we describe as the capacity for 'marginality'.

Chapter 10: Core Skills: The Joining Skills

Using a broad distinction between 'joining' and 'intervention' skills, in this and the following chapter we identify a relatively small number of core skills required by workers using the approach outlined in this book. The joining skills we see as essential in helping workers align sufficiently with other people for the formation of problem solving partnerships, and without which any attempts at bringing about change will be compromised. The intervention skills then build on these to help workers and others involved in direct problem solving and change activity. The essential joining skills are the capacity of the worker to behave congruently or with authenticity, and to be able to communicate empathically with a wide range of people. All these skills are necessary to help the worker retain the position of marginality identified as crucial in Chapter 9.

Chapter 11: Core Skills: The Intervention Skills

Workers need the joining skills described in Chapter 10 to understand other people's situations and how they experience them. They should not hide behind a professional mask or role. Particular situations may require further skills for change to be possible. Here we identify and discuss four of these: social entrepreneurship, reflection, challenging and reframing.

Chapter 12: Epilogue

This chapter summarises the main assumptions and presents some concluding thoughts.

2

Reinventing Social Work: Key Themes and Tasks

In Chapter 1 we introduced the idea that problem solving in partnership with people in the community requires workers to be able to reinvent their practice: that is, to help create new sets of solutions for unique situations. We emphasise *re*invention in acknowledgement that while there is knowledge and practice experience to draw upon, and while each individual, family or other social grouping is unique, there is also common ground between us all, and thus completely 'original' invention is unlikely to be either necessary or possible. In this chapter we return to and expand on the story of Carol and Gary, in order to ground subsequent discussion of some of the key themes and issues implicit in the idea of reinventing practice which the book as a whole addresses.

Carol and Gary's story: an illustration of promoting family and community social well-being

Carol, a 24-year-old white woman, is referred by a health visitor to a local social services area office in a large city. The referral states that the health visitor suspects that Carol has been abusing her 4-year-old son Gary, causing injury by physically chastising him. They are allocated to the local children and families team and subsequently approached by Mrs A, a social worker. Mrs A starts her intervention by talking to the health visitor who initiated the referral, ascertaining that she has general concerns about the vulnerability of Gary and his mother rather than very specific evidence of serious abuse. As she puts it, 'all the signs are there', but without physical evidence of serious harm. The worker also checks to see if the family has been referred before and if there is other information about them.

At their first meeting, Mrs A explains to Carol why she has been referred, the statutory and legal responsibilities of the social services

---

13

department and the obligations that these place on the social worker. Some time is spent sharing information.

Understandably anxious, suspicious and beginning to be a little hostile towards the social worker, Carol guardedly explains her situation. She is particularly vague about her parenting of Gary. He joins and leaves, but mainly interrupts, as he periodically tears through the conversation or demands something from his mother. Like most children of his age, Gary is a bundle of energy, curiosity and mischief, constantly demanding interaction. Depending on how *you* feel, he is an annoying, stimulating, boring, amusing, exasperating, interesting or irritating little boy: a typically exhausting child.

Carol says she doesn't know anybody in the area and is uncertain of her neighbours. Like many people in the city she thinks of the neighbourhood as a 'rough' one, and has been apprehensive about talking to people in the street since she moved some months ago. She was evicted from her previous home for rent arrears following separation from her partner. The worker detects that Carol is by no means sure that she will herself be acceptable to her relatively new neighbours. A routine check of Carol's benefits shows that she is receiving her entitlement.

The eldest of a big family, she moved a long way from them with her ex-partner. The worker recognises that Carol has plenty of experience of looking after young children even if she now has little confidence that she is being a 'good mother' to Gary. As the exchange develops, Carol is given information about various resources available in the neighbourhood, including projects related to the work of the neighbourhood team. She is invited to bring Gary to a playgroup, to see if she would like to be a volunteer helper. The trade-off will be that if Gary likes the group she will be able to leave him some mornings after he has settled. She will also meet other mothers in the neighbourhood who help at the playgroup and meet for coffee when they bring their children. The worker knows that Carol will always be with others at the group and that with this supervision she will be no risk to her own or other children attending.

Without denying the seriousness of the situation or her authority and responsibilities, the social worker has reframed some dimensions of the problem. Her first exercise of judgement is that she has enough initial information to be clear that there is a low risk of immediate danger to the child. She knows enough about the dangers of being catapulted unnecessarily into collecting evidence of abuse, which can leave the situation worse than before if no further action is taken (DoH, 1995; Platt and Shemmings, 1996). She also knows that she can reinforce the negative stereotype of Carol that Carol herself shares. Aware of the many factors that could contribute to the risk to Gary from Carol's relatively isolated position, the worker explores the support available to her but also looks to identify the strengths that Carol brings to their situation. The worker continues to share information with her, recognising and suggesting the use of Carol's own resources in such a way as to help Carol make use of others without confirming or reinforcing her feelings of failure and further building a 'problem' identity. Reframing or redefining the nature of the problem in this way is not just a linguistic ploy or another useless piece of professional jargon. It involves recognising different dimensions of the situation and different ways of looking at them, and is often essential to ensure the formation of a collaborative, problem solving relationship between citizens and workers.

Based on her understanding and experience of what mothers in Carol's situation have to face, the worker explores different questions once she is clear that Gary is not in acute, immediate danger. She has defined the task as family support, but at the same time is asking herself, 'how can this woman help us with the work we are doing in this neighbourhood?' This question is as important as trying to identify what the family member's needs are and who might help meet them, and how problematic behaviour may be changed. The assessment must look at both these areas to find ways which will be mutually beneficial and to reduce the risk to Gary. Carol's continued social isolation would increase the danger of stress, which could lead to neglect or abuse. Any one of her problems might be compounded by the combination of being socially excluded because of her status as a lone parent, her poverty and the demands made on any parent caring for young children. The reframing of the problem is implemented by the worker acting in a different way, which in turn opens up the possibility of alternative responses from other people involved, including how Carol sees herself and Gary.

To be able to make this response, the worker and her team colleagues have engaged in a variety of other community- and neighbourhood-based activities. They worked in the neighbourhood to study local needs and develop local resources. This involved a range of activities aimed at:

- identifying the composition of the local community, including age structure; ethnic, cultural and religious composition and norms; family, household and employment and unemployment patterns;
- analysing the prevalence of different social problems and the ways these are currently being managed and responded to;

- identifying the relevant resources that exist in the area: the strengths of families and neighbourhood networks; the capacity, policy and practice of other organisations in all sectors; the self-help and independent living groups;
- identifying how people in the neighbourhood relate to each other, to local institutions and to people in their wider social networks and communities of interest.

This work provided the team with information on:

- what relationships are part of the area's social problems and need to change;
- what people and groups are resources and so part of the usual formal solutions to problems in the neighbourhood, including specialist organisations for minority ethnic groups;
- how people and organisations can be mobilised to be part of new solutions.

Carol and Gary's situation, in common with many others in the workload of social workers, is a social problem, and the worker's engagement with the people involved is set in a context of statutory and legal responsibilities and the organisation's remit. The response includes using some of the same information and repeating the same responses which are relevant to other people in the same community in similar situations to Carol. At the same time it is unique, dynamic and fluid. Although we would all like simple guidelines, practice theory has to be complex enough to chart and understand what is happening in the different facets of Carol's life and in the local community, how this relates to the role of the worker and the responsibilities of the different organisations involved, some of which have a statutory basis, and how all of this informs the worker's action. All too often we focus on a single dimension or relationship, such as seeking only to protect the individual child, without also thinking through the long-term impact on family relationships, or allying with one parent or relative (Parker, 1995). Crucial facets of the problem begin to be excluded. This could overlook people as potential contributors to a solution, a failure which could be both expensive and contrary to what many of the central people want to happen.

Social work should make a significant contribution to a whole approach to social problems rather than be a particular activity or series of activities, and we need tools which recognise this. A holistic approach to and theory of practice demonstrates the necessity of seeing such difficulties as Carol's and the apparently distinct activities – direct work with her and her family and all the indirect development work – as different aspects of the same problem and the same strategy for resolution.

The worker's interventions with this particular family and the team's work in the area will need to be reinvented to maintain its relevance to the changing context and local and central policies. Key participants and their relationships change as part of ordinary everyday events or because of the team's interventions. Perhaps in the future we will be able to convey these changes in practice with 3D images on computers. For the present we can propose metaphors. Taking the common one of a music score for an orchestra, it would be a mistake to think that the fluid relationships involved in social work practice could ever follow a fixed pattern like the score for a symphony, predetermining when each person plays their part. Even the wide variation allowed arising from the conductor's interpretation and the quality of individual performances that make up the whole does not mirror the flexibility required. Social work is more like a jazz performance: the performers agree to play the same basic theme with its underlying chord sequence; beyond this, they may agree on certain parts where their playing is closely synchronised and sometimes agree in advance when to stop. But each performance is based on improvisation around the theme. In good performances, the players 'play off each other', linking phrases to those played by their partners, either building solos on each other's playing or dovetailing collective improvisation into a series of unique ensembles, agreeing to end when they judge that each has finished their contribution.

A holistic approach to social work practice needs to provide a set of connecting principles and strategies which allows us to see *how* working with different methods, different groups of people and within different organisations and legislative frameworks, are all aspects of the same task. We can then see how we can dovetail all the different practical activities of workers in the social care organisations and those in other organisations and in the community. Without a coherent theory of practice some essential tasks will not get done, others will tend to cancel each other out and unintended and undesirable consequences of particular interventions may remain unnoticed.

An effective and useful theory for practice provides *the mind of the enterprise*. In the rest of this chapter we outline some of the main themes of the approach developed in the book as a whole which we hope will help social work staff to reinvent their practice, draw their own maps of all the areas of intervention and service delivery, and continue the transformations involved in the evolution of their practice.

Development and not aid alone

All over the world, care is provided through individuals, families and others in their immediate social network. In the UK, the general Household Survey (Rowlands, 1998) reveals that, not including parents looking after children, there are 5.7 million carers providing support for adults. As many as 1.7 million carers devote at least 20 hours per week to the task; 24 per cent of all carers have been so for at least 10 years; and 18 per cent are caring for more than one person. Of these, a minority (41 per cent) had regular contact with the health service (doctors, health visitors and community nurses). Even fewer are in regular contact with the personal social services: of whom 22 per cent received home help, 8 per cent meals on wheels and 7 per cent saw a social worker. (Regular is defined as 'at least once a month'.)

It is well known that poverty and discrimination undermine the dependability of social situations. There is only a 1 : 7000 chance of a 5–9-year-old child with two parents, living in an owner-occupied home with more rooms than people and no more than three siblings, coming into the care of the personal social services. These odds shorten dramatically for a child living in poverty with poor social support. Of children between the ages of 5 and 9 living in families receiving income support, one in 10 is admitted to care (DoH, 1991b). Older people with sufficient resources are very unlikely to be referred to social services for assessments before they enter residential care. They or their families can pay for any services they choose to use. Potential residents of care homes, or recipients of home care services, are only referred and assessed if they need to draw on public finance.

Social, cultural, economic and political changes all affect the identity of social work. What does not change is that those who use, and are required to use, social work services continue overwhelmingly to be poor and disadvantaged. The last decade has seen both an increased understanding of the impact of race, culture (Ahmad, 1990; Butt and Mirza, 1996; Cross *et al.*, 1991; hooks, 1991), gender (Hanmer and Statham, 1999; Dominelli and McLeod, 1989), disability (Morris, 1993, 1996; Morris and Lois, 1995; Cambell and Oliver, 1996), sexual orientation (Cosis Brown, 1992) and learning difficulties (People First,

1994a, 1994b; Williams 1992) on the different ways in which people usually tackle their problems, and the development of appropriate ways of offering support.

Central to working with people in the local community is the necessity for workers to develop understanding of the ways in which the usual resources of care and control work in our communities, identify them, sustain them when they begin to falter or fail, and contribute towards their expansion without undermining them. In the story of Carol and Gary the work of the team members in understanding the community in which they operate, for example seeing the potential of Carol as a resource, is crucial. Our development role requires a capacity to tailor responses to complement and supplement often highly specific local patterns of social support and control. In the short term we may have to rescue individuals from their immediate circumstances, just as aid agencies deliver food and water at times of acute crisis. But in the longer term we also have to work to make social situations more dependable for those who live in them, acting more like development agencies working to build irrigation schemes, improve food production and the local economy and health services. When the activities in local communities are mapped, there is often surprise at the range of services which aim to reduce the number of vulnerable groups and communities and divert people from needy services by making their circumstances sufficiently dependable (Hardiker, Exton and Barker, 1991; Butt and Box, 1997) and supporting independent living (Cambell and Oliver, 1996).

Social work: beyond the individualisation of social problems

Social work is an integral part of the society within which it is practised. It is one dimension of the way that social problems are managed – one way in which individuals and families with particular problems get support and resources, and members of the community 'get something done' about the people they think need to change or receive help. As with social care, the vast majority of people are subject to the social controls exercised informally within the community and do not become involved with social care organisations or the criminal justice system. Of those who do get involved, the majority of first offenders do not return to court.

Usually social work is peripheral to the way that we solve our problems and manage the care of children and adults who need assistance or are at risk. Most of us have problems but live in situations that enable us to cope with them without welfare services. This position can dramatically change when we are faced with problems which go beyond our own resources and those of our networks. As one disabled person said to a group of non-disabled people, 'You have to remember you may be looking at your future selves'.

The demand for services is conventionally said to be based on the level of need in the community – thus we have 'needs-led assessment' as a cornerstone of current community care and children and families policy. In practice, this has maintained a focus on the needs of the individual adult or individual child, and at best the immediate carer. The vision of turning away from service-driven provision towards working with people's strengths (Griffiths, 1988) has largely been unrealised. Many assessment procedures introduced after the National Health Service and Community Care Act 1990 and subsequently revised in the context of financial constraints have had to pathologise people if they are to meet eligibility criteria for allocating limited services (Statham, 1996; Platt, 1996). Extensive use of investigation procedures (DoH, 1995; DoH, 1991b) has often been at the expense of working in partnership with service users, their carers and other people in the community to arrive at new solutions to problems of unmet need. Ironically, the focus on putting together 'packages of care' has reinforced the focus on service provision as the solution to people's problems (Caldock and Nolan, 1994; Hunter, Brace and Buckley, 1994).

In Chapters 4 and 7 we specifically describe frameworks to help workers and managers think about assessment and intervention in ways which go beyond criteria of eligibility for services and individual need. Moreover, by clarifying that there are many, often conflicting, 'users', the discussion in these chapters also helps identify how to respond to social problems in ways which are likely to be more genuinely user- or carer-led.

The individual child or older person may be the immediate subject of concern, but many others will be affected by any intervention: family members, neighbours, friends, employers; other organisations such as health, housing, education, the police; the media; and the general public as either taxpayers, or as people with personal responsibility for the identified person, or as potential or actual victims of their behaviour. We are all stakeholders either individually or by virtue of some combination of these overlapping roles. We may all be directly affected now or at some time in the future. We may be unwittingly and unwillingly excluded from taking responsibility by social work staff and their organisations if they take over rather than renegotiate different people's or organisations' contribution and supplementary support. This problem is compounded by lack of information in the community about the possibilities of help beyond the immediate family (Audit Commission and Social Services Inspectorate, 1997) and the fact that many requests for help come at the point of crisis when family carers feel they can no longer cope. Words like 'client', 'user', 'consumer' reflect the fact that the stakeholders in any social situation are multiple and not singular. All expect attention to their perspective from the workers who become involved.

Social work, social care and change

Modern societies are noted for their ever-increasing division of labour. We are used to industries that divide and subdivide tasks. Increasingly over the last few generations this has been applied to all aspects of life, as some of the functions of the family and kinship have been replaced by exchanges within the wider community. Care for people by the community is a relatively recent addition, with the growth in care work and more recently the introduction of market mechanisms replacing reciprocity, public service or charity as a basis for becoming involved in the lives of others. Social care provision now provides employment for large numbers of people. Estimates are in the region of one to two million (Local Government Management Board, 1997). Many more people are employed in social care than ever before. Until the late twentieth century this was an activity engaged in by few, provided only to people who were either very poor or vulnerable and certainly stigmatised, or purchased privately by families who were rich enough to supplement or replace their own care resources.

As we move towards reducing stigma and an increasing emphasis on building on people's strengths, changes are taking place in how we see support provided from outside the family. The division between caring and 'tending' is a key feature in social care. Parker (1981) describes 'tending' as the task of looking after someone's personal and intimate needs without entering into the emotional relationships of loving and caring. This does not imply that all family care is based on loving, or that those tending do not sometimes become fond of the person they are working with. 'Tending', as opposed to intimate personal care and nurturing based on kinship and reciprocity, is undertaken by people who are employed to carry out these tasks. Within the Disabled People's Movement this relationship is redefined as 'personal assistance' (Evans, 1995). This rejects using caring as the basis for the relationship and replaces it by one based on the support necessary to live independently. The Community Care (Direct Payments) Act 1996 gives public recognition to this change of status and provides the means for state funds to be used by disabled people to directly employ their own personal assistants.

Social care, traditionally understood as the care, tending and personal assistance provided through residential, day and domiciliary services, is part of the whole task of social work, part of the community's response to certain kinds of social problem. The range of services characterised as social care is one kind of possible solution, one way of dividing the labour of social care and control in the community. Such divisions often have unintended and unforeseen consequences, most significantly the fragmentation of services and increasing need to coordinate potentially conflicting activities across a range of individual, family, social and organisational boundaries. We discuss this both in the UK context and that of the USA.

The UK: our history and the present context for practice

In the UK there has been a long-standing awareness of the need to pull together the different parts of the social problem solving organisations in society. The Seebohm (1968) and Killbrandon (1966) reports argued for the unification into the generic statutory social services and social work departments of the then separate children's, adult and welfare departments. In Scotland this unification included the probation service, while in the rest of the UK social work with adult offenders remained court-based in the probation service. These major changes have been followed by a continuous series of policy statements and guidance documents stressing the need for organisations and workers to work together. The Barclay Report (1982) on the role and tasks of social workers, through to the Griffiths Report (1988) and the 1989 Children Act and on to guidance from the Department of Health, all emphasise partnerships between workers and parents, carers and other members of the public, including their involvement in the development of strategic plans for children and adults.

The requirement for collaboration is occurring at a time when there is increasing diversity of providers in the social care field. This aims to provide choice but is also fragmenting services. The mechanism to cope here is care management. While many packages of care are simple, some are extremely complicated: 24-hour care can involve several different providers (Levin *et al.*, 1994). Collaboration and partnership between key actors and organisations is seen as a basic requirement for good service delivery, yet the aim of 'seamless service' remains elusive in the 1990s. The results of the health and social services reforms and the strategic planning role of local authorities in the late twentieth century have yet to take general effect.

The USA

We have chosen to look at the USA because it has had a profound effect on social policy in the UK. Its philosophy, like that of the UK, has been based on individualism and eligibility rather than the European concepts of citizenship and social inclusion (Cannan, Berry and Lyons, 1992; Connelly and Stubbs, 1997). Now, both in the UK and the USA, there are moves in the opposite direction towards community-based practice and collaboration rather than a competitive market approach to health and social care, and towards greater flexibility of budgets. In the USA the number of organisations providing services has increasingly been seen as a problem. One of the authors of this book visited a family involved with 19 different social work organisations. Case management was introduced to resolve this, with one worker taking an overall management role to coordinate the activities of many others, but this has proved insufficient to cope with the degree of fragmentation.

Two major strategies are being adopted. The first is managed care. This is being introduced in health care, and social services are beginning to follow. Instead of services provided and paid for on an incident-by-incident basis, care is provided to a whole population. At present individuals of working age receiving health and social care are billed every time they receive treatment or a service. Depending upon their insurance arrangements, a proportion of this cost is paid directly by the patient and the remainder passed on to the insurance company. Under managed care a whole population, a workforce for example, is insured through one payment system and the insurance company pays for all treatments and services. Under this system there are large savings in administration costs, and changing priorities can be taken into account. It is further argued that individualised insurance arrangements favour high tech interventions while managed care will provide an incentive to promote health and preventative strategies.

The other strategy is based on the recognition that funding particular categories of care or service has led to the development of a rigid service-driven system, within which service users have to be fitted into what is available – rather than services being able to respond flexibly to meet local needs. If the foster placement budget is spent, then children may be placed unnecessarily in residential care if resources remain in this category of funding. This has led to a series of programmes designed to decategorise funding, or 'decat projects' (Adams and Nelson, 1995).

A practice response to fragmentation: a holistic approach

Given these levels of diversification or fragmentation on both sides of the Atlantic, what are the connecting principles that will hold together the different parts of the social welfare systems?

Many of the arguments for collaboration and partnership are self evident and uncontroversial. Many organisational factors perpetuate poor collaboration and there is little shared understanding of the nature of the whole enterprise of social work. Over recent years there has been considerable emphasis on organisational arrangements for delivering services and a continuing focus on the individual service user's needs, but much less attention has been paid to developing a holistic framework for practice.

The reasons for developing such a framework are:

● to promote knowledge-based practice as an alternative to 'mindless eclecticism' which draws on any theory or model of intervention or care that is convenient at the time, irrespective of inconsistencies, lack of supporting evidence or any understanding of how it might relate to the activities;
● to move beyond over-reliance on one or two specific models of practice or ways of working which, while valuable in themselves,

are a part not the whole of social work. Such models include cognitive behaviour programmes for juvenile offenders, family therapy for children's problems related to family relationships, group and individual counselling for sufferers of post-traumatic stress syndrome, using foster or residential care, establishing credit unions for families living in poverty, the development of self-help groups, and so on;

- to counter the sense of helplessness often induced by changing, apparently intransigent, multidimensional social problems, where people have different, conflicting perceptions of and responses to both the problems and their possible solutions;
- to address the nature of social work delivery in all situations, and provide a framework within which particular models of practice can be used in appropriate circumstances. Examples include social inclusion, community development, user involvement and programmes for independent living as well as care management and therapeutic work;
- to underpin the worker/service-user partnerships and collaboration within and between organisations that is essential to bring all the requisite specialist dimensions of the personal social services and related professions into a coherent effort to resolve the multiple layers of social problems.

Reinvention and knowledge-based practice

We endorse the movement towards knowledge-based practice while also recognising that our understanding of the nature of professional knowledge is itself the subject of critique and reinvention (Schon, 1983, 1987; Eraut, 1994; Thompson, 1995). Our approach is consistent with those perspectives which recognise and validate the importance of the tacit knowledge and 'know-how' carried in people's life and work experience. This is not to say that all such knowledge is valid and useful: the outcomes of worker interventions should be evaluated so that the most effective and relevant forms of practice can be identified and diffused to become widespread practice. Not all the knowledge and know-how required for social problem solving is contained in codified form (Eraut 1994; Thompson 1995). The more tacit understanding can be reflected on and exposed to explicit 'reality testing', the more we can move towards identifying the most effective modes of intervention for specific situations.

We also recognise that the management of these change processes should be based on the available research on the diffusion of innovations and the management of change (Rogers, 1996; Smale, 1996, 1998). Our goal is to describe a holistic approach to social problem solving at local level that helps workers and managers in different settings make sense of the overall enterprise they are engaged in. Social workers draw upon many different specific methods for bringing about change, such as different styles of counselling, group work, family therapy, family group conferencing, community action and so forth. Decisions about which to use should be based on the best available evidence of effectiveness, and at the same time recognise the difficulties of designing effectiveness and outcome studies which go beyond treating service users and others as essentially objects of study and concern, rather than as full participants in the joint discovery of the best means of tackling social problems (Smale, 1995).

Over the past 15 years we have been working in different parts of the UK and in some USA states with innovative workers and managers from a whole range of settings and sectors: statutory, voluntary and private. They have practised social work with different groups of service users, carers and parents, in rural, urban and inner-city areas. Testing and revising their approaches in the light of their day-to-day experience, these workers and managers have been reinventing practice to address the changes in people's lives, employment and communities. A common thread is the way they constantly work in collaboration with people to resolve problems, rather than applying standardised methods or predetermined solutions. This approach has been running well ahead of any explicit practice theory. Here we have used what we have learnt from them to describe a holistic approach to practice, connecting the activities of the different staff involved in tackling social problems at a local level.

The need to continually reinvent practice could be taken to imply that social work has no theoretical base apart from a few techniques or methods. This would never be proposed by other occupational groups such as the doctors or psychologists with whom we work, who see the merit of practice being reinvented in response to research evidence and experience.

The idea of reinvention as applied to social work conveys the uniqueness of each social problem and the encounters between the people concerned. It does not imply either 'making it up as you go along' or that there is no theoretical base or legal framework. Our aim in using the term is to demonstrate that social work, in common with other tasks, can never be a routine activity effected by simply following procedures. In our personal lives we change the way we confront problems as we gain more knowledge and experience, and as our repertoire of skills, wisdom and expertise grows. We become more effective in using our personal resources to fit particular circumstances, the strengths and weaknesses of our social networks and the specific patterning of the support available from family, friends, paid assistance or provision from social care organisations. If reinvention is part of our day-to-day existence, it is even more so in social work, where the worker is involved only because a social problem has gone beyond the usual approach to problem solving and the current resources, skills and support of the people involved.

Ideas influence actions and thus have significant implications for the people who use services. The consequences can have profound effects on their future relationships and their liberty. Whether we are aware of them or not, we use theories to shape and understand our world, and all too easily apply them to understanding the world of others. Accountable practice requires that the frameworks we use are not only explicit, but also tested and revised. Assessment, analysis and action are shaped by practice theory which provides a disciplined and rigorous way of thinking about people and social problems.

The application of practice theory is reinvented on a daily basis in the many interactions individual staff have with service users, carers, parents, workers in other organisations, local people, politicians and, increasingly, the media. Together they negotiate and renegotiate the nature of social problems being jointly addressed and the options available for tackling them. This process provides the impetus for the development of theory over comparatively short periods of time. The dynamic nature of practice is recognised in the continuing need to carry out research, and in the responsibility of workers and managers to update their knowledge and skills and to evaluate their own practice.

Skills for practice: a synthesis of knowledge, behaviour and values

Practice is neither based on theory nor on research evidence alone: the worker's knowledge of 'how to go on', how to behave helpfully in often complex social situations, is not based just on the kinds of knowledge easily codified and conveyed in lectures and textbooks (Schon, 1983, 1987; Eraut, 1994; Thompson, 1995). What a worker actually does is the product of the dynamic interplay between codified knowledge, tacit know-how, behaviour and values, which are used to understand and influence the behaviour of the people involved in patterns of relationships that precipitate or perpetuate social problems. These different components inform and frame the judgements and decisions that workers make, and the actions they take as circumstances change over time. The core skills we identify in subsequent chapters are themselves each a synthesis of knowledge, behaviour and values.

What the worker does when he is with other people is as dependent upon the behaviour of these others as their behaviour is on the worker's. This is not to suggest that there is equality or parity of influence, authority or power, but to acknowledge that all parties to an interaction are just that, and they each have some control and power over different aspects of the relationship, decisions, indecisions and judgements that influence subsequent outcomes. If workers can make choices and act on their judgement in these relationships, then so too can the other people. What people *do*, whether they are the traditional 'clients' of workers or those with the power to change their circumstances, will be limited by their repertoire of behaviours, what they perceive as constraints on their decisions, and will be guided by the experience and judgements that they make over time.

Our approach to social work is directed at explaining how people make their decisions and sustain or change their contribution to the behaviour patterns formed with *all* the people involved in a social situation. People's behaviour is not only determined by influences and 'causes', including the interventions of workers and others. It is also guided by the decisions or indecisions people make, based on their judgements of the situation. Understanding how decisions, or lack of them, are made involves at least six areas of understanding:

• insight into the recurring patterns of relationships between people, groups and organisations that precipitate and perpetuate social problems or those that promote the well-being of most participants;

• how to enhance people's ability to identify who should do what, with whom, to bring about positive change or to sustain effective relationships;

• the way different people construe their worlds, how they think and feel about others and react to events – specifically what they see as 'social problems', be it certain kinds of behaviour or 'unmet needs', and what they would consider appropriate solutions and responses;

- reconciling the inevitable conflicts that arise in the different perceptions of social situations and social problems and how to manage different vested interests;
- how to negotiate and renegotiate with people about who can do what to resolve social problems and to manage the coordination of the resources required;
- how to work with people to increase the choice and control they can have over their lives and expand their behavioural repertoire so that they can put new solutions into practice if they choose to do so.

All acts are necessarily social, involving other people who are themselves participants in all the wider changes of the modern world. Consequently a holistic practice theory reflects the variations of context, culture and power, including access to resources such as money, housing, employment, transport and information. Rather than being overwhelmed by fearing diversity and differences of opinion, we recognise that both are a rich resource, and inevitable. They present opportunities to test and revise our vision of practice and what it can achieve.

The whole enterprise: promoting dependable social networks

The whole social work enterprise is about promoting the development of dependable communities and other social networks, as well as confronting specific social issues, such as the care of vulnerable children and adults, and the social control of people whose behaviour is seen by society as 'a problem'. It is not just that social work is more effective if carried out in collaboration with others: achieving collaboration between all those involved in social problems is an integral essential part of the task. It can only be carried out through partnerships with others: through teamwork with many people in the community and with other organisations and institutions. We cannot do the work on our own, any more than an individual can have or be labelled as a social problem in isolation from other people.

Social problems are not the exclusive province of social work. Partnerships with others, often with many others, are involved. It would be perverse to stand alone as an occupation at a time when more orthodox occupations are recognising that their boundaries have to become more permeable. Nor can we claim to have clear-cut answers on how to tackle all these problems. Practice is a problem solving process, not a simple matter of the application of ready-made solutions. We have much to learn in each set of individual circumstances, and in the relationship between individual circumstances and the major social problems of the day.

A holistic viewpoint cannot be described by a simple linear theory where we assume that A causes B and could be put right by C. People's lives, including our own, are often messy, frequently illogical and subject to many factors beyond our own control. Those who use social services often have multiple interacting difficulties and are socially excluded through stigma and discrimination, and resource deficits. All these factors reduce the control we have over our own lives. Thus the *process* of practice will rarely be straightforward and will require changes in direction to stay relevant and effective.

The rest of this book develops and enlarges on these themes, starting with a discussion of the necessity for social workers and the organisations they work for to begin to see themselves as much as development workers and development agencies to communities and other social systems, as providers of 'aid' to individual social 'casualties'.

3

Formulating the Task: Aid or Development?

Introduction

In the previous chapter we discussed changes in the wider social context which necessitate rethinking the place of social work in the spectrum of responses to social problems, and outlined the major issues which a holistic approach seeks to address: in particular, the need to develop a view of the task which coherently encompasses its many seemingly diverse dimensions. In this chapter we discuss directly the fundamental purposes of social work.

Social work is not and could not be an all-powerful force that solves the social problems of individuals or the communities and societies they live in. Many people and organisations are engaged in the task, from central and local government, private and voluntary organisations, to every individual citizen. We have stressed that many of the same problems that social workers become involved in are managed or resolved by individuals, families and their immediate social networks, without intervention from any organisation. Social work is typically involved when the usual ways of providing care for ourselves and others are insufficient, break down or are carried out by parents, relatives or others, in ways which place vulnerable people at risk of harm. The task is not to take over from the predominant care-and-control mechanisms, but to add to these ways of resolving social problems, contributing particular expertise where problems persist, become intransigent and require a third-party intervention.

A holistic approach to practice helps workers and their managers strike a balance between:

- doing things *with* people
- doing things *for* people

- doing things *to* people on behalf of others, and
- *enabling* people to do things for themselves.

These four possible relationships between workers and others have always been central to social work practice, but have to be reconsidered and reformulated to be relevant to modern social, economic and political conditions. To highlight some of the tensions currently experienced in practice we will build on the analogy introduced in Chapter 1 of the distinction between the provision of aid and of development.

Aid and development

Aid downstream or development upstream?

Issues about who should care for whom, how it should be done and the balancing of empowerment and social control and conflicts of interests run through the practice of social work the way a river runs through a valley. When to intervene is as important as what we are getting into and what we aim to do.

Aid can be given to individuals, families, groups, or to whole populations. Development work has to include working with groups in communities – people who may be in a similar situation to Carol and those potentially in her social network. There are limitations to what can be achieved through social work governed by statutory resourced provision focused on individuals. In addition, this provision can be oppressive and undermining for people who are poor or experience structural disadvantage or discrimination. For example people living in poverty, black, ethnic and other minority groups and disabled people, find some social work interventions and social care services profoundly unhelpful (Beresford and Turner, 1997; Ahmad, 1990; Butt and Mirza, 1996; Butt and Box, 1997; Cambell and Oliver, 1996; Cambell and Lindow, 1997; Oliver, 1990, 1993; Morris, 1993, 1996; People First, 1994a, 1994b). The resources that people living in these communities have developed have very different priorities and philosophies from those of workers and statutory organisations (Harding and Beresford, 1996). Aid can range from being useful and supportive, to undermining and ignoring the resources and experience of those receiving it, either because of what it is or how it is delivered.

River rescues or upstream work?

Preventative activity or development is sometimes referred to as 'upstream' work (Egan, 1994). It comes from a metaphor likening crisis work to rescuing drowning people. Lifeguards jump into the river to rescue first one person, then another and then another. When the fourth appears they realise that somebody has to go upstream to try to stop these people getting into the water or to find a way for them to get out before both they and the lifeguards are exhausted or overwhelmed.

In the USA the categorisation of funding for different client groups, and increasingly in the UK the growing practice of creating different categories of problem based on specialist services, leads to the image of a row of lifesavers lined up on the river bank, each with a different colour of hat. None of them can enter the water unless the drowning person wears a matching colour. If their lifeguard is busy, people have to change the colour of their clothing to get saved. People without clothing that matches a coloured hat do not attract attention and are not rescued. Because they, or their organisations, only get paid when they enter the water, none of the lifesavers go upstream. Upstream work becomes truly heroic. First, it will probably be impossible to prove that you saved any lives; second, you won't get paid; and third, you will lose the friendship of all your colleagues downstream, robbed not only of some or all of their income, but also of their more obvious heroism.

This metaphor highlights only a particular part of the story. Lifeguards do not stand alone in the task of handling crises. When most people get into trouble they are kept afloat or helped out by others in their social network. We have seen in Chapter 2 that, although crucial to some, social services are peripheral to most care in the community, just as the justice system is to most social control, or health services to health (Graham, 1984; Glendinning and Millar, 1987). Consequently practice should start from recognising the need to work *with* these people. Wherever possible it should not take over what responsibility or control people already have. Where responsibility and control are taken away, efforts should be made to ensure that people regain control over their situations as quickly as possible, and are then once again assumed to be responsible.

Sending emergency aid to people in need, while often essential, is insufficient as a long-term solution to persistent problems. In the first place, resources for food production and appropriate changes in social, political and economic conditions will enable people to provide for themselves and engage in the give and take of social relationships.

Secondly, the way emergency aid is provided to individuals and populations can in itself contribute towards the difficulties of developing and carrying out longer-term strategies towards the goal of self-sufficient interdependence *with* others rather than dependence *on* others. Past histories of the relationships between countries, such as colonialism, and existing power relationships can influence the assessment of what is needed and how it is perceived once the initial crisis has subsided. The provision of aid and development resources is complicated by always being part of wider processes of change in which 'providers' attempt to exert influence or control over 'receivers', perhaps through intermediate organisations. In international aid and development these are the United Nations, the World Bank and the International Monetary Fund. In short, aid and development are aspects of control, with one or more countries trying to 'do something' about what is perceived as the 'needs' or shortcomings of another. Experiences in Bosnia, Somalia and other parts of the world illustrate the complex relationships between aid, development, conflict resolution and control. Implicit in many of the relationships between the 'developed' North and the 'developing' South is the false assumption that 'they' should be more like 'us': that the path of progress is for all societies to become industrialised, use intensive agriculture for food production and 'modernise' their economies.

Balancing aid and development

Similar questions about purpose and outcome exist for social work. Our assumption is that the *primary* task is concerned with:

- protecting vulnerable people at risk of abuse;
- maintaining people in their own homes when their need for support exceeds the dependability of their immediate social situation through providing services;
- creating systems which enable more people to have access to resources so that they can organise their own support for independent living;
- working to reduce the incidence of discrimination and social exclusion;
- supporting and helping individuals, families, groups and communities to become more dependable by enhancing their capacity to prevent people needing rescue or direct services from outside organisations;

- providing accommodation with social care support when it is either temporarily or permanently not possible for a person to live in his or her own home or with relatives or friends;
- exercising authority on behalf of the wider society to make sure people discharge their own responsibilities for caring for others appropriately;
- intervening in people's lives to change self-destructive or anti-social behaviour;
- working in communities to reduce the incidence and impact of such anti-social behaviour;
- developing the resources of the community to care for more of its members by reducing the burden on carers through introducing more neighbourhood support.

Inevitably there will be conflicting perceptions about the balance to be struck between resourcing immediate aid and longer-term development work in terms of both the broad purpose of social work, social care and provision, and in the response required in individual instances. It is impossible to do everything. A balance will also need to be established between care functions and exercising social control. Formal social control is exercised through the authority and mandate of the duties placed on the organisation through statute, or in the voluntary and private sector through contracts with a statutory body. Just as in education where there is a hidden curriculum through which the norms and values of society are passed on to children by teachers, so in social work organisations in all sectors there are hidden social control agendas implemented through the practice of social workers and the priorities of their organisations. The rationing of resources, whether through a policy such as targeting the most needy or through local priority setting, implicitly or explicitly declares that some service users are more deserving than others. Care and control functions are inextricably locked together.

Gary and Carol's story illustrates the questions about what balance should be struck between:

- **Providing emergency aid** – this can take various forms: money, advice and information, provision such as day care, counselling or group work, and so on.
- **Using the organisation's authority** to rescue Gary who could be provided with good enough alternative care and have minimal or no contact with his mother and the rest of his family. Alternatively,

there could be shared care where Carol remains an integral part of Gary's life, since we know that most children in Gary's position return home in a relatively short time after they have been on the Child Protection Register (DoH, 1995).

● **Development work with local parents** including individuals like Carol, their families and neighbours and locally based provider organisations, to create local resources so that they can meet their own needs without further emergency aid or rescue.

● **Development work with mainstream organisations** such as health, education, housing and transport to promote social well-being and social inclusion.

More generally, the development work and emergency aid that workers are involved in includes:

● Supporting carers indirectly by expanding the range of people involved in providing support for adults, through attempting to involve wider family members and others in the neighbourhood.

● Working with staff in other organisations to change their attitudes towards identified service users or carers of children or adults who, because they are stigmatised, find it hard to change.

● Entering into negotiations with people not typically seen as involved in social care, but whose attitudes and behaviour have a considerable, if indirect, impact on the perpetuation or resolution of social problems. Examples include using social policies to promote employment, through discussions with local business managers who might change their employment conditions so that people in situations like Carol's can take up work. Other actions could include advising policy makers and other organisations involved in tackling social problems on the impact and consequences of their policies; or setting conditions in contracts for bus companies that require easier access for people with mobility difficulties, or carrying heavy shopping or children.

● Negotiating with people who have conflicts of interest and different expectations and identifying how far the organisation's mandate for social control extends.

Social control

Currently the social control dimensions of practice and the centrality of working with conflicts of interests are masked by describing everything that workers do either in service delivery language or by that ambiguous term 'care'. This has meant that in social services as opposed to criminal justice organisations, the social control and conflict resolution functions are often implicit rather than explicit in discussions about how the work should be done. This contributes to the complexity of and misunderstandings about the task.

The social control functions are complex. When asked, service users frequently describe social workers in particular as agents of social control. For example, the image of the social worker as one who judged parents and took their children away was dominant amongst those who were offered and received help following the Hillsborough disaster (Newburn, 1993). This image persisted even amongst those who appreciated the help they received. They simply thought that their social worker was an exception to the rule. Acts of Parliament give authority to workers in statutory organisations to act to protect children and adults from abuse of specific kinds; to work with offenders of all ages and people with specific vulnerabilities such as mental health problems and learning difficulties; to protect certain people 'at risk' from their own behaviour. In these instances the social control function is explicit. Less obvious is intervention in the form of assessments of need and care management when an older person is referred by a third party and faced with leaving their own home for residential care 'for their own good'.

Power and powerlessness

Many users or carers have already proved to be outside the usual social control mechanisms, for example those who abuse or neglect children or adults; individuals engaging in persistent, dangerous or self-destructive behaviour; young and adult offenders. Government has the power to exercise sanctions over these people and the worker often has the authority, shared with courts and other workers, to take or initiate action. But nobody has the power to make these people do what society wants them to do. Social workers, together with other agents of social control, often take turns in attempting to do something that will make a difference, or at least contain such problems. This is graphically illustrated by the way that a small number of children and young people whose behaviour causes great concern are passed round the education, health and social services systems: a process that has been described as 'accommodation pinball' (Brown, 1996).

Paradoxically these same individuals who seem so beyond anyone's control may themselves feel powerless. They may also appear powerless to others who perceive them as being caught up in a predetermined set of responses to their situation that perpetuates both the problems they seem to make for themselves, and the problems they cause others. Some will choose to act in a way that risks society's sanctions; others will be deprived of real options or believe themselves to have 'no choice'. We are not suggesting that these processes always, or even often, involve rational choices. Most often decisions to act, or failures to do so, are based on the mixture of perceived facts, feelings, assumptions and beliefs that guide us all.

It is not uncommon for *all* parties to feel powerless, while appearing to others to be powerful. Workers can feel they have no power over the behaviour of parents and others, and so 'have no choice' but to act to rescue a child or an adult who is vulnerable. In doing so they appear all-powerful to parents and children, adults and their carers, who themselves may feel that they have no control over their circumstances. The 'objective truth', even if it could be defined, is less important than the different perceptions and expectations involved in perpetuating such relationships (see Chapter 8). The change agent's task is to help participants shift the way they see and act towards each other to enable them to participate in new patterns of behaviour that will open up new options, reduce or remove risk of harm or improve the levels of support available.

Empowerment

Empowerment is easy to talk about, but harder to achieve. From the 1980s onwards, the literature of social work is permeated with the term. All too often it means different things to workers and to people who use services. Empowerment is about people participating in the choices that affect their lives, and gives them greater control. The Disabled People's Movement speaks of independent living as a key factor in empowerment (Morris, 1996). When social control features as a major dimension of intervention then empowerment is about helping people regain as much control over their lives as possible, even when choices are circumscribed. Service users contributing to the Citizen's Commission on the Future of the Welfare State saw empowerment as arising from being seen as citizens contributing to society as opposed to being a liability to it, and from an increase in the opportunities to move out of welfare through education and training (Beresford and Turner,

1997). Essential though work with individuals is, it is rarely sufficient on its own. Change can only come through unlocking reciprocal relationships that bind people in their current unhelpful situations or antisocial behaviour. Any moves to facilitate the empowerment of some people are likely to lead to conflicts of interest with key members of the relationships they are in. These arise not only from personal relationships, but from some groups seeing others as scroungers or irresponsible, as 'not like us' or 'other' (hooks, 1991).

Managing conflicts

The management of conflict, along with managing transitions and change, is at the heart of social work. There will always be conflicting interests and perceptions about the nature of the problem, possible solutions and who has responsibility for what. These differences will easily lead to different and often conflicting emphases on the need for aid and who should provide it, for development work and who should be encouraged to make people's situations more dependable, and who should exercise what form of social control to change unwanted behaviour. Similarly workers need to understand what their responsibilities are, if any, for changing social conditions which exclude people through poverty and discrimination or oppression – what levers can be used or partnerships formed to promote social inclusion.

Gary and Carol's story as an example of identifying and managing conflict

The story of Carol and Gary's family contains a cluster of conflicts which the worker is attempting to help manage and mediate in. They involve a complex balance of different dimensions of conflict; for example:

1 Conflicts of social exclusion and inclusion
2 Conflicts through discrimination and oppression
3 Conflict in or between social networks
4 Conflicting assumptions about what is appropriate parenting behaviour
5 Conflict between parents and children.

Conflicts of social exclusion and inclusion

Carol is poor, unemployed and has few friends locally. Increasingly access to resources, income, and reduction of social isolation, is achieved through employment for women as well as men. Carol may feel excluded from the benefits of having adequate resources as an individual and a parent, and may feel less committed to social values and aspirations than the worker thinks appropriate for her own well-being, or Gary's in the future.

Her sense of exclusion can arise from something as basic as the food parents can afford to buy. The very poor have 'little room to manoeuvre' in seeking to provide a healthy diet for their children even though they may want to conform to social injunctions to do so (Dobson, Beardsworth and Walker, 1995; Lobstein, 1997; Kempson, 1996).

Carol and Gary's family are enmeshed in the fundamental social conflicts that exist in any society around the distribution of resources and the rights and duties of individuals, families and the wider community.

Poverty is not a reason for taking care proceedings, and most people living in poverty are good parents. But as we saw in Chapter 2, children in Gary's situation are far more likely to be taken into care than children living in families with more money and better housing. The worker balances:

- helping Carol with income maintenance issues;
- acting as a service provider;
- being a gateway to other welfare resources;
- working with Carol to see if she wants to find employment;
- ensuring appropriate care for Gary;
- assisting Carol to develop her self-advocacy and knowledge of her rights and entitlements;
- connecting her with local sources of support and friendships.

The worker and her team may well be involved in tackling poverty on a wider community level, working with local credit unions, food cooperatives, welfare rights groups, local job centres and training programmes. Without this work, much of the back-up support families living in poverty need will be unavailable. Carol and Gary are among many others in the local community who are poor.

Conflicts through discrimination and oppression

> Carol is a single parent and was known to social care and health agencies before she arrived in the area.

Discrimination, at individual, institutional and social levels, is often both the cause and the effect of conflict. Gary and Carol could experience discrimination because she is a single parent and dependent on income support. Had Carol been black or from a minority ethnic group, or disabled or mentally ill, this could have formed another source of discrimination which would interact in complex ways in her own and Gary's life and in the organisations they come into contact with. Pressures on her as a woman, single parent and newcomer to the area could also act as a focus of conflict. The worker, her colleagues and partners in other organisations would have a significant mediating role in such conflicts where they formed part of the social problems faced by Carol and Gary. The value base of social work which opposes discrimination (CCETSW, 1995) provides a touchstone against which policies and practice are judged.

Discrimination often forms the backdrop against which people live and they struggle daily with it. These issues frequently have to be tackled at the level of social policy, through the community and groups within it, including institutions such as schools and social care organisations. While work at the individual and family level is important as a means of reducing exclusion and discrimination, it has to be backed up by work in other areas and in collaboration with other organisations and workers. It is not only the individual and his or her relationships which are at issue, but the very context in which they exist and by which they can be distorted.

Conflict in or between social networks

> Carol has recently moved into the area away from her own family. She wants to make friends but does not want to be negatively judged, so she holds back from neighbours and appears to be rather withdrawn and guarded. This easily gets interpreted as standoffishness by those who would be her friends.

How professionals respond to this sort of embryonic conflict of expectations may be crucial to the capacity of Carol and her family to function independently. It would be easy to apply 'aid' type solutions, such as the provision of home support, day care or even respite care, or longer-term fostering for Gary, without recognising how this may undermine the usual development of both Carol and Gary's social networks, and the time and effort this might take. Hoffman's novel *Seventh Heaven* (1992) graphically illustrates how one divorced mother negotiated her way through prejudice, suspicion and bullying into new neighbourhood networks. In Carol's story, the worker involved Carol in a local group for mothers and children. A longer-term view might also consider training for employment, access to leisure and adult education.

Conflicting assumptions about what is appropriate parenting behaviour

> Carol was suspected of physically chastising Gary to a degree that the health visitor was concerned that it could be abusive.

In Gary and Carol's story the initial focus is on a parent using physical chastisement as a means of controlling her child. It is important in assessing the difference between appropriate force and abuse to remember that no culture accepts the physical abuse of children but that expectations about what is acceptable physical punishment differ significantly within the same society (DoH, 1995). The framework within which these judgements about limits are made comes from child protection legislation, local procedures and the wider cultural norms dominant at a particular time. In some countries, Sweden for example, physical punishment of children is illegal irrespective of who administers it, including parents. Except in clear instances of physical abuse, the worker has the difficult task of making judgements on behalf of society and mediates between different attitudes and expectations, including the varied perceptions of the various groups within the local community, different professionals, other key individuals and the family. Carol will have her own views, some of which will have been based on her own experience of being hit when she was a child. She may well be feeling bad about failing to live up to how she herself wanted to behave towards Gary, or she may feel that what she has done is no worse than anyone else she knows, or she may be fearful of getting out of control when she hits Gary.

Conflict between parents and children

> Gary is a bundle of energy, curiosity and mischief, constantly demand-
> ing attention. Depending on how *you* feel, he is annoying, stimulating,
> boring, amusing, exasperating, interesting or irritating.

The nature of Carol's conflicts with Gary may not be essentially
different from common parent–child conflicts. Others may manage
them through one partner letting off steam to another, or getting a
break by leaving the child with the partner or a relative, friend or
neighbour. These opportunities are unavailable to Carol for lots of
different reasons. Because these options have not been available for
some time, very ordinary parent–child conflicts have escalated into
potentially harmful patterns of mutually reinforcing behaviour which
are becoming more difficult for either of them to change. Expanding
Carol's social network, specifically being able to share the care of Gary
with competent others and get some time for herself, is a major function of family support. Like any intervention, aid may be necessary
but insufficient. If Gary and Carol are locked into a dysfunctional
relationship, then intervention will have to focus on changing perceptions and behaviour within the relationship. Had the risk to Gary been
greater than the probability of change, then, of course, more drastic
intervention would be necessary to secure his short-term safety while
longer-term changes are worked on.

Conflict resolution

Many of the social problems at the local level that social workers are
called upon to work with involve different levels of conflict resolution and decisions about when to intervene and with whom. Do the
lifesavers go upstream and stop people getting into the water – if so,
do they put up railings or engage in public education, or changing
the policies and practices of their own or other organisations? Should
they focus on saving those who are drowning? Do they start giving
swimming lessons and if so to whom – to all those who might get into
the water? Or should they improve the lifesaving techniques of those
who usually get people out of the water before they come downstream
drowning?

Many of the people who are the focus of social work have interrelated problems. These typically interact and intersect with each other. In our example, the worker's practice acknowledges this by:

- providing 'aid' through specific services;
- helping Carol and others develop their capacity for meeting their own needs for social support and socialisation;
- appropriately using the authority invested in her by her organisation;
- using her own credibility within the processes of negotiation.

Negotiations, shared perceptions and conflicts

Negotiations involving the main actors will work towards developing common perceptions of both shared and conflicting interests and goals so that necessary compromises and changes can be made by everyone. A more precise picture of the exact nature of the worker's task and role emerges by putting the exchanges between Carol and Gary and the worker within the wider framework of conflict mediation. Tasks include:

- identifying different levels of conflict
- setting expectations about Carol's parenting of Gary.

Real contradictions are often experienced by workers. For example, it is not uncommon to lose the trust built up through providing 'aid' to members of a family such as Carol's, and thus the possibility of further development work, when the same worker subsequently initiates social control through a legal action for child abuse based on what she has learned of the family through the 'aid' relationship. Workers unable to provide much hoped-for respite care to a daughter looking after her elderly mother with dementia might also face rejection if they attempt other forms of support. Service users and other members of the public enter into partnerships on a conditional basis, just as workers and their organisations place conditions on the delivery of their work.

The marginal worker

Increasingly the task is to create, recreate and support relatively temporary multidisciplinary networks of workers and others to tackle specific social problems, and then move on. People, like countries in our analogy, do not want to be or remain dependent on the aid, development or social control activities of social services, whether from the statutory, voluntary or private sectors. The danger of not going beyond an 'aid' response is that the recipients of aid will not have been helped to maintain, gain or regain greater control over their lives, and thus the provision of aid will become a permanent necessity. In the vast majority of instances this is something neither party wants (Beresford and Turner, 1997; Evans, 1995).

A mediating role

The importance of the mediation role of social work is reinforced by the effects of geographical mobility, divorce, employment patterns and the impact of poverty and fluctuating incomes on people's support systems. Networks may be characterised by different features than in the past and be less able, because of either geographical distance or their fragility, to provide the support expected of them. With increasingly sophisticated divisions of labour in society, and the propensity to pay for the social functions which traditionally were carried out by people's own social and kin networks, the need for such mediation, sometimes over substantial geographical distances and between conflicting demands, may well be increasing.

Polarisations: beyond illusions of opposites

Work with Carol and Gary included activities that have been called 'casework', 'social support', 'counselling', 'individual needs assessment', 'child protection', 'care management' and 'service provision'. The approach described also included activities variously described as 'community development', 'community action', 'neighbourhood work', 'user empowerment' and 'social care planning'. These different ways of describing dimensions of the whole task have often contributed to unhelpful polarisations, in which one aspect of the work is seen as incompatible or in competition with another. When this happens, or particular activities are put in a hierarchy according to presumed status, essential tasks may not get addressed. This undermines a holistic approach to the social problem facing Carol and Gary. Without the development work which created the playgroup, there would not be the resource which Gary and Carol can then both use and contribute to.

Polarisations have in the past set in opposition:

- community work or community development versus casework or work with individuals, groups and families;
- voluntary and private versus statutory services;
- family, friends and local helping networks versus worker intervention;
- social care planning versus counselling;
- the volunteer versus the paid worker.

Each phase in the history of social work has been characterised by these debates, typically based on different starting points rather than substantial clashes of evidence (Timms, 1983; Harding and Beresford, 1996). This growing list of polarisations does not need revising; it is in urgent need of rethinking to change the way we consider these problems and their possible solutions.

The opposition between working with the community or social network, and working with the individual and family, is rooted in more fundamental and equally misleading orthodox divisions between psychology and sociology. Although recognition of the way social problems cross traditional boundaries around health, education, housing and income support is now enshrined in legislation, many underlying polarisations still remain. These structure the worker's actions and can maintain divisions at the expense of the interests of people who use services. We have to break out of these illusions of opposites. If workers are really going to work in partnership with parents, families, other organisations and workers, the framework is that of people as citizens sharing with social work the usual way they tackle their problems and accepting its contribution.

Spuds or potatoes: an illustration

Watzlawick *et al.* (1974) illustrates such illusions of opposites with a story of a resistance movement's activities in prewar Nazi Germany. The National Socialists put up posters with the slogan 'National Socialism or Communism?' The resistance movement added a sticker saying 'Spuds or Potatoes?' A significant effect of the characteristic polarisations found in social work has been encouragement of an emphasis on the individual client and/or the immediate family as the focus of most, if not all intervention. Even where it is recognised that a holistic or ecological perspective is required, there is a tendency to regress to the individualisation of social problems under stressful circumstances. A holistic approach to practice helps workers and others retain an equal focus on the individuals involved in social problems, and the patterns of relationships between those individuals which add up to the problem itself.

Social work is not a compromise, a collection of activities lumped together to suit the convenience of the day and the current trend in organisational philosophy. A holistic approach to human behaviour and social problems explains why sometimes our intervention is not required, while in other situations the same problems are resolved by our interventions, while yet again the same problem presented in very much the same circumstances resists all our efforts to bring about change. Conventional segmentalised approaches are significantly incomplete.

Unintended consequences: beyond the good intentions of aid, development and social control

The belief that our interventions are inevitably either helpful or at least neutral in their effects is no longer tenable. It has in addition been shaken by scepticism about 'professionals' in general (Schorr, 1992), by specific, high-profile scandals within social work, and research which demonstrates the negative impact of some interventions (Cheetham *et al.*, 1992), especially in the user-led research (Cambell and Lindow, 1997; Morris, 1996; Beresford and Turner, 1997) and research on child protection. There is also sound evidence of positive contributions (DoH, 1995). Just as the behaviour of the worker is crucial in determining the quality of a service (Harding and Beresford, 1996), their judgements about how to intervene can also be as much part of the problem as part of the solution. An earlier episode in the story of Carol and Gary illustrates how this can happen.

Carol had moved to her current address following eviction for rent arrears. She had left her home town a year or two earlier, where she had referred herself to the social services asking for help with Gary because he was 'uncontrollable and aggressive'. The social worker recognised several different ecological factors influencing her situation, such as low income, estrangement from her parents, and her position as a very young mother. Nonetheless she accepted Carol's framing of the problem as being something intrinsic to Gary. This was demonstrated less by what was overtly said or done, than by the provision of aid in the form of 'direct work' with Gary.

The social worker had a student placed with her who wanted experience of direct work with children, and this seemed like a good opportunity to meet both some of Gary's needs and those of the student. The student arranged a series of sessions at a local clinic in which she used 'non-directive play' with Gary and skilfully established rapport with him. He generally enjoyed the sessions, although on more than one occasion expressed a wish to go home early. Carol continued to say that Gary's behaviour at home was unacceptable, and gradually began to withdraw from involvement with the student and her own worker.

Carol was at the same time being seen by a health visitor, who reported concerns about Gary being 'unhappy' and 'emotionally neglected'. It was at this time that Carol left the area. This health visitor's notes followed Carol to the new area and contributed to the second health visitor's concerns.

The way in which workers assess or construct a social problem can turn them unwittingly into contributors to its very existence. The response reinforced Carol's problem with Gary. Workers are not simply external, objective applied social scientists, reporting and responding to the facts of the social situation. Accepting, or imposing, a definition of the problem as being 'in Gary' is not to respond to an objective fact, but to contribute to the way his behaviour and hence he himself is constructed as 'the' social problem. The workers are as much part of this definition of the social problem as are Carol, Gary or anyone else. This is not a negative to be eliminated from the scene but a fact to be recognised. The construction placed on Carol and Gary's situation and the resources brought to bear on it were very different in the two independent interventions. Not a great deal had changed in Gary's behaviour by the time the second social worker became involved.

The different organisations' statutory and legal responsibilities and aims contribute to the problem being defined and redefined in quite unpredictable and often unexpected ways. This produces unforeseen and unforeseeable consequences for everyone. The good intentions of offering 'counselling/play therapy' to Gary had unintended consequences, contributing unwittingly to Carol feeling increasingly unable to cope and deskilled as a mother, and hence increasingly resentful towards Gary.

Does the provision of aid, development and social control need expertise or can it just be left to commonsense and good will?

For many years there have been debates (Payne, 1996) among the general public and in social work itself about whether commonsense and personal experience alone are sufficient to do many of the things that social workers do. Our view is that social work comprises skilled and complicated activities, which Chapters 7, 8 and 9 explore. Here we will identify the nature of the expertise through Carol's story.

- Carol and the worker spend some time sharing information. To do this purposively it must be possible to establish a relationship of trust, especially in those situations where one or more people have reason to be suspicious if not hostile. The worker must be able to demonstrate that she and her team colleagues understand the predicament of the other people: 'see the world as they see it'. They must also know about their statutory obligations, the services available from the organisation and the potential resources obtainable from all aspects of the community, and be able to communicate these to the people they work with.
- The here-and-now relationship between Carol and Gary is observed by the worker, and she must be able to judge the degree of risk to Gary and understand the nature of the relationship, how it has developed from the past, and make a judgement about how it is likely to unfold in the future, and how intervention might change their reciprocal behaviour for the better.
- The worker has understood and reframed some dimensions of the problem to turn the insoluble into potentially achievable tasks, to recognise opportunities where only deprivation, limitations or hopelessness are perceived.
- The worker and her team colleagues will have engaged in a variety of other community-based inter-organisational activities to develop resources and make the neighbourhood more dependable.

All of these activities look like the kinds of things that many people do as part of their usual family, social and working lives. But social workers, like 'professional' singers, are paid: talent, training and skill should make them better than many amateurs. But we recognise that this is not always the case, for some amateurs are naturally extremely talented and there are also many informal ways of developing skills and knowledge. There are also many styles of singing which are learned in different ways, just as there are many approaches to helping people resolve problems. When social workers are involved, we, the public, have a right to expect them to perform at a consistently high level. Workers should also conduct themselves in certain ways to meet ethical standards, to protect those they work with and fulfil their obligations to the public they serve and the organisations that employ them. By this definition there is no distinction between a home help and a qualified social worker or a head of a residential home or senior manager. As citizens we may or may not be good at tackling social problems, just as we may but do not have to be able to sing. Social workers and their managers may engage in activities which are not essentially different from the stuff of usual social interaction. In the vast majority of instances they are only involved when the usual support systems have failed or given up because the problem has become too complex for them to handle. However, workers and managers are accountable to the public they serve, and on whose behalf they exercise some dimensions of social control that directly affect some people's liberty and rights as citizens. This requires them to be able to describe the components of their expertise and meet the standards expected of them.

Social work education is grounded in theoretical understanding of the activity, the disciplined acquisition and rehearsal of practice skills and the acquisition and constant updating of relevant knowledge. The coherence of social work is more than just an incremental list of skills, methods, values and knowledge. Social work and its management is grounded in a fundamental and developing knowledge of and skills in the tasks of confronting social problems and the parts played by the different key players. There is a stated value system governing the way workers relate to service users and carers and an ethical code about behaviour to guide interventions in other people's lives (BASW, 1996; SCA, 1989). These values point not only to the role of social work in aiding people in distress, but also to a long history of promoting personal and social change.

Conclusion

In this chapter we have identified some key issues which a holistic approach to the practice of social work addresses, and have illustrated these through the analogy between the nature of social work responses to social problems within a community, and the responses of more 'developed' countries to the social, economic and political problems of the 'developing' world. We next move beyond these metaphors of support and control, and address directly ways in which contemporary social problems can be understood and tackled through a reinvention of the 'traditional' ideas and practices of social work.

We shall do this by presenting a framework which synthesises the different key tasks teams need to address, and which describes the key stages of negotiation necessary to achieve the task in partnership with all those involved in particular social problems.

4

Mapping the Task
and Processes

Introduction

We have argued in the preceding chapters that community-based practice requires a synthesis of often artificially polarised activities, and illustrated this through discussing the distinction between aid and development approaches to tackling social problems. The task of social workers is not unwittingly to take over and become central to people's problem solving through 'aid' activities, but to contribute to the usual ways that the community, family and individuals solve their social problems. In this chapter we present a way of coherently framing the diversity of typical social work activities, and a way of framing the characteristic processes of negotiation involved in building community-based partnerships.

Most social care is provided through the partnerships and support systems which we form through our personal and family relationships, our links in our workplace, the groups to which we belong and religious organisations. Social work activities evolve through partnerships between paid workers and other people in the community, including a variety of citizens and workers from other organisations and services. Social workers are but one participant, often only temporary, both at the general level of care within the community and in the specific situations of people who use services. Although complex and changing, it is possible to map or signpost the social work task in terms of:

- **Content and outcomes**: the key tasks which members of a team must address in partnership with others, in order to be sure of desired outcomes at all levels of particular social problems.
- **The process over time**: the key stages of negotiation through which team members arrive at the specific aims and methods relevant to

the social problems being addressed within central, national and organisation policy and local circumstances.

A map of the content of social work

The main areas of activity are illustrated by the story of the Jones family.

The Jones family

The Jones family includes Mrs Jones, her daughter Shirley and son-in-law Colin. Mrs Jones is in hospital following a fall. She is referred for residential accommodation by a hospital doctor who has spoken to Shirley. Shirley and Colin have said that they cannot have her at home. An assessment is called for. The worker introduces himself to Mrs Jones, explains why he is involved and seeks permission to talk to members of her family. The worker considers conducting a detailed interview with Mrs Jones, but having ascertained that she expects to go home they decide together that the worker should check out what is happening at home: to check on the dependability of Mrs Jones's home situation. The worker also plans to arrange for a discussion with Mrs Jones and health staff, possibly involving Shirley and Colin, to reach a shared understanding of Mrs Jones's immediate and potential level of mobility and what support she needs during the day and night.

During these first encounters the worker carefully explains that he is not necessarily there to provide services but to offer help through identifying what people want and to see who can do what to help so that their needs are met wherever possible: to help balance different, and sometimes difficult, choices that they may make to arrive at a sustainable situation. He will also provide information about the services available from his own and other organisations, and about the eligibility criteria that exist.

When he meets Shirley and Colin and hears them describe their situation and the events leading to the referral, the worker learns that they feel unable rather than unwilling to cope with the demands of supporting Mrs Jones. They know that Mrs Jones wants to get home as soon as possible. Their needs are:

- Time to sort out their feelings and what they want to do. They felt under pressure from the doctor, who has pressures of her own, when they said that they could not have Mrs Jones at home. They have not yet 'really discussed it with Mother'.
- Help in sorting out what they want and what they can realistically offer Mrs Jones, because they have strongly conflicting feelings.

> • To have Mrs Jones out of Shirley's way for at least part of the day. Mrs Jones, a gregarious woman, needs company. Colin does not want this always to be Shirley. Shirley feels she will need some relief from the caring tasks to avoid further damaging her relationships with her mother and husband.

The worker's involvement up to this stage has been an example of:

• **direct intervention:** an engagement with individuals and their immediate family and networks to tackle problems which directly affect them.

The worker is aware that if he launches straight into the complicated process of assessing eligibility, finding and drawing up contracts for an appropriate service, it is easy then to slip into taking over from and ignoring the resources that have already been coping right up to the referral. These resources may have become overstretched rather than have disappeared altogether.

The worker uses the knowledge he has built up of the neighbourhood. For example, he suggests that Shirley and Colin contact a local carers group. Another member of the team helped set this group up – but the group members are now wanting to be more self-sufficient, and the management committee are making plans to become a not-for-profit provider organisation. This development is a priority identified in the social services department's community care plan. The initiation of this group is a typical example of:

• **indirect intervention:** work with wider community groups and other organisations to tackle problems which affect a range of people including the individuals involved in direct work.

The initiation of the group required some complex negotiations between a member of the worker team, two local health visitors and their manager, members of the committee of two different local charitable organisations, a Caribbean community group, and the worker's own manager. For the formation of this carers group to succeed, some of these people had to change some of their priorities and expectations and reach agreements to allow yet other people to become involved and provide various resources. In short, a number of changes had to take place in the way people perceived and responded to some aspects of the social problem of older people and their carers. The member of the adult care team worked with a small group of carers of people receiving department services to initiate, facilitate and follow through the development of this group. The indirect interventions of the staff involved with the carers group have been, and continue to be, of two kinds:

- **change agent activity**
- **service delivery.**

Change agent activity

This is work to effect change in the ways people relate to each other that precipitate or perpetuate social problems at individual, family, group and community levels. It includes the way resources, such as the worker's and the team's time, are allocated and accessed by other organisations, local groups, individuals and families.

If the carers group did not exist, one of the resources which would prove to be helpful to Mrs Jones and her family would not have been available. It could not have been created just for them. Investment in the development work necessary to ensure resources are available when required is as much a central part of the whole task as is any direct work with individuals and families, and often involves bringing about complex changes in the ways in which people are currently tackling particular problems. Social work is more than administering and gatekeeping current resources; it requires the support and recreation of existing resources and the creation or commissioning of new resources to meet new and developing needs in the community. Currently in the UK social care organisations are developing their strategic planning, purchasing and commissioning roles as a growing proportion of direct provision of services is coming from the private and voluntary sectors. The employment bases of workers are much more diverse than in the past, with a growing number employed directly by disabled people as personal assistants. Being able to map out the aim of a specific contribution, that of their own and other organisations and community activities, becomes a core task.

Service delivery

This work involves the maintenance of certain social situations by the provision of services in order to maintain people living in their own homes or in residential care. These complement care home services to reduce risks to vulnerable people, overload for carers and parents, and avoid further distress or unnecessary and unwanted admission to care homes.

The carers group has been supported through the provision of a range of resources from the social services department. It has received financial support for organising links with a voluntary 'sitting' service for some very frail older people who cannot be left alone, the use of local authority accommodation and some administrative help. The group provides a range of services, such as a lunch club. Support for the policy of the redirection of organisation resources from provision of direct care came directly from legislation and change to the statutory responsibilities of the organisation.

The significance of direct work with Mrs Jones remains. This is change oriented. The worker does not take responsibility for the problem. He recognises that changes in views and in the patterns of relationships are needed if the care network is to be reshaped, supported and extended. In just the same way, the worker and his organisation do not take responsibility for meeting all the collective needs of carers in the local area, but work with them and a range of others to receive support from an extended network of care.

The worker counsels Mrs Jones, who is grieving for the loss of physical capacity and independence and relives many of the experiences of the death of her partner. This is direct change agent work. Changes in Mrs Jones's expectations of herself, of others, and in her understanding of how others perceive the problem, may be a necessary part of the negotiations needed in her network in order to change the pattern of who does what. Options are identified and discussed: residential care or home with certain conditions. Neither was originally Mrs Jones's choice. She, like most of us, cannot get all she wants – but she can remain in as much control as possible over what happens.

A visit to the lunch club run by the carers group three days a week is suggested to help Shirley further. Mrs Jones agrees to a trial period, and in addition accepts the use of a bathing service provided through the social services department. The former is an example of an indirect service for Mrs Jones; and the latter, a direct service to her and the carers involved. The arrangement of these services at the individual and family level is for essentially the same purpose as at a more communal or organisational level. Policy support (Carers (Recognition and Services) 1996 Act) for the right of carers to a separate assessment and services recognises their central importance in the lives of the people they support, the role they play as the backbone of care in the community and the wisdom of building on, and not taking over from, the usual patterns of care.

The carers group helps the social services team indirectly maintain people in the community. The direct provision of services to individuals such as Mrs Jones achieves the same purpose. The unit of assessment is the social situation as a whole, and this approach at the same time meets formal requirements for separate assessments for Mrs Jones as the service user and Shirley as her carer.

The importance of process and time

The story of the Jones family could go on to describe the different interventions and arrangements that have to be made, as changes in any one person's contribution or circumstances have repercussions on the other people and services involved. Implicitly or explicitly negotiation has to take place with all these people to monitor who is doing what and who is prepared to do what under what circumstances. These negotiations are often complex and very detailed. Failure to take sufficient time, or not attending to the process, can lead to arrangements which are not dependable or services which do little, are irrelevant or even make the situation worse. Mrs Jones, Shirley and Colin will be directly involved in some of these relationships as they unfold over time, and indirectly in others; but should be kept involved in, or at least abreast of, all the discussions the worker engages in. People's circumstances change over sometimes quite short periods of time, and further change agent activity may be necessary both directly with Mrs Jones and with her immediate family. The family's relationships with workers from organisations may alter, involving changes in the services provided directly or indirectly by the social work team. What happens in this family and other situations like theirs may result in identifying other social problems requiring longer-term development work in the area, the commissioning of new services, or reframing existing ones to meet new needs and changing expectations.

This amount of interacting detail can become confusing and overwhelming. The worker can lose the picture of the whole – not seeing the wood for the trees – unless he uses practice tools such as the map to chart out the different forms of activity that took place to negotiate the support available to Mrs Jones.

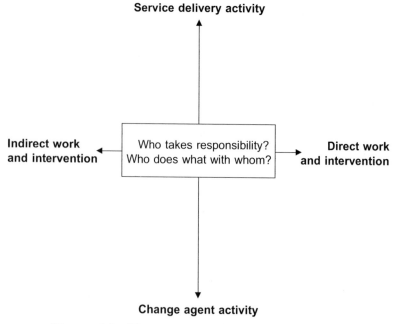

Figure 4.1   The content map of social work tasks

Although not appropriate at this point for Mrs Jones, the team had also undertaken change agent activities with, for example, the local housing associations which were moving to supported housing with care, and a private care home providers' group to offer respite care on a flexible basis; as well as joint work with the primary care group on promoting the health of older people in the community.

The content of the task using the map

The diagram is a map, not an axis along which things can be measured: there is not a 'continuum' from 'change agent activity' to 'service delivery'. A map is a device for finding our way around. Features are abstracted, given symbols and plotted to provide 'landmarks' for planning a journey or locating the position of one feature relative to another. There are several other important points to bear in mind when using this map to analyse social work and social services activity.

Work in each of the quadrants is equally necessary
A major tension in current policy and practice is between strategies for targeting highest need, and preventative strategies aimed at providing

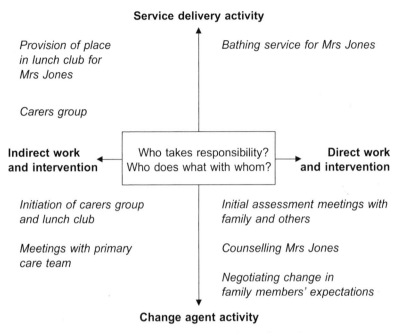

Figure 4.2 Mapping the specific tasks

non-stigmatising help at an earlier stage to prevent, or at least delay, people falling into the 'most needy' category. Yet there is evidence which shows the positive impact of support at an early stage for carers of people with dementia (Levin *et al.*, 1998). Similarly, young offenders requiring secure accommodation in their teens have been identified as children with problems during the primary years of their education (Falshaw and Browne, 1997; Crowley 1998). We have illustrated this tension in Chapter 3 with the metaphor of people falling into the river and the need for upstream work. This map assumes that both levels of work are necessary, and it can be used to identify how they are integrated into practice.

Where to intervene, whether to engage in direct intervention and aid or to engage in indirect development work, will depend upon many factors, including an understanding of the consequences of our interventions. It is often easier to think through issues by stepping outside our own frameworks, and drawing upon analogies and parallels from elsewhere (Watzlawick, 1993). Our next metaphor, our 'as if', is drawn from ecology.

Greenfly can be tackled with a chemical garden spray. Besides being expensive such interventions can cause their own problems. If the insecticide kills the ladybirds which eat the greenfly, then even more insecticide will be needed to kill the next crop of greenfly. Our understanding of ecology, and specifically the interrelationships between different species and their place in the environment, has changed the way we intervene in these problems. We can take more sophisticated action by inventing new insecticides which do not have harmful unintended consequences, or change the balance of relationships between parts of the ecological system within which the problem occurs: we might now introduce ladybirds rather than use insecticides at all. In many fields, such as agriculture, time and money in large quantities have been spent on understanding and developing solutions to such problems – more than is spent on research and development in understanding social problems.

An ecological model of both social work practice and provision provides an understanding of the detailed way in which parts of the whole social system relate to each other. There is a growing recognition of these dimensions of social problems. For example, the diversion approach to juvenile justice attempts to tackle offending behaviour without increasing the risk of offenders becoming entrenched in the long-term criminal behaviour associated with taking on a criminal identity (Children's Society, 1989). Similarly the emphasis on family support aims to maintain children with their families rather than risk further harm being caused through the separations involved in 'taking children into care' (DoH, 1995; National Commission of Inquiry into the Prevention of Child Abuse, 1996). Investment in the future as well as the present as a contribution to developing the community infrastructure for social care (Statham, 1996; Smale, 1996) is a priority for politicians, policy makers and senior managers.

Work in one quadrant of the map will have an impact on work in other quadrants

Work in one quadrant inevitably has consequences for work in the others, and managers and workers need to be able to decide how best to allocate resources and divide labour so that the impact on the *whole* task is maximised.

Teams recognising the significance of their work in all four quadrants of the map will monitor their **direct interventions**, both in relation to individual clients and their families as well as to the totality of their direct work, and the relation between the two. Sexual abuse was an issue in 10 families for one team. Monitoring was carried out at the individual family level, but also included monitoring of these families as a group and in relation to other populations. These activities can provide crucial information on what changes are necessary to support specific groups such as minority ethnic families (Bernard, 1994, 1997). The team also monitors their **indirect interventions**: their 'upstream', preventative, resource and community development work. This includes activities to improve working relationships with other organisations, workers and service providers. Managers have the task of finding out about what is going on in these task areas, both from within the team and from other organisations involved in the direct work. Teams adopting this approach have found it essential to develop workload management strategies as compared to focusing on caseloads as a measure of individual time available and the team's staffing needs (Law, 1989). Staff and management time has to be explicitly allocated to successfully develop schemes and projects involving either community groups or other services and organisations (Crosbie and Vickery, 1989). Some social services departments have implemented the changes proposed in the National Health Service and Community Care Act (1990) by introducing locality planning and commissioning units to focus on these areas of work, as a means of taking forward their strategic planning role within the local authority and with the health service.

Work will be going on in all four quadrants at once

There is a danger that the work of staff, or the organisation as a whole, is concentrated in one quadrant at a time without integrating work in all four quadrants, whether undertaken within the team or by managers, partner organisations and service providers. It is not uncommon to find that individually orientated workers and managers define direct work as 'real work' and see other tasks as peripheral or even an irrelevance. Indirect areas of practice are also increasingly seen as part of front-line or middle management work (Levin *et al.*, 1994), but to be effective have to be a part of everyone's responsibility if a fragmented approach is to be avoided. Segmentalising of the task can go even further. The tendency to make alliances with one person within a child's network to the detriment of others involved (Parker, 1996) can make things more manageable, but inevitably distorts the picture of the lives of the people we are working with and the resources they have or need access to. Carol's and the Jones family's stories illustrate how important it is to have a framework which takes a broader view of practice. The effectiveness of the division of labour relies on the way that the specialised contributions are coordinated. From this perspective social work is no more an individual enterprise than a social problem is an individual condition.

Changes in perceptions of the situation will change the location of the work

A worker may begin by engaging in some direct work, such as counselling a parent concerned about his child's behaviour, but in the process could become sufficiently concerned about the care of the child that he feels it necessary to move into direct service provision in the form of initiating care proceedings to provide the child with alternative care. It is crucial for the worker and his manager to notice that work relevant to one particular situation is likely to be going on in all four quadrants at once. Often work at different levels is undertaken by different organisations without reference to each other. Inter-organisation joint working is notoriously difficult to achieve and maintain (Audit Commission and SSI, 1997). Community care and children's services plans, followed through to the level of practice, should provide a means of focusing on the whole task in the social services field and not primarily the specific remit and priorities of a single organisation, as should community safety and juvenile justice policies. One task is identifying when there are blocks to using resources, including budgets, flexibly across organisations in order to bring together the means necessary to tackle a specific social problem in the local community.

The work of the Canklow team in Rotherham's Social Services Department in Yorkshire, England, illustrates a successful use of this starting point (Eastham, 1990). The team recognised that a large public housing estate produced a high percentage of the children received into care while housing a relatively small percentage of the children in the local authority area. They began by setting out to improve relationships with residents and other organisations and identifying how they could form partnerships to make a more effective response to the high level of referrals. Resources were provided to community groups and other organisations on the estate which provided support facilities and alternatives to high-risk activities. Other indirect change-agent interventions established relationships with extended families and wider community networks, encouraging people to help those who might otherwise have been individual referrals.

The task requires team work
The smallest unit which can undertake the whole task is a team, not an individual worker. The *whole* task may be all the social problems in a particular locality, or all the social problems associated with a particular user group, or the whole social problem of a particular family and social network such as the Joneses. Irrespective of the scale of the whole task, it will always require a team response.

Groups of workers are assembled to work with a particular focus. These teams may be geographically based, for example all the child protection problems in a particular locality, or all the juvenile justice problems in an authority; or may be teams assembled to address several different social problems in a given locality or community. Team members usually have different skills and expertise, often called 'skill mixes', which are required for the task in hand. In criminal justice, for instance, the team might include the probation officer, a psychologist, ex-offenders, an adult educationalist, secretarial and administrative support.

We define a **team** as 'all the people needed to accomplish a task'. There are:

1 **Agency-based teams**: By this definition workers grouped together under a manager or team leader comprise only one of the teams that the workers will be involved in.
2 **Multiple teams**: These organisation based teams are individual workers who will be members of other teams put together for a particular task: some will be time limited, others have longer-term remit. We have called these 'multiple' teams because their membership comes from diverse sources. They often have no clear line management structure and include people over whom the coordinator has no direct authority: who cannot as a last resort be either instructed to take action or to provide resources. These can include membership of:

   • inter-organisation or inter-profession teams
   • local community management committees
   • safer community groups
   • community regeneration teams
   • care package providers.

In Mrs Jones's case, the team is:

- Shirley and Colin
- social worker
- social care worker (bathing)
- carers group
- carers group support worker

- Mrs Jones
- GP
- volunteer driver
- hospital social worker
- community nurse.

Team work is like handling the baton in a relay race. If the team members do not achieve smooth and effective changeovers, synchronised and fully understood by each member, then it does not matter how fast each individual runs: they cannot perform well. Understanding and coordinating, let alone leading such teams, means constantly managing the tensions between relationships. The worker will be involved in a multiplicity of such teams – sometimes as leader, in others as coordinator or member. Those engaged in this collection of roles are sometimes called 'network entrepreneurs' to emphasise the need for someone to put time and energy into initiating and sustaining the network existing, extended or built around these situations (Smale, 1996).

The allocation of responsibility

Who takes responsibility for what provides the critical distinction between service delivery and change agent activity. To engage in change agent activity is to deliberately *not* take responsibility for the problem or its solution: for the change agent the task is to work with other people, helping them bring about change. The worker will have responsibility for facilitating processes of change, but not for the content of decisions made, services provided, or ongoing care and control of people.

Change can be brought about through mediating the conflicts of perception, expectation and interests between people which underpin many social problems. Conflicts will often centre on questions of who has responsibility for what in a social network, whose judgements and perspectives are or should be given priority, and what statutory authority the worker and others involved have in these negotiations. The characteristic activities of any change agent, described in Chapters 9, 10 and 11, include negotiation, persuasion, education, consciousness raising, problem solving, resource provision, information sharing.

To deliver a direct service is to acknowledge and accept some responsibility for a problem or its solution

This means providing something to help solve that problem, often by maintaining the status quo or preventing further deterioration in a person's situation. A clear example of this is the statutory process by which local authorities assume the care of children who have been abused, or are perceived to be at risk of abuse. The local authority staff accept responsibility by providing substitute or supplementary care. The children are in the public care (Utting, 1991) and the local authority is the corporate parent, and, as such, responsible for ensuring they receive adequate education, health and social care, and are safe from abuse (Utting *et al.* 1997; Kent, 1997).

The change agent/service delivery dimensions often overlap

Currently most discussions of social work activity implicitly assume that the task essentially consists of providing or arranging the delivery of services. This obscures very significant social control, conflict resolution and process dimensions of the whole task. Framing the task primarily in terms of 'assessing individual need and purchasing services to meet the need' can make much social work activity invisible because it is not just service delivery (Kearney, 1995; Platt, 1995; Rowlings, 1995). There are many ways of tackling social problems other than the provision or commissioning of direct services.

Mapping the content of the whole task – the main areas of activity which together make a coherent response to social problems – is a key feature of a holistic or ecological approach. A second is the characteristic social and interpersonal processes which ensure that team members' work is consistent with other key players, and in partnership with service users and other workers and organisations. The next section outlines a map of the crucial stages over time of negotiation and renegotiation which workers have to go through to define and redefine the problem and its possible solutions in partnership with all the other key actors.

Mapping the process of social work over time

Introduction: the spiral of negotiations

Although process is something which ill fits with an emphasis on measurable outputs, it is highly valued by the people who use services

(Harding and Beresford, 1996). This means that user-centred services and practice require the means to identify stages in that process and the means to analyse and review them.

The process map takes the form of a spiral, representing continuous, recurring activities that overlap because of the cyclical nature of social problem solving. Workers are aware that both they and the people who use services are involved in recurring activities. It is easy with this degree of complexity to feel at the mercy of events. At one moment all is calm, at the next all is in flood; but this process can be analysed and structured to support practice. The components which contribute to these changes include:

- physical and human development;
- the passage of time, sometimes over quite long periods for young people in the care system, for example, or for individuals, families, groups and communities where there are chronic and recurring problems;
- the stages in progressive illness or conditions;
- public attitudes to particular behaviour;
- social and economic conditions;
- the value base of social policies.

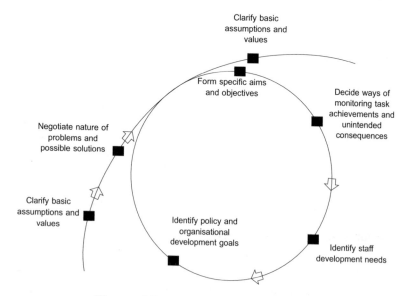

Figure 4.3 The spiral of negotiations

The spiral of negotiations: the process map

The process map signposts the basic steps a group of people take to negotiate and renegotiate definitions of the problem being addressed and its possible solutions. 'Negotiation' here means to 'settle by discussion and bargaining' and 'to pass over or through an obstacle' (*Shorter Oxford English Dictionary*, 1980). Collaborative social problem solving consists of involving all key players openly in decisions on who should do what for whom, and overcoming conflicts of perceptions and interest through discussion and bargaining in both social care and social control work. The content map is a flat two-dimensional picture which enables workers to chart out the territory. The process map provides a tool to describe the key points of the journey that has to be taken through that territory over time.

The image or metaphor of a spiral of change is not uncommon. For example, David Kolb (1984) describes a learning cycle that people follow in tackling problems; Charles Handy (1990) renamed this cycle 'the wheel of learning', with the four stages of deciding, doing, reflecting and connecting, each returning on themselves as the learner moves round the cycle; Giles Darvill (1997) uses this image in describing how workers and managers can develop new ways of working by 'breaking' established patterns of circularity. Similarly, many readers will be familiar with the idea of reflective practice and the reflective practitioner (Schon, 1983), and will recognise a congruence between the idea of reflection-in-action and the processes of negotiation which we outline here. In our use of this metaphor we emphasise the spiralling nature of circular processes of change – we may go round and round the same stages several times, but if the appropriate work is undertaken at each stage, then these circulations will also create forward progress, as with any spiral. In addition, we emphasise that it is teams, or networks of people, who negotiate their way round the stages of the spiral, not just individuals; and that this complexity needs to be taken into account.

It is useful at this point to review what assumptions the content map and the process spiral have in common. Both assume that:

- Social problem solving requires a team approach which usually involves a mix of skills and organisations, because no one individual worker or organisation could undertake this continuous spiral of negotiations any more than they could cover the whole territory.

- Task teams are composed of whoever is needed to complete the task and will include service users, carers and key people in the local community. The composition of task teams is likely to change over time as the task changes, and will tend to break down the boundaries between organisations, and between the people who use, provide, purchase or inspect services.

- Each individual has his or her part to play in concert with other members of the organisation or inter-organisation teams and all the other people with whom they are working.

- Boundaries between organisations and other social systems will have to be crossed and broken down continually, particularly when there are insufficient, inadequate or malfunctioning structural supports for this activity.

- Negotiated changes can begin at any stage and may require activities to be undertaken across the spiral, not just in the logical and sequenced steps depicted.

An essential feature of social problems is that there are conflicting aims, assumptions, priorities, working practices and interests between the different people involved in their formation and possible resolution. This underlines the need for a framework which can encompass the full range of relationships. These may be between social workers and the public they serve, or within their own organisations: between themselves, service users, other citizens, other workers in the health services, education, leisure, housing, social security, in provider organisations including those outside the traditional boundaries of social welfare such as transport and the environment.

The process map is a way of making explicit and visible the process of continuing negotiation involved in identifying all the different perceptions of the problem, and its possible management, in attempting to resolve conflicts of interest, expectations and behaviour. Making these conflicts more overt and explicit will often be a necessary, but not sufficient, prerequisite of honest dialogue, renegotiation and changes in the pattern of care or changing inappropriate and antisocial behaviour.

Work with the Applemores provides an example of process.

Peter and the Applemores

David and Jane are a couple in their late thirties. They have been married for several years, and it is a second marriage for Jane. Carol and

> Wayne, Jane's children by her first marriage, live with them. David and
> Jane are foster parents to 14-year-old Peter, who had previously lived
> with several foster families. Peter told a teacher that David had sexu-
> ally abused him.
>   Following initial enquiries, Peter was moved immediately from the
> foster home and placed in a specialist residential unit for boys. David
> was arrested by the police pending further investigations. The joint
> police/social work team negotiated with David and Jane for David to
> live away from home at a relative's during the enquiry and while on
> bail. David was subsequently convicted, sentenced to a short period of
> prison detention, and later became involved in a therapeutic group for
> similar offenders set up and run by a specialist voluntary organisation.

The range of tasks involved at any one time can be mapped on to
the two axes of the content map. For example:

- **direct work and intervention**: to protect Peter and the other children
  in the family, provide information about child protection procedures, to bring about change in the relationships between
  different members of the family and others; to help different actors
  manage the results of unexpected changes imposed upon them
  through statutory requirements;
- **direct provision of services**, such as residential care, to substitute for
  that being provided by the foster family;
- **indirect change and development activity** by staff of the probation
  service in facilitating the formation and work of the voluntary
  organisation working with sex offenders which David began to
  attend;
- **indirect services** provided by the independent sector residential
  home for Peter, and the group for David.

Mapping the content provides a way of analysing one part of the
task, but leaves out the timescale and the ways in which these activities
will change over time and the processes through which changes in task
and activity have to be negotiated by all the people involved.

Stages in the spiral of negotiations

There are key stages through which negotiations between the key actors
are conducted. Many of the parameters of these negotiations will be set

out in law, statute, social policy and organisation procedures. Some will be strongly influenced by local custom and practice, by 'how it is done here' (Marsh and Fisher, 1992), and by what 'people round here' will accept. These will not be negotiable on a case-by-case basis, but can be changed over time. Any intervention with someone like David, who acts 'as if' he intentionally rejects socially accepted norms, necessarily involves attempts to negotiate with him, and others like him, how they are to live within existing social norms. The main stages of negotiation and renegotiation involve all four quadrants of the content map over time and include:

1   Clarification of basic assumptions and values
2   Negotiation of the nature of problems and possible solutions, through consultation with all service users
3   Forming specific aims and objectives, and identifying who needs to do what
4   Identifying ways of monitoring outcomes for those involved, including unintended consequences
5   Identifying team and staff development needs
6   Identifying policy and organisational development goals.

Stages in the spiral of negotiations

I   Basic assumptions and values about:

- sexual relations between adults and children;
- how offenders should be punished and how they are treated in the community;
- people we know, live with and love;
- political and public views on abuse and how abuse should be handled (who abuses, why, and what should happen to them);
- the type of care most appropriate for children living away from their parents;
- the powers of social workers and how they are used;
- what knowledge, skills and methods are appropriate;
- whose responsibility it is to keep children safe from abuse and harm;
- the role of social work and its value system.

2   Nature of problems and possible solutions:

- investigating whether Peter is a victim of abuse or not;
- reconsideration of why Peter is being fostered in the first place, and what should be the long-term plans for him;
- identifying issues for Jane in keeping her children together;
- identifying best sources of support for Jane and the children to cope with their own reactions and those of relatives, friends, school and employers;

- identifying causes and change options for perpetrators of sexual abuse;
- how to ensure effective partnership with allied organisations and agreement of immediate action plan;
- how to make keeping children safe from abuse and harm everyone's responsibility.

3 Specific aims and objectives: who needs to do what:

- to complete the enquiry and subsequent action plan;
- to provide emotional and social support for Peter, Jane and her children;
- to keep Jane and her children together by providing David with alternative accommodation and support;
- to investigate, in accordance with the agreed policy, the allegation of abuse;
- to develop a plan of longer-term work with Peter, Jane and her children, including provision for re-entry of Peter into school and for Jane to return to her job;
- providing Peter with specialist support and accommodation;
- to prevent or reduce the likelihood of David abusing other children.

4 Monitoring task achievement and unintended consequences:

- the actions and outcomes of interventions by workers and allied staff;
- the actions, responses of and outcomes for children and young people, families and relatives;
- the experiences of Peter, David, Jane and her children of the interventions;
- direct and indirect interventions: in relation to individual families and abused children, and their families and perpetrators as a population;
- the policies, actions and provision which might prevent child abuse or support children and families who have experienced it.

5. Team and staff development needs:

- to ensure staff have adequate skills and knowledge to undertake the work;
- to provide support for staff in carrying out stressful and complex work;
- to provide forums for service users and carers to share their experiences with workers and to be involved in training at all levels and with other organisations;
- to provide inter-organisation and multidisciplinary forums which promote mutual understanding and joint practice and policies;
- to ensure staff regularly update their knowledge and keep abreast of skills and methods and developments, including multidisciplinary work.

6   Policy and organisational development goals:

- to carry out statutory responsibilities;
- to work with other organisations and local groups to ensure that the range of provision is available to support abused children, young people, families, and treat or control perpetrators when there is alleged abuse and when it has occurred;
- to ensure abusers have more access to treatment;
- to identify what direct and indirect provision is available locally and regionally;
- to promote developments that fit identified groups in relation to different levels of prevention;
- research on success/failures of treatment for abusers;
- community safety policies and procedures for released convicted abusers.

Basic assumptions and values

Social work is characterised by conflicting values and assumptions, at the individual and family levels, and the organisational and political levels. The facilitation of dialogue within this contested field is an essential dimension of the task. In our example members of the team engaged in dialogue with a range of people in working with the Applemore family. These dialogues are not open-ended, since much of the framework for the intervention is already shaped by statute, employers' policies and procedures, and taxpayers and their representatives who ultimately sanction and resource social services. When social control is at issue these assumptions and values enter directly and powerfully into the workers' interactions with Peter and family members. All prescribe essential components of the values which are integral to the work with the Applemore family.

The consequence is that the negotiation of basic assumptions and values does not just inform work with the Applemore family, but often constitutes much of the main task of facilitating change. For the Applemores, the main areas of basic assumption and values which were negotiated included:

Relations between children and adults: David's basic assumption that his behaviour was an acceptable, if secret, activity, began to be challenged first by Peter, then by the actions of the teacher, the police, magistrates and the social worker, and subsequently by his peers and the workers within the offender group. These challenges all contributed towards a renegotiation of David's basic assumptions about the boundaries of sexual relationships, the nature of the problem within the family and different people's roles and responsibilities.

Assumptions about the people we know and love: Jane's basic assumption at the investigation stage was that her husband could not have done what he was accused of. She angrily attempted to negotiate this perception with Peter and the workers involved in the early stages of the investigation process. Subsequently her son from her previous marriage, Wayne, said that he too had been abused by David and this changed Jane's basic assumptions about David and the nature and purpose of social work interest in her family, and thus her capacity to engage in further stages of the spiral of negotiations.

Assumptions about responsibilities of organisations: Different members of the family engaged with different staff, each implicitly or explicitly negotiating the nature of their involvement, their mandates and purposes. Similarly, different staff negotiated through formal systems such as the joint enquiry and the case conference, but also through the face-to-face contact in the family and their social network, including David's colleagues at work, the parents and children at the local schools. Some of these negotiations about the nature of different responsibilities towards members of the Applemore family contributed to wider developments such as the joint development of groups for offenders. Most of the enquiries into tragedies in child care highlight failures or breakdowns in communications between organisations in carrying out their different responsibilities (Butler *et al.*, 1995; DoH, 1991c). Knowing what these responsibilities are, and their impact on decisions and actions, is crucial to practice.

Assumptions about what is important: In the past some social workers have tended to underestimate the importance of a young person's education, health and employment in overcoming the difficulties they face, and the damaging effects of multiple moves whilst they are accommodated in care. Increasingly, research and listening to young people's own experience have to inform a base-line against which standards of practice are developed (Aiers, 1998).

Assumptions about the value base of social work: The value base of social work takes a clear stand on opposing discrimination and oppression on the grounds of race, gender, social class, age, sexuality or disability. This stance does not extend to sexual abuse of children because of

issues of the imbalance of power between children and adults. However, the value system distinguishes between the act and the person,
between condemning the act and not the whole person; and this enables
work with David to change his criminal behaviour. Although there are
many doubts about the success of treatment for perpetrators the
worker has to proceed with hope, at the same time as working with
others to protect children and trying to find new and effective solutions.

Negotiation of the nature of problems and possible solutions
There is often an implicit assumption that assessment and investigation of situations such as that of the Applemores is essentially a process of 'objective' enquiry which can discover the 'truth', or get a
picture of reality, through questioning the child and others involved.
However, there are different perspectives and perceptions within the
family and the wider network about the meaning to different individuals of what happened and what they want to happen. For example,
while children want the abuse to stop, they equally may want to stay
within their family and to remain in control of what happens to them
(Macleod, 1996; National Commission of Inquiry into the Prevention
of Child Abuse, 1996). A process of negotiation and renegotiation over
the definition of the problem and possible solutions is essential in order
to reach a stage of shared understanding, even in a clearly abusive and
unlawful situation. In this case, the abuse was eventually admitted
by David and confirmed by Wayne, but this was the end point of a
process in which there were competing views about the nature of the
problem and possible solutions. There are many cases where enquiries
prove no abuse has taken place and others which are never 'con-
clusive'. All investigated families continue to live with the long-term
consequences of the enquiry which has often had profound effects on
relationships within the family and outside of it (Platt and Shemmings,
1996; DoH, 1988).
   Negotiations about the very nature of the problem and thus possible
solutions may involve conflicting assumptions about the available
knowledge base. In child sexual abuse, for example, controversies range
from the very existence of 'ritual sexual abuse' to the reliability of
diagnostic interviewing techniques and the effectiveness of treatment
methods for convicted perpetrators. Whilst this makes the task sometimes controversial, it does not remove the responsibility to make
judgements on the best available evidence.
   To work together effectively and across organisations, and with
others in the community, basic assumptions about the very existence

of certain phenomena have to be negotiated. Different theories exist about what constitutes abuse, about the causes of child sexual abuse (National Commission of Inquiry into the Prevention of Child Abuse, 1996) and the 'best' therapeutic or investigative procedures available to tackle them. A group of staff very committed to a particular theory, for example a psychodynamic or systemic family theory model, or a particular perspective of practice, cannot assume these models are shared by others in the same organisation, let alone those outside of it. These include the public, elected members, trustees of charities and directors of companies and other groups. If partnership is the objective, theoretical assumptions need to be identified, conflicts recognised and opened to explicit negotiation. Otherwise they remain hidden, but often powerful, forces in the intervention.

Understanding the implications for practice of research outcomes is as essential as the use of expertise and skill developed within particular approaches. All have to be used as part of a coherent plan which addresses the whole task. The absence of a range of approaches leads to an inappropriate over-reliance on one. This often means failure because it is difficult to engage in work in all areas of the content map since different kinds of partnerships are necessary for the range of tasks. This will inevitably require flexibility and openness to the different basic assumptions of others, the skills and knowledge and expertise they bring.

Similar controversies about community care for people who have mental health problems or who are persistent young offenders highlight the impossibility of operating within this minefield without understanding the available knowledge base for practice, how it relates to personal and workplace value systems and the worker's own practice, and how it relates to other areas of skill in the teams of which the worker is a part.

Forming specific aims and objectives, and identifying who needs to do what

Team members, including members of the family and their wider social and kinship network, have to negotiate a shared identification of the main tasks to tackle the problem as they see it. In the Applemore situation, some of them involved indirect interventions aimed at providing the specialist residential unit used by Peter, or the offender group which David joined. Negotiations also had to take place about direct work, which involved addressing such questions as:

- What information should be available and to whom?
- Should David leave home while investigation takes place, or should Peter, and who should make this decision?
- What are the boundaries set by statutory responsibilities on full involvement in decisions?
- Who is most likely to be able to establish a good rapport with Peter and how much should his biological mother be involved in the investigation interviews?
- What support might Wayne and Jane want?
- Which worker from the different organisations involved should lead negotiations with Jane, Peter and others about Peter's ongoing care?
- What are the best strategies and tactics for negotiating with the members of the offender group a plan for effectively tackling their problems?
- What are the wider issues about children's safety and foster care policy which need to be addressed?

The different levels of objective setting are interconnected and not separate, compartmentalised activities. This is not just a theoretical exercise. A synthesis is necessary for the work of staff in different organisations with different responsibilities and priorities to form a coherent approach for Peter and the Applemores and more widely for protecting children from harm. For example, working directly with David through setting up and running the group for perpetrators had an effect on some of the specific objectives of direct work with other members of the family. David's high level of resistance in turn affected wider thinking about local policy and practice for working with this particular group of people. Local inter-organisation groups reviewed how they could contribute more widely to greater safety for children and young people, renegotiation of how current staff and other resources were being used, and the need for those working with children and families to have closer links with staff working with perpetrators of abuse.

Identifying and applying ways of monitoring outcomes and unintended consequences
Who is monitoring whom? Monitoring takes place on a number of levels: through formal organisation procedures, by local groups and communities, by other workers involved, and by individuals and families who use or are required to use services. Most frequently concentration is on formal procedures and complaints, but other

sources of information are no less important in monitoring how relevant practice and service provision is in the lives of people and their communities. For example, black and minority ethnic groups and disabled people, mental health survivors, people with learning difficulties, have all campaigned for provision and practice which has greater relevance to their own lives and expectations. This gap between what is available and what makes a positive difference in their lives was identified primarily through their own experience, actions and research (Ahmad, 1990; Butt and Mirza, 1996; Butt and Box, 1997; Morris, 1996; Cambell and Oliver, 1996; Cambell and Lindow, 1997; People First, 1994a, 1994b). Explicit monitoring systems need always to be built in, but as these will centrally involve some people monitoring the behaviours of others, these systems need to be jointly negotiated, and then renegotiated, as perceptions of the problem, or the range of people involved, change over time.

Formal monitoring should include the people who use or are required to use services as well as workers and local groups, to ensure that the different perspectives each may have are properly negotiated before decisions are made (Platt and Shemmings, 1996; Amphlett, Katz and Worthing, 1997). To achieve this requires people who use services to be fully involved at all stages, from policy to planning, implementation and monitoring (Harding and Beresford, 1996).

People who use services: Workers' behaviour is informally monitored by family members and others, and at times this becomes formal, such as when complaints procedures are used. For example, Wayne, David's stepson, monitors the effects of Peter's disclosure both on the family and the workers involved. On the basis of his assessment of how this is being handled he feels safe enough to disclose his own experience of being abused. The value placed on the style of the worker and the relationship they establish is often underestimated in formal organisation evaluations. This is not the case for the people who use services: they place great emphasis on this as an indicator of quality (Harding and Beresford, 1996); as do carers, if they are to feel confident about organisation provision for older relatives (Neill and Williams, 1992).

Workers also need to monitor the direct and indirect impact of their involvement, and in particular any unintended and unforeseen consequences. At the direct-work level Peter was initially very concerned about David's welfare and state of mind. Despite having been abused by his foster father, he was still attached to and fond of him, and at times became angry with and resentful towards some of the workers involved. None of these reactions of Peter's were 'intended' by the workers, but needed to be noticed and responded to appropriately; and this in turn involved the renegotiation of monitoring arrangements.

Workers and teams monitor their own practice: Deliberately attempting to bring about change in social situations or in the behaviour and attitudes of people is not an exact science. Involvement with families such as the Applemores has to be seen as 'experimental' in the sense that knowledge, skill and experience have to be reinvented to fit each highly specific situation that workers encounter. There are clearly times when mistakes are made. Consequently effective monitoring of both intended and unintended consequences of action is crucial. When this learning is pulled together across the organisation it will include information at team and interdisciplinary levels about workload and resource levels; about what solutions and services are being applied to what kinds of social problems; and what are the outcomes of these services and interventions, at both individual and social levels. The content and methods adopted for these different monitoring processes need to be negotiated by those directly involved if they are to produce information which is meaningful to everyone and influences practice (Pottage and Evans, 1994). To be useful at the front line, information needs to be collected to understand and inform the changing nature of the organisation's task, and the tasks of individuals within it.

Other organisations and workers also make formal and informal evaluations: There are formal means of monitoring inter-organisation and multidisciplinary working, such as case conferences, specific monitoring groups, joint commissioning organisations, local action zones on such issues as health, mental health, school exclusion or crime prevention. These are always complemented by informal monitoring and evaluation which does not necessarily become formalised, but which profoundly affects working relationships at street level and official levels. The Cleveland Inquiry (DoH, 1988), for example, describes relationships between the police and social workers which were fraught with problems and contributed to escalation of the difficulties in which the children were enmeshed.

Identifying and meeting team and staff development needs
Monitoring and evaluation will identify new team development needs because:

- basic assumptions and aims are changing or are challenged;
- new skills, knowledge and ways of working are required;
- social policy or organisational structures and culture create new demands and expertise.

There are several distinct modes of development in addition to individual and team supervision which might be necessary, including:

- awareness raising
- skills training
- reorganisation of the knowledge base or acquisition of new knowledge
- team building
- organisational development
- evaluating/researching team practice.

These are more fully discussed in Chapter 6.

Responding to social policy changes at the local level

At specific points in time in the UK, national government, European and local policy guidelines have to be integrated into practice. During the late 1980s and early 1990s, community care and child care legislation produced a vast amount of detailed guidance and recommendations, which transformed the way provision was structured and practice carried out at both the strategic and individual level. These provide a framework but cannot be mechanistically applied, because they are part of the process of negotiating task definition. Ignoring this process ends in a growing gap between policy statements and what happens at the front line and the experience of people who use services.

Impact of research into child protection: One example of such a renegotiation is research which promoted a change in emphasis from child protection investigation towards family support. Separate research initiatives contributed to a substantial programme which concluded that:

A more balanced service for vulnerable children would encourage professionals to take a wider view. There would be efforts to work alongside families rather than disempower them, to raise their self-esteem rather than reproach families, to promote family relationships where children have their needs met, rather than leave untreated families with an unsatisfactory parenting style. The focus would be on the overall needs of children rather than a narrow concentration on the alleged incident. (DoH 1995, p. 55)

The change of emphasis implied by this research has significant implications for how workers view their task, the skills and knowledge they require, and points to significant changes in how the work itself is organised and evaluated in terms of individual examples of intervention and the work of both organisations and allied workers. But whatever factors are the catalyst for change, these are only steps in the processes of negotiation about the very nature of social problems, the forms of organisation best able to tackle them, and the skills and knowledge to be given priority. Everyone involved needs to be engaged in these processes as they are issues of public as well as professional concern.

Conclusion: implications for practice

Any practice tool used in a limited or rigid way is doomed to the twin failures of ineffectiveness and unintended negative consequences. The task is to find and adapt frameworks which grapple with the infinite choices, causes and uncertainties that shape social situations, and the value judgements we have to make. New patterns will be identified, judgements made about their ethical desirability and the effectiveness of approaches. So the spiral goes round again. Public expectations are that we should be explicit about standards of practice, able to explain what we do and why to the people who use our services, to politicians and to the general public. Promoting social well-being is far more than a job for one type of worker or organisation. Social work has its niche in these patterns, and in interactions that revolve around personal and social care. The particular nature of this endeavour places responsibility on all of us:

- to struggle for an awareness of how patterns in our social relationships work, how they disadvantage particular people and perpetuate undesirable behaviour and responses;
- to be fully accountable to the people we work with and for;
- to explain and be accountable to the public for what we do;
- to test responses and intervention against the value base of social work;

- to contribute to the development of practice and standards, in partnership with the people who use or are required to use services.

In this chapter we have mapped out the different levels of work required by teams of workers if they are to move beyond the provision of 'aid' and contribute to the usual ways that the community, the family and individuals solve their social problems. We identified that this will be done through expanding the numbers of people involved in informal support networks to underpin the efforts of the usual patterns of care givers; by helping families expand their problem solving repertoires; by contributing absent resources; or by some combination of these approaches. Only in extreme situations where all those involved have failed to produce change should we take control and responsibility for vulnerable individuals. In these circumstances we should still be working towards a more dependable environment, since most children and many adults return eventually to their families and local communities.

Implicit in the approach taken here are particular perspectives on the very nature of social problems, the central position of social control activities in social work, and the nature of social change. In the following chapters we discuss the theoretical concepts that underpin this approach to practice, the basic knowledge and the skills required. We begin in the next chapter with an analysis of the patterns of interaction through which particular social situations are defined as 'social problems'.

5

Social Problems, Social Control and Patterns of Interaction

Introduction

The family and the community are the source of most care and control. Just as the major job of caring for people with support needs rests with families and others in the community, so too does day-to-day socialisation and social control. However, in modern societies with increasingly specialist divisions of labour, there are widespread expectations that workers can, and should, take on responsibilities which in practice can only be discharged by people as members of the community in their day-to-day lives. The dilemmas this poses for all of us are illustrated by what happens at the meeting between the policeman and the villagers.

The policeman and the villagers

The chief inspector gets to his feet and looks at his audience. The local councillor has explained the parish, district and county councils' parts in the problem and its possible solutions. The meeting has been called to discuss traffic calming in a small country village, following a fatal accident. The road through the village has become a 'rat run', a short cut linking two main roads, leading to greatly increased traffic moving at high speed during rush hours. The policeman starts his speech by directly confronting the whole audience. 'How many of you have come the short distance from your homes in your cars?' he asks. 'How fast do *you* drive? People who use their cars for convenience and drive too fast are not a different kind of person,' he says. 'They are people like you. Unless you change your behaviour, tragedies like the recent one in the village will continue to occur, no matter the number of police or what

---

kind of traffic schemes are introduced.' He explains the options, the costs, the limitations on the budget position and the objective facts about the village's traffic problems relative to other potential accident sites. He concludes that the village is a low priority and nothing is likely to be done.

The villagers are surprised: they expected him to be defensive and that they would have to put their case strenuously. But they did not expect this turning of the tables: the police are there to solve such problems, not to tell the villagers that *they are the problem* and the solution is partly in their hands. But they do not protest, although they continue to press for action. They accept that all the policeman says is true, as indeed it is. There are lessons here for the way we should tackle many social problems, as well as road deaths.

People come in contact with social care organisations in different ways. Some ask for help for themselves, others through participation in local community groups, through voluntary work or through the experiences of a relative, neighbour or friend. However, the majority of service users are referred, or sent, because somebody else is concerned about their welfare or their behaviour: for example, the doctor or health visitor who suspects nonaccidental injury or child neglect; neighbours who call the police expressing concern for a vulnerable person; the courts who refer a child for offending. A person's behaviour is seen as 'mad' by somebody, who then tries to get a worker to 'do something' about it. Often people are referred by a family member, for example relations who think an older person needs residential care; or a neighbour who thinks an isolated older person needs more social contact (Levin *et al.*, 1994), or is concerned about the welfare of a child, who then becomes the centre of concern (DoH, 1995).

Identifying all the key people

Attempts have been made over the years to find a word to portray accurately the relationship between social workers and the people they work with. All such terms differentiate between the identified 'client' and other members of the public or other workers. The latter, however, are often as much stakeholders, both in the solution and in achieving change, as the people identified as clients (Pincus and Minahan, 1973; Specht and Vickery, 1977). Similarly, the apparent division between 'client' and worker is often a false one, since we ourselves may at other points in time or in other parts of our lives use or be required to use services.

The term 'client' has largely been replaced by such terms as 'service user', 'carer', 'consumer' or 'customer'. All of these give the impression that the significant relationships are directly with individuals, or an individual and his or her family: it is assumed that the focus will be on assessing the need for and providing services or support. But as we have seen in mapping the content of the task, workers and related staff are not just concerned with providing and gatekeeping resources and services to individuals. The control function, although most explicit in the criminal justice system where work with offenders is aimed at reducing offending behaviour, can also be central in other relationships even if obscured. For example, it is present in children and families work involving neglecting parents, where people are subject to compulsory admission to a psychiatric hospital; in the response to a relative who wants someone placed in residential care; in referrals for care for older people, which rarely come from the older person himself. None of these situations are straightforward service user or customer/provider relationships. Lack of clarity about what and who brought the relationship into being can lead to underestimation of the differences in perception of a problem and what is necessary to tackle it. There are likely to be at least three definitions of 'the problem' and what is needed in any one situation; those of:

- the person who 'sends' someone for help;
- the person who is 'sent';
- the perspectives of the other stakeholders involved.

Different people see a social problem and its potential solutions from their own perspectives. 'Needs' are often described in terms of what is thought to be the most appropriate solution to a problem. An older person may be described as 'in need of residential care' by a GP who perceives the person to be 'at risk' because she needs more care than the primary health services can arrange. Perhaps the nearest relative can only just sustain care at the cost of suffering significant stress. Maybe a neighbour's contribution is at the limit of what they can offer. The older person may not perceive any of these problems; indeed they are not 'hers'. She may not think there is a problem at all. The risks she is taking are acceptable to her: she wishes only that she could still get about more, that her daughter lived nearer, that she were a little less lonely. If something happens to any of the other people to exacerbate the seriousness with which they view 'the problem', a referral could be triggered.

Most people enter residential care because of their social circumstances and not only as a result of their individual characteristics. Levin *et al.* (1994) found that the crucial factor when older people suffering from dementia went into residential care was not the degree of dementia but either the death of a carer or the fact that he or she had not wanted to provide care when initially interviewed. In the UK, the National Health Service and Community Care Act (1990) acknowledges that the majority of people entering residential care do not want to be there and that many could have been maintained in their own homes with a relatively small amount of additional support from others (Sinclair, Parker *et al.*, 1990).

Residents in care and nursing homes are not necessarily more dependent on others for help with self-care tasks than many living in the community (Levin *et al.*, 1994). Social factors such as housing, income, support for carers and the availability of intensive packages of care are crucial determinants of whether admission to residential care takes place (Levin, Sinclair and Gorbach, 1989; Levin *et al.*, 1994). The Carers National Association (1992) estimates that 33 per cent of carers receive no help or support even when they are providing intensive and intimate personal care; only 36 per cent have received information on advice about caring from social workers, 32% from GPs and 28% from district nurses.

Children also enter care because of their social circumstances, not their individual characteristics. Two of the main findings of research on placements of children in care are that:

> The level of family discord and fragmentation which is reported indicates that practical services alone will often be insufficient and help with family relationships may be essential for effective preventive services.

> The availability of functioning family and social networks seems to be a critical determinant of the need for admission and thus a necessary focus for preventive work. (DoH, 1991b, p. 34)

It is common that the person defined as 'the problem' in such situations is the one with the least power over others: children, frail older people and individuals seen as different from those around them.

Often the child who is abused is taken into care, away from home and the people he or she loves, while the perpetrator remains; the older person is taken into residential care, rather than others looking for ways to provide sources of support for immediate carers under chronic stress. Frequently 'the problem' can be described as several people's problems.

The nature of social problems

In the same way that the vast majority of people's needs are met by families and carers in the community without regular social work intervention, so the maintenance of social order is through families, neighbours and universal provision, such as that of schools and religious organisations. All contribute to the socialisation of young people and other control mechanisms for adults.

People have many problems whose causes are located in different facets of their own attributes and behaviour, in those of other people and systems in their environment, or in the often complicated interaction between the two. Individual problems become social problems when they cannot be resolved by the individual or others in their family and social networks, or when needs cannot be met by people in the immediate social environment. Focusing on the individual service user or identified client and his or her needs alone ignores the resources usually called on in such circumstances, and the problems that others may be experiencing. People are social beings whose behaviour can only be understood in the context of their relationships to others. Intervention is required because somebody defines a situation as one that should change. This can happen on an individual or group level. We give two examples.

A frail, older woman who has difficulty feeding herself, is fearful of being alone, and has no one with whom she can share her depression about her physical condition, clearly has 'problems'. Some may say these are an inevitable 'fact of life': a feature of 'ageing'. If she is referred to a social care organisation or the situation is seen as a 'social problem', this is more a comment on how her problems are, or are not, being dealt with by others, than on the condition itself. Being old, even old and frail, is not a serious problem, any more than being a baby. Being either without appropriate resources and relationships with others, however, *is* a social problem. People's needs, whether as a service user or carer, young person or parent, only become a social problem when these are not met.

In an inner city area with a high proportion of young people from minority ethnic groups, schoolchildren travelling by bus were being racially harassed on their way home. The harassment was organised by a local right-wing group who knew school-leaving times. One 'solution' was for the young people to be met by parents, or the youth workers who became involved. Another was for the worried bus drivers to drive on when there were black young people at a bus stop. Such reactions implicitly define the young people as 'the problem', not the people racially harassing them. An alternative would be for parents, youth workers and the schools to negotiate with the bus company to try to find a different solution, while also collaborating with the police to tackle the organised abuse.

Social workers and other social change agents typically become involved as a consequence of somebody saying that someone should care for a vulnerable person, or exert some form of control or influence over a person behaving inappropriately. Members of the network may be too overwhelmed in their own lives or not want to become involved, and wish to shift responsibility on to others whose job they think it is to solve the problem, or at least take responsibility for it. Such expectations may be enshrined in the duties placed on social services, social work and education departments and the NHS by statute, or through a charity's aims. It is not just service users, therefore, who can become dependent upon welfare to tackle their problems. Many members of the public and institutions such as schools and the health service are dependent upon social care organisations to take social problems away from them.

These referrals can be described as people responding to social problems by extending the user's network to include social workers or other organisations' staff, and sometimes delegating the problem to them. On occasions this is a choice not to accept responsibility for family, friends, neighbours, pupils or patients. However, more often than not it comes about when those offering help have become overwhelmed and exhausted, as in Mrs Jones's story. Even when this necessitates an older person living in a care home, many relatives seeking residential care do not want to discontinue their responsibilities, but to renegotiate what these responsibilities are. They become very concerned if care staff 'take over' areas which are not part of this negotiation (White, 1997). Alternatively, the situation may be that there are no people known to the person needing support who can provide it, or that such support is deemed insufficient or inappropriate.

Beyond the individualisation of social problems

'Service user', 'client', 'user', 'carer', 'patient' or 'customer': all such terms define people through their relationship with the worker or service provider. The implication is that the person has less knowledge, information, expertise or resources than the worker and that he or she is 'appropriately' the object of concern and hence merits attention and intervention. Other people, such as relatives, neighbours or other workers, whose problems are solved or reduced by the intervention of social workers, are by contrast not always seen as legitimate objects of concern or intervention.

The individualisation of social problems encourages, although does not justify, seeing the identified individual or family as less able than those who 'do not have the problem'. A range of systemic and ecological perspectives recognises that social and personal problems lie in the relationships between people and systems (Pincus and Minahan, 1973; Goldstein, 1973; Specht and Vickery, 1977). But it is no more satisfactory to assume that all participants, rather than just one, are deficient. Shifting the emphasis from the individual to the family has pathologised many families, and at the community level contributes to labelling whole areas as 'bad neighbourhoods', or entire groups in society as the 'underclass', or the 'uncaring community'.

The community: problem and solution

The community has often been seen, optimistically and over-simplistically, as the main source of solutions to many social problems. This is based on the view that there are untapped resources in communities and neighbourhoods which could be mobilised to support those in need. These are seen as similar to reservoirs of oil under the seabed: all that is needed to develop them is to locate the oil and build a pipeline to areas of need, thus providing support (Smale *et al.*, 1988). The frequent experience of failure to locate such resources in communities and channel them for productive use has led to a more cynical, or at least more sceptical, view of the potential of community in the modern world. However, we need to go beyond this polarisation of hope and doubt about the value of community by developing a more practical perspective on the patterns of the social relationships involved.

The 'untapped oil well' model of looking at networks, communities, their needs and resources, overlooks the fact that these communities or networks can also be said to cause or at least perpetuate the problems workers are called upon to resolve. The community is not just a potential solution to social problems – it is part of the nature of the community that such problems lie within it. The racial harassment of schoolchildren on buses was the result of tensions in the local community which escalated beyond the control of any individual passenger or bus driver. People contribute to the creation of their communities and networks by the ways they behave, and the ways they 'misbehave', in their environment. These sets of relationships are as often dying as developing. As they change they create, and perpetuate, the same problems that they are called upon to cure or resolve. Social problems are part of the very fabric of networks and communities. Networks and communities, therefore, cannot be applied as external cures or supports.

The problem of crime illustrates this. Young and adult offenders are part of the community. One way of looking at this is to see them as the cause of crime in society, for without them it would not exist. Some argue that they are in turn the product of negative influences in society: of poverty, bad housing, unemployment and social exclusion, certain approaches to parenting, or the lack of it, of too little or misguided education, and so on. Others claim that the cause of crime is genetic, or a manifestation of original sin, or the malevolent, selfish choice of the individual offender. Increasingly, many argue that the causes of crime lie in some combination of all of these factors and the social circumstances which exist at the time of the event. Whatever the cause, most people assume that something can be done: that crime, the behaviour of young offenders, will be affected by the responses at national and local community levels. The choice of cause will influence the chosen responses, ranging from special education, psychological treatment, social work intervention of different kinds, employment schemes, combined with tactics such as closed circuit TV and neighbourhood watch, on to penal approaches such as locking up young offenders until they grow out of it and 'three strikes and out', leading to life imprisonment.

All such responses are designed to influence crime rates by changing offending behaviour. It is implicitly recognised that the perpetuation, if not the cause, of crime is a feature of the pattern of relationships between all the people involved in a community, or in society as a whole; and that offending behaviour changes when other parts of the system themselves change. The significance of this framing of the problem of crime is that it includes the whole spectrum of the law and order debate from 'hang 'em, shoot 'em and flog 'em' through to 'love them and let them off'. All these responses demonstrate the belief that what 'we' do makes a difference to 'them': that we are all part of the same system within which crime persists.

When the community is called on to offer more support to certain people, to be 'more caring' or 'tougher on crime', we are not just seeking to change individuals but to change patterns of relationships that can only change if *all* the significant players change. The resources of the community – the potential helpers in a social network – are people currently busy doing other things. Formal helpers, using traditional methods, take on certain responsibilities for the problem in place of others in the community. Potential helpers, be they next-door neighbours or relatives, are busy with their own lives, even if they 'wish that they could do more'. There is no evidence to suggest that there are queues of people sitting in a social vacuum waiting to help.

Many people are in networks which ignore, neglect, reject, persecute or in some other way cause them stress, or leave them alone with their pain. Most people are in communities and networks where resources are unevenly distributed, and some feel powerless relative to others. Often people known to workers are in networks that label them as 'clients'. The worker will deliberately, or unwittingly, but nevertheless inevitably be part of these processes.

The idea of community

Community is a concept used to describe social relationships defined by geography, kinship or common interests. All people are part of social relationships which we, or the others involved, might call a 'community'. Taken in its widest sense, a person's network, the set of relationships between people, can mean all the contacts that person has, from the milkman they never see to their closest relative. More specific networks can be identified, such as family or kinship, work relationships, religious and other particular interest groups and friends. Most people are members of different interlocking or overlapping networks. It is impossible to imagine anybody who is not part of a network. Knowledge of such a person would be proof that somebody, somewhere, has some form of relationship with her.

Increased levels of care or social control do not arise spontaneously. People identified as the community's resources have to change if they are to meet the needs of others. Workers and family carers have developed, and need to continue to explore, new forms of practice to achieve change. Examples include campaigns to recruit foster parents linked with older people isolated from their families in a grandparent role; recruiting volunteers to act as mentors to socially excluded or disillusioned young people; opening a school to adult learners who need qualifications. Initiatives are realised through creating partnerships and agreements with new combinations of people, to involve them so that existing patterns of care and control change for the better. This includes reviewing, and where necessary changing, the part played by people who currently control other resources such as finance, access to buildings and transport. Often the worker aims to change the way the people in a network define a particular social problem, in order to enlarge and change the network of people who might contribute to its solution. It is possible to be optimistic about the potential of the community, if we are realistic about the nature of the changes required. But becoming more realistic means addressing the question of who is the customer or user of services.

The individualisation of social problems involves identifying a person, typically the least powerful, as the 'problem' and so the object of concern. Meanwhile others in the network, by defining their problem as 'the person', have translated their 'problem' into the problems of that person. This is not a malevolent process: it is a conventional way of defining problems in a society that emphasises the separateness of individuals at the risk of underestimating their interdependence.

People who use services are citizens

Moving beyond the individualisation of social problems necessitates an alternative framework which retains the status of the people who use services as citizens.

A simple way of giving people who use services the power to become customers is to give them the financial resources and information to gain direct access to the services they want. This is the approach used in making direct payments to disabled people to purchase their own support or employ personal assistants (Community Care (Direct Payments) Act 1996). In other instances this simple solution is complicated by confusion over who the customer is. Is the social service offered to a particular person just for him or her, or even for that individual at all? Is it not the case that others always benefit directly or indirectly from the intervention, not just the identified service user?

Carers, as recognised by statute, are also customers with needs of their own, and like others in the network will be relieved to know that the social care organisation has taken at least some of the responsibility for what might have been identified as primarily their problem. This position becomes particularly evident when the interests and needs of the carer and cared-for conflict (Pitkeathley, 1995).

Many other people can see their needs and those of another as in conflict, particularly when a person's behaviour causes concern: relatives and neighbours who are relieved of anxiety, pressure and exhaustion, the hospital doctor whose beds are freed, the policy makers whose responsibilities are discharged.

Customer satisfaction with social care is not something that can be easily measured in the same way as for consumer goods. The provision, or withholding, of a service may satisfy one or more of the possible customers, but only directly or indirectly at the expense of others whose needs or interests may be in conflict with those of the 'satisfied customer'. There are always multiple customers or service users and often conflicts of interests and perception between these different people. Workers inevitably have to mediate between different and sometimes conflicting interests and norms within any social situation. Using this broader framework, many people can be reframed as customers, service users or stakeholders. These people or groups are neither 'dependent' nor 'in need' in the way that these terms have traditionally been applied. Recognising that *all* these people are a legitimate focus for workers' attention, and that it is the relationship between them that is the target of intervention, may help us to be less patronising to some of the people we work with. This wider perspective does not mean widening the net, putting up the tariff or creating impossible demands for increasingly scarce resources, but reframes the nature of the task and hence the use of existing human and other resources. The option is not easy but it is the one that is most likely to lead to lasting change.

Deviance and social control

If deviance is behaviour by one or more people which is contrary to the norms other people believe should govern behaviour, then it is a central issue in social work activity. To say that people's needs should not be neglected is another way of saying that those people who could be meeting them should be behaving differently. This assumes that it *ought to be* possible for neighbours, relatives, friends or staff in the social and health services and other organisations to behave in ways which enable unmet needs to be met. This is an implicit value position: stated explicitly, it proposes that to neglect a neighbour deviates from the assumed norm that neighbours should help each other. This norm is demonstrated when people say how guilty they feel about not helping more because of other commitments. Norms are an integral part of our diverse culture. They express a variety of different expectations about who should care for whom and who should take what kind of responsibility for others, both personally and professionally. For instance, older people have views about what personal assistance is acceptable to them: intimate personal care given by a neighbour, as opposed to a close female relative or by a spouse, goes against the 'norm' (Sinclair, Parker *et al.*, 1990). Expectations can alter over time, for example with changes in gender roles and greater cultural diversity. But the fact that some deviance is very common, such as speeding or petty dishonesty, makes little difference to the belief that this behaviour *ought to be* different.

Norms and their impact on practice

Social work is one of the mechanisms for promoting and implementing conformity to certain types of norms. Seeing social work simply as a service delivery activity, or as a form of social care and support, avoids the necessary open discussion of the norms that social workers are implicitly, if not openly, encouraging people to adopt. It is, therefore, important to identify the norms which are:

- generally accepted and embodied in laws condemning their contravention, for example those prohibiting abuse of children, racial abuse, theft and violence towards others, the self or property;
- contentious and ambiguous, for example in relation to substance abuse where the norms of young people may be very different from those of older generations or the criminal law;
- only enforced through the grey area of social convention, for example the expectations that we have about the care of each other, what constitutes good enough parenting, about what is and what is not appropriate or normal behaviour. These have cultural, gender and class dimensions and are rapidly changing, causing marked differences between the generations and social groups holding to the traditional values of their cultures and others.

In complex and rapidly changing societies like our own, there is often no general consensus about what norms should be upheld, except when there is a legal definition. This gives rise to conflicts and differences of opinion and emphasis between people, and much confusion. These differences increase the closer they relate to the details of day-to-day living: the context for much social work practice. For example, whilst there is general agreement that child abuse is wrong, there is much less agreement on whether physical chastisement is acceptable (Gulbenkian Foundation, 1995; DoH, 1995). This leads to different practices in various social organisations and institutions, and to changes over time in opinions about whether physical chastisement is acceptable in childminding. Attitudes among individual parents can differ radically, and until the late 1990s there were different rules in the UK for private and state schools on corporal punishment. In September 1998 the European Court ruled against parents who had physically punished their child, making public the whole debate about such punishment in the home.

The pivotal position of social work

No one occupational group or organisation has, or is likely ever to be given, power to define what we, as citizens, mean by 'deviant'. Definitions are the product of a wide range of negotiations, understandings, debates and political processes. However, social workers often occupy a pivotal position as mediators in such negotiations. The lack of consensus on the application of norms concerning the welfare of children is a major reason why workers are 'damned if they do and damned if they don't' intervene in many situations. Pivotal positions are uncomfortable to occupy, particularly in relation to life-threatening risks, or judgements which affect the life and liberty of citizens or intrude into the privacy of family life; or in relation to social norms about which there is dispute or disagreement. It is often assumed that the complexity, ambiguity and uncertainty inherent in the worker's pivotal position could be removed if appropriate procedures could be found to guide decisions and action. A more realistic position is to recognise this lack of certainty as an inevitable and integral dimension of the role of the social change agent. The task is to balance these different perceptions and reconcile conflicting behaviours. Ambiguity, confusion and complexity are not problems to be solved before the job can be done: working towards their resolution *is* the work.

Authority and personal style

Social workers in statutory organisations have formal authority vested in them by society through the statutory powers of their employer. They exercise this as part of the social response to deviance, and through gatekeeping public resources. Workers can appear to have unbounded formal power over the lives of people who use services, even though this is circumscribed by statute, and usually involves other organisations or workers.

Status and power derive from knowledge, skills and access to information as well as to resources, but are expressed through the personal style in which the worker provides personal assistance and support. In their practice workers have to remember what is likely to be the perception of their powers and address this, particularly in initial and early contacts: the literature and research of people who use services make abundantly clear the importance of the worker's style. They report the humiliation and even actual harm caused by lack of respect, by disregard of individual dignity through prejudice; by being stereotyped because of race, age, religion, disability or sexuality; and by the very inappropriateness of how the service is provided (Morris, 1996; Cambell and Oliver, 1996; Ahmad, 1990; Butt and Mirza, 1996; Beresford and Croft, 1993; Harding and Beresford, 1996). Change which endures is brought about not through the exercise of formal power, but by the worker interacting with the service user or carer and understanding the nature of their experience. It is important to extend such skills more widely.

Six premises for understanding patterns of interaction

Our first premise is that human behaviour is best understood through circular causality, and our second is that punctuation is a key concept for understanding social relationships.

Ecologists and other systems thinkers have shown us that a strategy of producing change through social interaction goes beyond the simplistic view of causality as a linear chain of cause and effect, where events shape the person or community as if they were lumps of clay (Capra, 1997; Watzlawick *et al.*, 1967, 1974). Simple cause-and-effect explanations of individual or collective behaviour ignore the essential inter-relationships between people. People act as well as respond, and others respond to these actions, provoking further response and so on. Watzlawick and his colleagues point out that:

> There is strong evidence that in the interaction between organisms there is a circular pattern: cause produces effect, and effect feeds back on cause, becoming itself a cause. (Watzlawick *et al.*, 1974, p. 93)

This can be represented with the following diagram. In this we can see how the behaviour of A leads to B's response, which in turn produces the next response from A and so on.

In an interaction such as this A makes sense of the other's behaviour by focusing on the sequence B.1, B.2, B.3 and so on, and B focuses on A.1, A.2, A.3. To say B.3 was caused by A.3 is to understand the interaction in a certain way, just as a plausible alternative would be to say that A.3 was caused by B.2. Such attributions are common phenomena and may be universal, particularly where each party to an

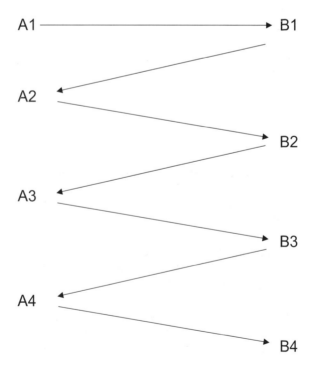

interaction blames the other or themselves for what is happening. Either of them may attribute different causes to the other's sequence of behaviour, blaming the other's personality, their past or whatever theory they use to make sense of human behaviour. Any of these explanations may be partially true.

Systems thinkers from organisation research and family therapy would see the attribution of individual blame within patterns of such interaction involving the reciprocal behaviour of several, if not many, people as a matter of 'punctuation' (Minuchin and Fishman, 1981; Watzlawick *et al.*, 1974). By this they mean that cause and effect is attributed to one person or another and is seen as being dependent upon the position of the person making the attribution. They see the attribution of 'cause and then effect' as being dependent upon where a sequence of behaviour is said to start, the way that full-stops frame a stream of words into sentences.

This analysis can illuminate the relationship between two or more people, as it can help make sense of the relationships between nations. For example, was the Cold War provoked by the West or the East? Did it start with the Russian Revolution, after the Second World War with the Allied occupation of Germany, with the Berlin blockade, the building of the Wall, or with Winston Churchill's famous speech declaring that an 'iron curtain has fallen across Europe'? Recognising the circular nature of such relationships, and how each side is using alternative punctuations of the other's actions, enables us to see how the behaviour of each perpetuates, or is a causal factor in, the response of the other.

Watzlawick has argued that in understanding human relationships, as in modern physics, the point of view of the observer is decisive:

> In contrast to objects, however, human relationships are not phenomena that exist objectively, in their own right as it were, nor is it possible to have a consensus about their properties. Above all, if there are differences of opinion about the characteristics of a human relationship, it cannot be proved that one of the partners is right and the other wrong, or, to anticipate one of our main topics [the author is applying systems theory to understanding mental health problems], that one partner is 'normal' and the other is 'crazy'. Relationships, the contents of our interpersonal, pragmatic reality, are not real in the same sense as objects are; they have their 'reality' only in the perception of the partners, and even this is shared only partially by the partners. (Watzlawick, 1990, p. 16)

Whether or not we agree that our perceptions of other people are not as real as of objects, we can see that Watzlawick and his colleagues provide us with a powerful insight into the nature of social relationships and particularly the perpetuation of some of their problems. For example, he points out that:

> Ordering sequences in one particular way or another creates what, without undue exaggeration, may be called different realities. This is particularly evident in certain kinds of human conflict. A mother may see herself as a bridge between her husband and her children: if it were not for her there would be no bond or contact between him and them. Far from sharing this view, the husband sees her as an obstacle between him and his children: if it were not for her con-stant interference and monitoring, he could have a much closer relationship with them. If we do not bear in mind that this is a punctuation – and not a definition of one way of behaving rather than another – we may become victims of the same fallacy as the two parents and consider one of them mad or bad, the typical charges made when communication breaks down as a result of the discrepant punctuation of jointly experienced sequences of behav-iour. (Watzlawick *et al.*, 1974, p. 62)

In artificially extracting the individual from his or her social milieu we do more than cut down on the variables. Time is also frozen: the person becomes a static object consisting of components made up of different historical or social influences, rather than a person interacting with others and so constantly changing. The innately human aspects of this 'object' are consequently overlooked. The result of thus objectify-ing people is that the proactive nature of the interaction, and the commonalties between us, are ignored. Each individual is subject to a 'life cycle', but all too often this is reduced to a series of isolated snapshots – birth, childhood, adolescence, young adulthood, maturity, retirement, old age, death – rather than perceived as a moving picture show with benefit of zoom lenses. The attraction of simple snapshots is that they reduce the probability of becoming overwhelmed by detail and complexity. But there are other tactics for surviving in this unpredictable swirling torrent of events, based on coherent principles which can help us pattern such complexity for practice.

We have argued that usually one person or group of people, often the least powerful, is held responsible for what goes on, particularly what goes wrong, in relationships or social situations. We can see this any time we enter a room where two or more children, or for that matter adults, are fighting. Schooled in the arts of punctuation and the attribution of responsibility, one or other of them, and normally both, will be quick to point out that the other started it. An observer entering the room enters the fight at an arbitrary point and inevitably forms an opinion of what has been happening based on this first sight: their own first punctuation of the sequence of behaviour. The wise observer knows that one person's retaliation is the other's provocation, leading in turn to their retaliation. Who actually struck the first blow – a significant, conventional punctuation – may be discernible, but even this is likely to have been in retaliation to a felt psychological and emotional blow: precise knowledge of the seeds of the conflict becomes lost. It is likely that an observer, unaware of their own prejudices, will punctuate events to perpetuate their own preconceived perceptions of one or other party in such disputes: he is a 'good boy' so is likely to be the victim, he is a 'trouble maker' so likely to be the villain. We are just as likely to punctuate many social situations in the same way. For example, an older person is likely to be seen as in need of support and a younger person as resourceful, whereas each might offer help to the other. They, and their relationship to the rest of us, will not be seen as the problem. The danger of such over-simplifications should be obvious, but they are often masked by the definitions of the situation assumed by those who refer individuals for social services, just as they are reinforced by the way that much social policy is framed to focus on individuals.

Disputes over punctuation are often serious and far reaching. Racial and sexual harassment provide examples of how punctuation of events can distort perceptions. The person who 'explodes' after putting up with months of harassment can be blamed and labelled as aggressive or violent, while those responsible for the persistent abuse can be seen as victims. Are street riots and demonstrations in urban centres following a clash between the police and local drug takers caused by 'police provocation', the effects of illegal drugs, 'unruly young people', 'their parents' failures', 1960s educational ideas, 'politically motivated minorities', 'unemployment', 'racial discrimination', 'underclass poverty and alienation', 'late twentieth century capitalism', 'the weather' or of preconceived and media perpetuated 'causes': the list is almost endless. The answer is often 'yes' for somebody in each case. These punctuations are often provided by prejudice, and voiced without any direct knowledge of the events. Even if none of the assumed causes is true, that is supported by a full analysis of events, they influence and sometimes determine what we see.

A theory which can cope with the complexity of multiple perceptions helps us focus on reciprocal interactions between actors and not simply on the actors themselves. We can recognise that effects are often causes which are then effects, and see the patterns which connect people and perpetuate their problems. We should also recognise that although all the actors will actually see events differently, some will lie about their perception if it suits them, and so further complicate accurate problem definition and resolution. This approach to social problems does not deny that individuals should be held responsible for their actions, nor that there is a distinction between truth and falsehood. But it does not seek to over-simplify social situations by only holding one person responsible, and so running the risk of perpetuating prejudice and the scapegoating of individuals or particular social groups. It also helps us guard against seeing only one person as 'being in need' and so perpetuating the myth that social services are only there to serve the interests of those who have come to be seen as 'service users'. It attempts to work towards encompassing the full complexity of events so that problems can be better understood and our attempts to intervene made more effective.

The idea of punctuation in social events enables us to recognise that the imposition of simple linear 'cause and effect' analyses on these situations is at best partial. It is typically not only *incomplete* but also *biased*. It may be the case that one party was at one time 'the cause' of the problem. But that becomes of only historical relevance: it is the pattern of relationships that has to change. Both parties need to change, and this of course also brings about unforeseeable changes in other relationships, which in turn require understanding and the invention of new solutions to the new problems that then arise. Tackling one, then the other, to achieve such change is ineffectual: the action of the second provokes the recycling of the pattern before work with the first can be completed.

Peter and the punctuation of events

The story of Peter, the foster child who was sexually abused, has been told *as if* it begins with his joining the foster family – as if all the difficulties he now has have been 'caused' by his being fostered, and more particularly 'caused' solely by his foster father's sexual abuse. This is legitimate, or 'right', from one point of view, but it is also quite arbitrary, and leaves out explanations of the prior steps which led to his being accommodated away from home in the first place. These have contributed to his current situation. Perhaps the solution to the problems with his own family, being fostered, has become the main problem and other options should have been explored for him. A similar, parallel spiral of events could be described to explain how David became the person he was when he met Peter. In a strictly scientific sense we do not know what 'the causes' of his behaviour are, but we have to act now. Peter's story illustrates the multiple facets of how these situations came about, how they are defined as being in need of change and so how change might be accomplished.

The Jones family story is told *as if* it begins with Mrs Jones having a fall – as if the fall, or the subsequent injury is 'the cause' of the present difficulty. But from the hospital doctor's point of view the cause of the problem she is acting upon may be very different. Her anxiety and actions may be provoked by Mrs Jones's social worker's reluctance to expedite admission to residential care quickly and free a bed, which in turn may be caused by cutbacks in the number of geriatric beds on her ward. The cause from Shirley's point of view might be her mother and father's relationship, which meant that when he died her mother was unable to function sufficiently independently because she had concentrated her life on the home and the family and had few contacts outside it.

All of these possible explanatory sequences of cause and effect are equally true. The definition which dominates the negotiations between the people involved will not do so because it is the only true one, but because the person or people presenting that perspective have been more successful than others in their, often implicit, negotiations over the definition of the social problem. Some people have more power or authority than others when it comes to defining the situation. Social workers and other staff are vested with authority to assess a social situation, but their conclusions will be only *their* way of punctuating events and attributing responsibility, and will be shaped by many influences, including their own and their manager's perceptions of the remit, responsibilities and resources of the organisation.

The role of the worker and other agents of change is to act as broker, as go-between in these punctuations, and not to initiate or join in the hunt for the one true cause of the problem. Instead the worker needs to understand that a particular punctuation may be contributing to definitions of the problem which make it seem insoluble. Equally importantly, she needs to be able to identify and validate punctuation which allows different options to be tried by the people involved, and to do this within the statutory and legal framework and the policies of the organisation in which she works.

This leads to our third premise: deviant behaviour, behavioural problems and other behaviour typically presented for 'help', sustains the concomitant behaviour of others within the same social network or system.

Since social problems involve more than one person, and problem behaviours are in part a response to a particular situation, symptomatic behaviour is in some senses appropriate behaviour: appropriate in the sense that it dovetails with that of others and often has the consequence of maintaining the pattern of people's relationships. In context it is survival behaviour: it *makes sense*, even when it looks irrational or 'mad' when taken out of context, or judged 'bad' by those using commonly accepted standards. The questions that need to be asked are: what sort of situation, what sort of sequence of behaviour, is perpetuating this kind of adaptation? The forces perpetuating the status quo may be experienced as resistance to change by those trying to help. Even if problems are not demonstrably initiated or caused by the interactions in people's immediate or extended network, they can be perpetuated by them. This is the reason that insiders in families, groups, communities, tolerate risks and behaviour which to an outsider look impossible. These interactions are hard to untangle and even harder to change or extricate people from, whether the problem is violence or abuse, drugs or alcohol, bullying behaviour in school, in the community or at work.

Punctuation and the organisation

John and secure accommodation

A young teenager, John, is being accommodated by the local authority. He runs away and returns to his father, who insists he has to go back to the children's home. Instead John wanders the streets, joins a squat, shoplifts and commits a burglary, for which he is caught and subsequently returned to the children's home. He is told he risks being placed in secure accommodation if he continues to behave in this way. He runs away again, commits another offence, and is returned to the children's home, from which he absconds again. His father is even more angry and rejecting on hearing of this behaviour.

At the same time, the social worker responsible presents his situation to a panel of senior managers in her department with a view to applying to the court for a short period in secure accommodation. The panel is the gatekeeper for this service, both to ensure that no other options are viable and to ensure the proper use of an expensive resource. They fulfil these functions by making sure that it is not used for those who do not 'need' it. The social worker's recommendation is rejected. When John eventually reappears in court, the social worker is asked by the magistrate what her plans are for John, and she reports on the rejection by the panel of her recommendation for secure accommodation. The magistrate adjourns the case and makes a point of informing the local press of the situation, so supporting the view that 'something needs to be done'. Subsequently, the panel reconvenes and agrees to a recommendation for a secure accommodation placement for John.

On the one hand this can look like a straightforward story of a young offender out of control: a young person who 'causes' all the care and social control responses which then ensue. However, true though this is, it is only one punctuation of the sequence of events, based on only some of the evidence, and one which masks the ways in which the behaviours of all the adults in the situation are as much the cause of the escalation of events as is the behaviour of John. Accepting one definition of these events overlooks much of the available evidence and obscures the fact that the behaviour of each sustains the concomitant behaviour of the other.

John's accommodation in the first place was precipitated by the social worker accepting the definition of John as the problem, which arose when his father remarried and John came into conflict with his new stepmother. The social worker recognised there was a relationship problem and that it was not all John's fault, but nevertheless saw the solution to this problem in terms of the provision of a service, residential accommodation, for John. This was reinforced by John himself initially seeing this as the solution, but becoming more and more angry at his rejection as he grew older. The social worker, looking primarily for a short-term solution to the immediate crisis, and overlooking the potentially harmful effects of entering the institution, was primed to provide the service that John and his father seemed to want.

Here we can see how, right from the beginning, the behaviours of the different actors mesh with each other, and thus sustain and escalate a particular punctuation of the problem and its solution, which then becomes the problem, although for the actors involved this becomes increasingly difficult to see. This process becomes a vicious spiral in which people who are meant to be working together towards a common end, such as the social worker and members of her management team on the secure accommodation panel, end up working against each other. Instead of constructively managing the problem they begin to contribute towards the perpetuation of John's behaviour and the escalation of his identity as a 'difficult delinquent'. All the efforts of the social worker in overcoming the resistance of the panel simply reinforce the labelling of John as 'out of control' and 'delinquent'. He reacts to this in ways which then reinforce the labelling of him.

Our fourth and fifth premises follow from the complementary nature of interactional behaviour. They are that: a change in an individual's behaviour or circumstances will cause change in the patterns of interaction of which it is a part.

Negatively stated, this emphasises the natural 'resistance' to such change: an individual's behaviour in his relationships with others can only change to the extent that other people in that set of relationships change their reciprocal behaviour.

In Mrs Jones's story, Shirley could have continued to behave as if she does not want to have her mother living with her. If she is not helped to voice her ambivalence, she might not dare to think about or say that she would have her mother at home provided she can get some respite and her mother can develop other sources of company. If Shirley never explicitly says anything about Mrs Jones living with her and Colin, both Colin and her mother may implicitly interpret this as meaning that Shirley definitely does not want this to happen. Consequently, not only do they not raise this as a possibility: they act as if this option is definitely out of the frame; and because they think Shirley may feel bad about it, talk positively about residential care. Shirley then interprets this as a genuine expression of both Colin's and Mrs Jones's preference, and so is even more reluctant to raise the possibility of her mother coming back to live with her on certain conditions.

Options are closed down and the solutions polarised as either more of the same or a residential care home. Thus the behaviour of each reinforces that of the other, so that one can change only if the others do also. Shirley, for example, might begin to voice her doubts about residential care, but Mrs Jones could hear this as just guilt masking Shirley's real preference, and so reassure her and thus maintain the status quo. For the pattern of interaction to change reciprocally, Shirley would have to be more persistent, or Mrs Jones to start voicing her own reservations as well. These processes are not mysterious or exclusive to social work. They are the common web of everyday life and the rich material of novels.

The role of the worker as a third party, marginal to self-perpetuating interactions, can be crucial in either reinforcing these processes, or establishing a change in the pattern by resisting the tendency to make an alliance with one person in a network, rather than seek to work with *the network as a whole*. How the worker introduces herself, whether she does or does not side with different members of the network, and how she continually locates responsibility with different people, including other organisations and workers, and encourages them to negotiate differently with each other, are all central to bringing about change.

This leads us to the sixth premise, to be discussed fully in the next chapter. There are different types of change in relationships: first- and second-order change. It is crucial for the worker to distinguish these and behave consistently with the order of change being promoted.

Understanding the nature of social and interpersonal change, the different orders of change involved, and how this understanding can be used, is crucial. We devote the next chapter to this topic, and build on this in Chapter 7 with a discussion of the nature of assessment and intervention.

6

Managing and Mapping Change

Introduction

In the previous chapters we have argued that bringing about change in social situations, through introducing innovations in the ways people tackle particular problems, is central to the social work task. Often such change activity is, appropriately, 'social control', and thus an area of conflict. Even at the level of the individual or family, there can be conflicts of interest and over who thinks who should do what. The worker may have a significant part to play in mediating between people and the organisations involved. This will also be reflected in any wider unresolved conflicts in the community which the social work team is a part of, and in which the workers involved have to be continuously seeking change.

The story of the police inspector which opened Chapter 5 is the story of a response to people's demands which seeks change in the behaviour and attitudes of members of the community as a basis for dealing more effectively with local transport problems. The policeman's challenging approach can be seen as just the first step in a longer-term strategy through which a range of more specific innovations can be introduced in the behaviour of ordinary people. These innovations include the way they use their cars and their speeding; the way workers respond to the public referring problems to them, particularly over what responsibilities they can and cannot accept; and possibly the reallocation of a range of material and personal resources.

The story of Gary and his family, with which we began this book, is similarly a story of workers becoming involved with members of a family because of wider concern about the care of a child; and of attempts to influence the behaviour of all those involved, including that of the workers who, by focusing on the strengths of the family and by engaging in 'upstream' interventions, are themselves part of a change process. All these dimensions are important if social work is to address issues of social inclusion when responding to individuals' needs. In this chapter we pick up from Chapter 5 the discussion of ways of understanding the crucial difference between different dimensions of change in relationships, and further our understanding of the nature of social change by offering ways of mapping some of the people and processes involved.

The theory of change and practice

A workable theory of change requires an increase in our own and other people's understandings of how:

- to bring about change in the relationships between individuals and groups in the community that perpetuate problems;
- the nature of the relationships between a whole range of significant people needs to be understood and changed, reunderstood and changed again.

The task for workers is constantly to reinvent practice through forming and reforming partnerships with all the people involved in particular social problems. This necessitates recognition of six key characteristics of change agent activity:

1 **Social workers move in an environment of different definitions and perceptions of the reality of social situations.**
2 **The formulation of a problem is always a joint enterprise between the people involved and the social worker.**
3 **Assessment, intervention and service delivery are essentially the same enterprise.**
4 **To achieve change, it is often necessary to reframe the problem.**
5 **Alternative behaviour has to be demonstrated.**
6 **Resources often have to be reallocated.**

*Social workers move in an environment of different definitions and
perceptions of the reality of social situations*

Practitioners gather information about who sees what as a problem
and what they see as potential solutions through their interactions
with people. Practice is not about collecting 'facts' in an objective
sense through responses to 'neutral' questions. What people say to a
worker about what they perceive as a social problem will depend upon
their changing perception of the problem, the level of risk or threat to
themselves or others, their response to the behaviour of the worker,
and their perception of the organisation which he represents. How
the worker in turn responds in the chain of responses will influence
both what he is told and how. The aim of facilitating the empowerment of the service user often fails despite the best intentions of front-
line workers and their managers because users are not involved from
the beginning in negotiating and planning changes as well as carrying them out. Empowerment is not a gift which can be bestowed or
withheld: it comes from having a central, not a peripheral, part in
the process.

Through the processes of intervention, feedback and hypothesis-
ing, balancing and negotiating the authority and responsibility of
the organisation against the rights and expectations of people using
services, a version of reality is negotiated by all those involved. This
may hold only as long as the specific interaction, or may form the basis
for longer-term work. Our intervention perpetuates or changes the
unfolding pattern of events. It is an essential premise of our approach
that no single reality exists for everyone, individuals or organisation. One may dominate because of factors such as statutory or legal
powers, organisational role, class, ethnicity, gender, age, disability,
sexuality, or mental health. For example, a disabled person comment-
ing on a training programme on community care said:

> I had never been on a course which was just for disabled people
> before ... I was completely surprised by how empowered I suddenly
> felt, being among people I didn't have to explain or justify to how
> angry I felt about years of oppression. (Hemmings and Morris, 1997)

Workers need expertise in understanding how different people
define their reality, and expertise in working with these different
definitions. People's experience and culture, their age, social class,
ethnic group, gender, religion, sexual orientation, whether they have

impairment or learning difficulties or mental health problems, all contribute to and are part of their view of the world. How they see themselves, the appropriateness of relationships and what they define as a problem, are all influenced by these frameworks. Although carrying statutory responsibilities and having the power of the organisation behind them, workers cannot define people's realities. Their job is to develop mutual understanding, particularly when the need for change, or the nature of the change required, is disputed.

The formulation of a problem is always a joint enterprise between workers and other people

Workers cannot avoid working in relationship with a range of other people, but can treat them negligently as subjects or objects of concern rather than as full partners. Partnership emphasises explicitness and openness, by sharing expertise and recognising differences and conflicts as well areas of agreement. Workers must include themselves and their intervention in the assessment of situations, examining not only how members of a network respond to each other but also how they respond to the worker. If the impact of his position and behaviour is ignored, it becomes easy for the worker to slip into using his own view of the problems and options as *the* defining one, and to believe that these have been worked out in collaboration with the service user (Marsh and Fisher, 1992).

Assessment, intervention and service delivery are essentially the same enterprise

The case examples we have used demonstrate that distinctions between assessment, intervention and service delivery, while a convenience for technical and theoretical analyses, cannot be made in practice without masking significant dimensions of the whole task. They are each a different punctuation of the same activity. Arranging foster care for Peter is to provide a service – to provide substitute care; but it is also a profound change in his life and that of both his family of origin and the foster family, with many unforeseeable and unplanned consequences. At the same time Peter, his experience, and his relationships with others is being continuously monitored and assessed, along with those of all the other people involved. This assessment occurs through the statutory monitoring of Peter as a child being fostered by the local authority, and through the whole process of reassessment which occurs following his report of being sexually abused. But these assessment processes are also services being provided, and furthermore are also interventions.

To achieve change, it is often necessary to reframe the problem

Some problems are perpetuated by people being locked into obsolete perceptions of situations, or of people's behaviour, or of each other, as we describe in more detail in Chapter 8. Problems are also sustained when people have a limited view of options and alternatives; where former survival strategies are no longer appropriate or become too high risk; or when they perceive themselves as powerless and unable to behave in any alternative way. Where there is overwhelming poverty and discrimination, what may seem like very small changes to an outsider can have great significance for those experiencing the situation, tackling the issues of day-to-day living with inadequate resources. Problems that are defined as insoluble clearly need to be redefined if change is to take place; workers need to confront existing perceptions of problems, including their own, where these serve only to maintain the status quo. In John's case, all the time that the problem is seen *only* in terms of John's offending behaviour, the only solutions available will be more of the same: those aimed at controlling him. These will inevitably tend to perpetuate the situation by encouraging his committed resistance to control.

Alternative behaviour has to be demonstrated

Patterns of dysfunctional behaviour can be repeated because of lack of other options or support to try them out, the absence of confidence, or low self-esteem. New behaviour has to be demonstrated and tried out in safety if the risks of change are to be confronted and behavioural repertoires expanded. The worker can demonstrate changes through his own behaviour within the existing patterns of relationship, by behaving differently from the expectations of some of the key actors. A key dimension of this behaviour is often to confront painful problems that others avoid, to act as if a solution can be found when others have given up hope. Another approach is to involve other people who have survived similar problems or difficulties and have regained or moved to greater control over their own lives, behaviour and relationships. There is clear evidence that people who have been through traumatic crisis or suffered long-term oppression do not want to be helped by those with no direct relevant experience (Newburn, 1993; Hemmings and Morris, 1997). Increasingly user- and carer-led groups and advocacy schemes, for example, are demonstrating alternative responses to care and control issues in ways which promote opportunities for independent living. The worker's skill and knowledge may be required for the complex task of helping people initiate and support such activity, but not in deciding how they should live.

Resources often have to be reallocated

Change in social situations can be brought about by:

- workers adding services directly from their own or a related organisation;
- accessing other resources in the community to meet needs which cannot be met by people currently in the immediate social network;
- intervention geared to changing the pattern of relationship within a social situation, including linking those with needs to those who could meet them and initiating and supporting community support projects; or
- some combination of all these which changes over time as problems change.

Resource reallocation may be achieved through existing mechanisms of distribution or a change in the patterns of resource allocation. For example, a team or organisation may access new resources through European or UK-wide funding or local agreements such as Regeneration Schemes, Mental Health Service Frameworks, Action Zones and Joint Commissioning arrangements. In these cases change is fuelled by finance, but attention to human resources is equally significant if such radical changes are to be made and sustained.

First- and second-order change

Most contemporary writers on change and the management of change distinguish between different orders of change: radical or routine;

revolutionary or evolutionary; incremental or fundamental (Nord and Tucker, 1987; Angle and Van de Ven, 1989; Beckhard and Pritchard, 1992). Such changes can also be understood as 'first' and 'second' order changes in the relationships between people (Watzlawick *et al.*, 1967, 1974) .

A first-order change is a change within the rules of a given social system, that is within the existing pattern of relationships between people. The nature of the relationships between people, the roles they play out with each other, stays the same even where specific tasks and particular behaviour change significantly.

We can illustrate this by looking at the example of a family where the parents are locked in struggle. The mother may lose out and be dominated by her husband; the children may form an alliance with the mother and, as they grow up, the father may begin to lose out to his wife. Things do change, for better or for worse, depending upon who you are and what is happening. However, the family remains a 'family locked in struggle'.

A second-order change occurs when there is a change in the rules, a change in the nature of the system, when the rules and the boundaries of a pattern of relationships change in an unprecedented way. The roles of each party in the relationship change.

For the family locked in struggle to move to a cooperative pattern would require second-order change. To increase the numbers of people receiving a service from an organisation, or to change some part of the service, would typically involve first-order changes within the organisation. But to change the way needs are met by organising a user-led or community-based group often involves a second-order change in key relationships. To alter existing child care procedures directed by policy makers would be a first-order change in the relationship between senior managers and staff. In contrast, to introduce child care procedures designed to change the actions of workers from focusing on investigations as the entry point into child protection, to early intervention directed at improving the social environment within which parenting is taking place, would require a second-order change in key relationships. There is no simple relationship between first-order change and providing services, or between second-order change and change agent activity. The latter is not just a larger-scale version of the former.

Second-order change aimed at altering the nature of patterns of relationships goes outside the current patterns of interaction within which the problems are locked. Typically workers have to change what they do, as well as what others do, in order to initiate second-order change where they have become an integral part of the relationships which need to change. In John's story, his offending behaviour was being exacerbated by the behaviour of the worker, John's family, other workers and the court. All would have to change their behaviours to change how they are relating to John and to each other, that is change the rules of the situation in which they are all enmeshed. John would also have to change his behaviour if a new pattern is to be sustained. Synchronising these reciprocal changes in behaviour is essential but it is also extremely difficult. As we shall see in Chapter 8, one or other party has to assume that the other will change in the future. Social workers using such approaches must expect pessimists to see such optimism as naïvety, when it is in practice an essential ingredient of attempts to effect changes in human behaviour.

Second-order change usually comes about through novel solutions, as compared to the usual or routine solutions available from within the assumptions held by members of an existing network. The ability to identify such solutions is the essential value of people in a marginal, third party position. For network members, even simple solutions can be difficult to perceive and difficult to achieve.

The practice of managing change means being able to understand and to use this theory of change in situations as different as that of a family like the Joneses, and of an organisation such as the department responsible for John.

Mapping change

Innovation is at the heart of social work activity designed to produce change in people's circumstances or in their problems. We have underlined the fact that most of the problems referred to social care organisations are resolved in many similar situations by the actions of other people. Sometimes the problem can be managed or resolved by adding a service or by linking those with unmet needs to those who can help. But where intervention is required to change the behaviour of an individual, or within a family or social network, or the relationship between key parties, the problem has usually already been addressed but failed to be solved or managed satisfactorily. Under these circumstances social work involves 'innovation', defined as the application of new solutions to problems (Rogers, 1996; Smale, 1998).

It is not unusual for workers to intervene in the lives of individuals, families and communities, using very implicit or incomplete models of the process of interpersonal and social change. No one theory or practice can guarantee particular outcomes, since no one person, or group of people, can have sufficient control over the complex processes involved or the ever-changing context within which they operate. But by making sure that the way we are managing change is consistent with the actual innovations being introduced, it is possible to avoid the worst unintended consequences that are often the result of our best intentions to reform practice. The Managing Change Through Innovation approach (MCTI) (Smale, 1996, 1998) identifies four strategic dimensions to be considered in managing the process of introducing an innovation, a new way of tackling a problem:

1   The foundations of change: what changes and what stays the same?
2   Planning through the Innovation Trinity:
    • mapping the people
    • analysing the innovation
    • understanding the context.
3   Negotiations between key people: individual, family, social network, community and/or inter-organisation development.
4   Feedback and monitoring consequences of change.

We shall discuss these four dimensions of change through an account of the ways in which some innovations in community-based practice were introduced by a social work team.

The foundations of change: what changes and what stays the same?

In partnership with other local organisations and user groups, members of a newly created locality-based team developed a profile of the community they served, and the range of resources and social problems characteristic of the area. The team identified that the bulk of their time and other resources went on individualised statutory investigations, family work and care management. It was recognised that they were in a 'vicious spiral' through which the demands and expectations made it impossible for them to undertake the longer-term 'upstream' work necessary for reducing these individualised statutory demands, and which could help create a more 'virtuous spiral' of informal, preventative partnership practice in the community. They wanted to implement what they saw as the potentially empowering spirit of both the NHS and Community Care and Children Acts by developing more effective teamwork within their own team, with other organisations and with people in the community. Over a period of some months the team members asked themselves, and others, the following broad questions:

- What needs to change?
- What should stay the same?
- For whom is the status quo a problem?
- Who wants change and for what reasons?

Two points are worth remembering. First, exclusive concentration on what we want changed can mean that things we want to hold on to get lost in the process because no one thought about them. Good practice, good parts of relationships, can get 'mislaid' in the rush to change things: hence it is crucial to identify what can and should 'stay the same'. Secondly, the perspectives of the people using services can be drawn in too late for them to have any real influence over what happens. The requirements of the organisation, and the expectations of other powerful stakeholders, can dominate so that service users are given merely token involvement. The end result for them can be things that do need to change either stay very much the same or get worse.

What needs to change?

By this is meant, what has to change in order to manage, or resolve, particular social problems. It refers to broad ideas about solutions to problems, how the mission of the organisation and its tasks could be more effectively achieved, and how people's circumstances could be improved. Some of the team's answers included:

- infrequent and unreliable public transport to rural areas of the locality;
- insufficient or inadequate crèche facilities on two of the public housing estates;
- insufficient or ineffective team involvement in local community development and in departmental-wide commissioning of innovative services;
- patchy inter-organisation system for recruiting, training and supporting volunteers;

- too many children on the at-risk register and/or accommodated by the local authority;
- unreliable and uneven recruitment and retention of foster parents;
- conflict in collaboration with the specialist mental health team;
- dominance of bureaucratic 'paper-chasing' in departmental models of assessment and care management.

What should stay the same?

Some of the current practices which needed to be retained included:

- the geographical boundaries, membership and management structure of the team;
- the contribution of team members to joint investigations of child sexual abuse;
- supervision of students from local DipSW courses;
- provision of a staff member on the management board of the local council of community service;
- financial support for existing voluntary groups;
- use of most of the existing not-for-profit provider organisations.

For whom is the status quo a problem? Who wants change and for what reasons?

The team developed an understanding of the importance of teasing out answers to these questions despite the complexities, and also came to recognise how answers change over time. Examples of the kinds of issues which they discovered needed to be addressed as part of the process of introducing specific innovations included:

- The scarcity of public transport to the rural parts of the area was seen as a problem by most local people. Anyone without a car had very restricted access to employment in the local town, problems getting to the hospital and shops where food was cheaper, or to adult education facilities. Some politicians in the authority saw it as a problem, but not others, with consequent implications for the need for sensitivity to the political consequences of how lobbying and campaigning might be conducted or supported by the team. Issues of transport for local people were seen as an appropriate focus for team attention by some senior managers in their department, but not others, who viewed it as outside their remit.

- Poor crèche facilities were seen as a major problem for some young single-parent families, and were thus a problem for team members who recognised that some of the stress being experienced resulted in referrals which otherwise would not happen, or which could be dealt with in a more informal way through good day-to-day contact between the team members, parents using the crèche and other workers. However, this was not seen as a major problem or priority for the local education department which controlled the most suitable buildings available in the area, or some members of the social services committee who saw the responsibility as lying with other departments.
- Local politicians and senior managers saw the high numbers of children on the register or accommodated as a necessary dimension of child protection. However, for the team members and families involved it was a problem, and there was a strong desire to change the status quo in this area of service, while at the same time neither putting children at risk of abuse nor team members at risk of censure. Offering only crisis intervention and preoccupation with a small number of families with acute problems engendered high levels of anxiety and absorbed virtually all available resources. Both workers and families recognised that a situation had to reach crisis point before help would be offered. By that time many problems had become much more complex and intransigent, the family and its members clearly labelled as a problem and all the pathological relationships more entrenched.

Planning through the Innovation Trinity

The **Innovation Trinity** is at the core of the MCTI approach. It helps change agents to identify the key areas involved in a new way of solving problems and the action and negotiations that have to be undertaken. The trinity is composed of:

- **mapping the significant people**, to identify who has to take what action with whom – and what relationships need to change;
- **analysing the nature of the innovation**, to plan appropriate action and recognise feasible timescales;
- **understanding the context of change**, to identify how key dimensions of the human and wider environment can be used to promote desired change.

The well established and still growing body of research on the diffusion of innovations (Rogers, 1996) and the management of change and innovation (Angle and Van de Ven, 1989) gives clear indications of the characteristics of key players and why some innovations prove to be more adoptable than others in certain circumstances. It is beyond the scope of this book to enter into a detailed discussion, but these factors are introduced here because they relate to central dimensions of the social work task.

Mapping the significant people – identifying the key players

Let us return to the social work team described above. Team members recognised that they would need to develop an overview, or map, of all the people likely to be affected by specific changes in order to introduce innovations in their approach to working with others to tackle local social problems. This would help them see who needed to be brought on board if a specific innovation was to have a chance of being successful, who could help, and who might make it difficult. This meant identifying all the significant people, or key players (see Figure 6.1), and relating them to the key roles played by different players as identified in the diffusion of innovations research (see Figure 6.2). Maps will be different for different innovations, but the team's map looked like

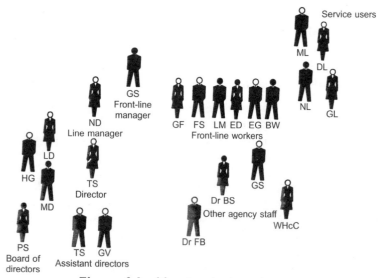

Figure 6.1 Mapping the key players

that in Figure 6.1 when they began their work on improving access
to transport.

The key players identified by research on the diffusion of innovations (Rogers, 1996) and tested with practitioners and managers in the
UK and in the USA (Smale 1996, 1998) include:

- **Innovators** who introduce a new idea for solving a problem or
  method of work. It does not have to be original, only new to the
  people they are working with.
- **Change agents** responsible for implementing the change, whether
  on a formal or informal basis: they might be workers or key people
  acting in the situation to bring about change.
- **Product champions**, a term used in marketing to describe those
  crucial people who both adopt new methods and take up the cause
  by spreading the message to others.
- **Early adopters** who take up the new ideas quickly and take the
  initiative to find out more.
- **Later adopters** who tend to rely on local experience and direct
  personal contact before they take on new ideas.
- **Opinion leaders**, people who have a significant influence in family,
  community or organisation or occupation about the way problems
  should be tackled or the methods and approaches that others use.
- **Gatekeepers** who control how much and what resources are used.
  It is important to recognise that all people are gatekeepers of their
  own resources of time and energy and their own cooperation.
- **Consultants**, those who provide a sounding board and support or
  professional supervision, a third-party perspective, whether they
  are employed for this purpose or are a trusted friend or colleague.
- **Legitimate initiators**, the people who are seen as having the
  authority to introduce change in organisations. In the community
  it is likely that different people will be seen as legitimate by
  different people: for example, some will assume that doctors should
  prescribe certain solutions, that community leaders should lead on
  some initiatives and that only people with direct personal
  experience have credibility on others.
- **Minders**, often those in senior management who support innovators when the going gets tough, or those in the community who
  offer support and protection to people taking the risk of
  attempting new solutions to their problems.
- **Opponents**, those who are against a particular change. They may
  disagree with the definition of the problem, or the chosen solution,

or be hostile to the people introducing it, or to the people who will benefit. The reasons may vary from being a genuine champion of an alternative proposal requiring the same resources to personal investment in the status quo, from prejudice against certain solutions or to people wanting a peaceful life.

- **Close collaborators** are the people change agents work closely with during implementation of a change. Analysis, strategies and tactics are discussed with them and plans made.
- **Network entrepreneurs** who work at linking people to others, initiating and maintaining links between people to 'make networking happen'.

It will quickly be recognised by those applying these categories to maps of the social situations they are concerned with that frequently people wear more than one of these hats. A product champion of one innovation will be an opponent to another.

When applied to colleagues, staff in other organisations, members of the local community or people in the user's or carer's network, the framework provides a way of thinking and planning specific changes. When mapped out, this second stage produces Figure 6.2.

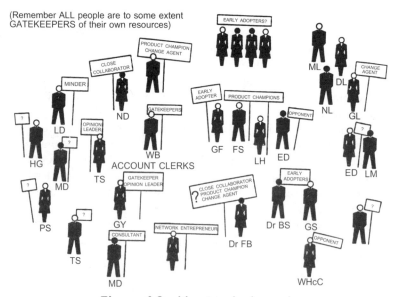

Figure 6.2 Mapping the key roles

The next stage is to ascertain the role each of these people is likely to play in bringing about change in the people involved (Beckhard and Pritchard, 1992, p. 72). Is he or she needed:

- to make it happen?
- to help it to happen by providing resources?
- to let it happen by not blocking the process?

What the innovation means for all the key participants will also be a crucial determinant of their attitude towards the particular changes suggested. For example, does the proposed change mean a significant change in identity for key players? These and other important dimensions of key players' responses are discussed elsewhere (Smale, 1998). A third map can be drawn to help identify the impact of the innovation of each of the relationships between key people. This is done in answer to the key questions:

- Within which relationships can the innovation be introduced without changing the nature of the relationship (first-order change)?
- Which relationships will need to change to adopt the innovation (second-order change)? (Smale, 1996)

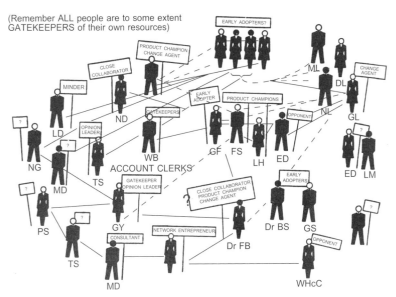

Figure 6.3 Mapping the impact on relationships

Some of what this mapping means in practice for a team can be illustrated by the example of introducing the idea of a locality based transport action group to monitor transport provision, and lobby and negotiate for changes in services.

Introducing a locality based transport action group

- The **innovator**, a local person with a long history of involvement in public transport, proposed the idea at a public meeting, actively promoted it and subsequently became chair of the committee.
- The **change agents** included the innovator himself and a community development worker working with the social work team who became involved in the project.
- The key **product champions** were a local councillor who became enthusiastic about the idea and promoted it in important forums, and a member of the board of one of the bus companies, whose elderly parents lived in the area and depended to some extent on the services of the competing bus companies.
- The **early adopters** included several local people who attended the original public meeting. A significant member of this group was a young disabled woman using a wheelchair, who drew attention to access issues which affected not only herself but a number of other people in the area. She was also a service user.
- The **later adopters** included managers of the major bus company serving the area who, not unreasonably, waited to see whether a local group could actually be formed and supported, then became involved, especially through direct contact with other transport staff and an interested member of the local chamber of commerce.
- The **opinion leaders** with significant influence in the different organisations involved included the team leader of the social work team, managers in the bus companies and the innovator who had considerable technical expertise on transport issues.
- The **gatekeepers** were many and various, including local authority transport officials, staff of the bus companies and the community development team.
- The main **consultant** acting as sounding board to the innovator was the community development worker. A long-term friend who had been involved in a similar project in a neighbouring authority also provided support.
- The **legitimate initiators**, that is the people seen as having the authority to introduce change, came chiefly from the bus

companies, but also from the local authority transport committee and interdepartmental joint committees.

- The **minders** included the team manager who was supportive of the involvement of the community development worker, and contributed the use of some of the team's physical resources, such as phones and meeting rooms. He was also willing to express opinions to the press about the impact of poor transport facilities on people living in the locality.
- The **opponents** were not always obvious. For example, early in the process the wife of the innovator became a significant obstacle. She correctly saw that the work might prove too demanding for him in view of his health. The community development worker involved picked this up in casual conversation and negotiated with both of them a package of support, including transport and an answerphone, and a readiness to talk to them both.
- The **close collaborators** were people in the innovator's local network who became members of the committee, and members of the team with whom the community development worker worked.
- The **network entrepreneurs** were the community development worker in particular, and one or two others on the committee who worked at linking people to make networking work.

The process of mapping all the people involved helps answer the question of who sees what as a problem, and thus helps those managing change identify and reconcile different definitions of the problem and possible solutions, and all the possible resources and obstacles within the whole social network.

Analysing the innovation
It is not enough to know what we want to change and the people involved: the next stage is to think through *what sort of change* we are trying to introduce, whether in a family or as a new form of response to social problems in a particular area of work.

It is possible to identify some of the main attributes of different innovations (Rogers, 1996; Stocking, 1985):

1 How adoptable is this innovation? Is it something that is welcome, or very different from anything that is currently going on? Knowing this will help thinking about realistic timescales.
2 What is the order of the change in the relationships involved? Are they of a first or second order? Understanding this will show who needs to change what behaviour and why.

3 What stage is the innovation at in its own development? Most
   innovations fail or take a long time to become mainstream. Ideas
   about involving the people who use services in decisions about their
   own lives and in planning the services they use have been around
   for many years, but are only now part of social policies. We still
   have far to go (Bynoe, 1997; Cambell and Oliver, 1996; Morris,
   1996; Lindow, 1994). Knowing how familiar a particular change is
   and what support it has locally, regionally or nationally, or from the
   individual, his or her immediate family and friends, or the wider
   network, is useful in analysing the information and experience
   available to us and others we are working with. This knowledge also
   assists in determining how persistent we will have to be.

Understanding the context
Community-based practice involves a different relationship between
front-line staff and the public. This requires second-order change in
many relationships, for example from one where it is assumed that
workers possess all the relevant expertise, to one where they are seen
as experts in some things, but all members of the community are
recognised as experts in their own situations and lives. Both bring
resources to the social problem solving table, rather than workers using
their exclusive resources to solve the problems of others called 'service
users' or 'clients'. Such changes underpin working in partnership and
facilitating the empowerment of people to have more control over their
own lives and social environment. These styles of working run counter
to the hierarchical relationships between managers and front-line
workers in large social care organisations. To be sustained, change in
the relationship between staff and the public requires change in the
relationship between managers and staff: partnership with service users
cannot work if managers regularly overrule partnership decisions.
    There may be factors in the context which:

• are compatible with the change;
• are going in the opposite direction;
• can be linked with the change to give it support in the family,
  group, community, our own or other organisations.

We do not have to, indeed cannot, be in control of all the factors,
any more than a brilliant juggler can have complete control of the
balls. But the more we understand what is happening, the more likely
are we to manage change successfully (Smale, 1998).

At the end of this process a realistic timescale can be drawn up: people become disillusioned when they expect change to happen quickly and this is not practicable. Major changes in social attitudes can take many years. Changing the law on homosexuality took generations. The mapping exercise allows us to identify whether there are significant gaps in the map of who needs to do what; what resources are available; and whether missing resources might be made available. For example, at the end of early consultations it became clear that the thrust for improved public transport was consistent with emerging policies in the newly elected majority local party towards reducing the use of the private car in urban areas. Different interest groups emerged: teenagers wanting a late night bus service, a small group of people with learning disabilities who wanted to use mainstream services. These different interests and perceptions needed to be negotiated and brought together to promote change. There is strong evidence that innovation takes place through a convergence of ideas rather than through conversion or coercion (Rogers and Kincaid, 1981; Rogers, 1996; Smale, 1998).

Negotiations between key people: individual, family, social network, community and/or inter-organisation development

Those engaged in adopting new approaches to social problems often need to acquire new knowledge and skills. If new skills are not to be quickly eroded by attempts to fit them into old customs and practices, organisations have to change to assist workers, managers, users of services and others to implement these new approaches. Most people adopt innovations in their general life or in their practice by copying peers, opinion leaders or 'product champions': a process of contagion rather than conversion. Where the introduction of an innovation means a change in the roles and relationships of those involved, then these need to be renegotiated. Training inappropriately used as a way of getting staff and others to accept management policy has become commonplace in many organisations and community groups. It is more effective and arguably more honest, as a first step, to *negotiate* changes in relationships, tasks and service conditions. Consequently, it is central to any change process to identify who has to carry out what negotiations with whom, to get agreement for changes in practices and changes in significant relationships.

Choosing an appropriate mode of education, training, group and organisation development should then follow such negotiations. In Chapter 4 we identified several such modes of development, which we shall elaborate on here.

Awareness raising

Simply raising someone's awareness of an issue, such as the impact on the social and economic lives of people in communities of inadequate public transport, or the impact of a person's behaviour on others, is a distinct development activity. We use the term in the broadest sense. It can range in scale from raising the awareness of an entire community or organisation about a particular issue, for example implicit discrimination against certain sectors of the population such as older or young people, minority ethnic groups, disabled and poor people, to alerting a parent in a case conference to the rights of a young person with learning difficulties. It could also be applied to helping people to recognise the consequences of their behaviour. Awareness-raising events, such as conferences, workshops and public meetings, are often sites for publicising innovations successful elsewhere, and become the first step through which the uninitiated and uninvolved become informed.

Knowledge acquisition and skills training

Awareness does not of itself guarantee the ability to act any differently as a consequence – other kinds of learning may be required before changes in behaviour become possible. It is no use for a parent to become aware of the need to change his behaviour in order to be a more effective father for his child, if he is not also offered the possibility of developing new skills and the support necessary to actually acquire and maintain new behaviours and take the risk of applying them. The same applies to workers and others involved in developing the transport action group, as it would in any other type of intervention.

For organisation or team, the task is learning more about the community and social networks in which they live and work. The important point is that not everyone needs to know and be able to do the same things – one or more members of the team can develop the necessary knowledge and skills. In the case of the transport action group, the local man who was the prime mover, or innovator, had considerable knowledge of transport issues and policy, but lacked knowledge of local political figures; the disabled woman was not aware of many of the transport policy dimensions, but was fully informed on issues of disability discrimination and access, and had her own sophisticated electronic communication systems which the group used and learned from.

Team building
Any collection of people working together on a common task will be involved in team building. Teams develop through shared achievement, disintegrate through failure. Much development takes place just through working together, but greater sophistication is necessary when there are likely to be particular problems in barriers to cooperation. Then team building activities need to be introduced related to a specific task or the overall working of the team. The informal relationships between staff members can be overlooked when considering staff development. Peer-directed learning is often underestimated in reviews of staff development, just as self-help support groups can be overlooked as a resource. Consultation outwith the team may be necessary to provide specific expertise to examine how team members relate to each other and other people, and to engage in planned change in the division of labour and the ways work is carried out.

Increasingly there is recognition of the importance of inter-organisation groupings, and groupings involving service users, carers and other community members – the creation of sometimes short-term 'virtual organisations' such as the transport group. These exist at a tangent from mainstream organisations, at the same time using some of their resources, alongside local people, politicians and experts in the particular area of the task in hand. People can be prepared by training, but it is more likely that practice will be changed when development work takes place within and between organisations, and directly involves service users and other stakeholders in the community.

Policy and organisational development
Task-led organisations, sensitive to their public, constantly evolve to meet changing needs. Skilled and informed training will involve not only staff but other key stakeholders to achieve organisational objectives and standards. While the education and training of individuals is important as one means of establishing standards, there remains an important task of connecting what individuals know and their skills to the policy and tasks of the organisation. Investment in individual training does not necessarily make a difference to practice and provision of services unless decisions are made about:

- how to connect individual expertise to the work of teams, organisations and the whole task;

- when it is appropriate for training to take place within the organisation;
- when outside expertise or a catalyst is needed;
- who should go outside the organisation for training and for what specific reason;
- how what is learnt will contribute to the practice and task of the organisation;
- how the organisation's standards, services or particular problems or plans change in the context of regional or national developments.

Feedback and monitoring consequences of change

Getting feedback and monitoring change continuously depends on communication with the key people charted on our maps, listening to what they say and observing their and our own behaviour. We can thus identify who is giving positive and who negative feedback, both about the change itself and about the way it is being introduced. The question of whether the change still addresses the problems it is supposed to has to be asked again: changes should be judged by their impact and not simply by whether they happen. People can – and do – persist with a change rather than lose face or status by admitting it was either a mistake or did not deliver what was intended. If you need people with political power to initiate change, perceived failure might affect their standing. You will then be under considerable pressure to achieve historically set objectives.

All actions have a range of consequences, positive and negative, intended and unintended, direct and indirect, which must be taken into account. Monitoring accordingly involves charting which consequences are:

$$\text{desirable} \longleftrightarrow \text{undesirable}$$

$$\text{anticipated} \longleftrightarrow \text{unanticipated}$$

$$\text{direct} \longleftrightarrow \text{indirect}$$

This enables us to identify the consequences of change for all the people on the original map and evaluate whether the change actually

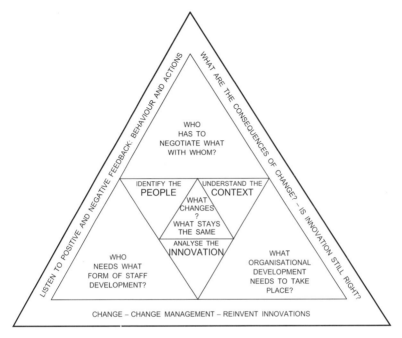

Figure 6.4 Managing Change Through Innovation (Smale, 1998)

resolves the original problem; and to identify the unintended consequences which will form the bases of the next round of change.

This whole process has been summarised in figurative form as shown in Figure 6.4.

Conclusion

There is no simple approach to managing change since the task itself is complex. 'There is always an easy solution to every human problem – neat, easy and wrong' (Mencken, 1958). The MCTI approach provides a coherent framework for organising and understanding complex social problems. Further key factors include:

- Many families, groups and agencies are inoculated against new solutions to their problems, new methods of work and approaches to service delivery by the way that change is managed.

- Different changes need to be managed differently.
- The methods or approaches developed to introduce an innovation can be replicated in other contexts, but not the innovation itself: other people's solutions to their problems may not fit your problems and situation.
- There will always be an element of reinvention when a change is adapted to fit another situation.
- It is more important that ideas and concepts are communicated rather than detailed prescriptions for practice. The ideas of roundness and axles are more helpful than fully designed wheels.
- Community-based practice produced through the relationship between local people and professional change agents can be reinvented, but never duplicated.
- The assumption of partnership with others means that there can be no internally generated fixed destination: community based practice is essentially about the processes workers engage in, the relationships they develop and how they maintain and change them.

In this chapter we have identified the importance for workers of having an explicit approach or theory for managing the process of change, and spelled out some of the main dimensions of this approach. In the next chapter we explore the implications of how workers tackle assessment of people's situations and the nature of expertise, before returning in Chapter 8 to consider further the factors that influence the patterns of interaction that perpetuate social problems, and suggest what has to be done to promote change.

7

Assessment and Intervention

The task

In the preceding chapters we argued that:

- The nature of social problems requires a holistic approach in which both aid and development activities are undertaken by social work teams.
- Change and social control tasks are central to the worker's role.
- There are ways of managing interpersonal and social change.

In this chapter we present the implications of our approach for how the tasks of assessment and intervention are tackled.

It is a consequence of the way we define the nature of social problems that problem resolution is achieved either through the provision of new resources to individuals, families and communities; or through bringing about change in the patterns of relationships which have created or help perpetuate problems; or some combination of these. These two broad areas could seem a rather narrow definition of the range of activities social workers typically engage in. However, they are in fact very inclusive. For example, in the case of Mrs Jones the worker might become involved in supporting her through a re-arousal of grief at the loss of her husband. This would not be undertaken primarily just for its own sake. After all, grief is not in itself, by definition, a social problem requiring intervention. The worker would undertake bereavement counselling or support as part of a process of managed change in the family and wider networks of which Mrs Jones is a part. The hypothesis might be that Mrs Jones is finding it difficult to respond to necessary changes in arrangements for her support because of valid preoccupation with her own sadness and loss and inability to share this with her own family and friends. Consequently supportive work with someone experiencing loss can, and should, be understood as part of the wider strategic process of 'bringing about change in the patterns of relationships which have created or help perpetuate problems'. It is crucial that these wider strategic purposes are understood otherwise it is easy for workers to slip into thinking, for example, that they are offering counselling to a bereaved person just because they are bereaved, and in so doing both pathologising normal experience and creating unrealistic expectations about what they can actually provide. All the activities which social workers engage in will be contributions to either service provision or changes in patterns of relationships, or both.

Workers have to develop an understanding of the nature of the particular social problem being tackled, and the feasibility of different kinds of solution and their possible consequences. Realistic assessment has:

- to address the whole of the task;
- to engage in ongoing negotiations with the full range of people involved in specific problems and their possible solutions;
- to address both the change, care and social control tasks;
- to go beyond the individualisation of social problems as the focus for assessment and intervention.

Alternative models

A worker can either take the role of an expert who, from the outside, understands the service user, the user's problems and what might be the best option; or she can work alongside the person and other significant people to arrive at a mutual understanding of the problem and negotiate who might do what to help, or who might best influence behaviour seen as undesirable or self-damaging. Both approaches may end up with the person getting what they want, or not, depending on whether resources are available or change is possible. The difference is in how power is used and its impact on the service user. Only the latter allows the citizen to be a fully involved partner in a process of negotiating the nature of his or her problem and possible resolutions. These two approaches lead to two different models of assessment: the Questioning Model and the Exchange Model. A third approach, the Procedural Model, a variation of the Questioning Model, is also described below.

The Questioning and Procedural Models

In the Questioning Model the worker is assumed to be the expert in identifying need. In the Procedural Model, it is assumed that the managers and policy makers who draw up guidelines have expertise in setting the criteria for resource allocation. To this extent they are the experts in how problems should be managed and resources allocated. By contrast, the Exchange Model assumes that the service user and other people in the situation, including the worker, all have valid perceptions of the problems, know what these are, where they cohere and where they conflict, and can contribute to the range of available options.

The example of the Jones family illustrates the distinctions. There are five people involved:

- Mrs Jones – the service user
- Shirley – her daughter and main carer
- Colin – Shirley's partner
- The hospital doctor – the referer
- The social worker/care manager.

Usually more people will, and should, be part of the network.

In the Questioning Model information is gathered from Mrs Jones as the service user and from Shirley as the carer, to make assessments of their needs or problems and to arrive at a solution. The worker's behaviour is dominated by asking questions, listening to and processing the answers, using the information gained to form an assessment, determine eligibility and formulate the requirements of a future package of care. The questions reflect the worker's agenda, not other people's. Embodied in the questions will be implicit or explicit perceptions of the problems that 'people like Mrs Jones' have, and preconceptions about the resources available to meet them.

This model assumes that questions can be answered in a straightforward manner, or that the worker is able to interpret accurately what Mrs Jones really wants even when she cannot or does not express it. The complexities of communication across cultural and other boundaries, such as race, age, gender, class, disability or occupational reference group and organisational allegiance, tend to be underestimated or even ignored.

The Questioning Model may suffice to identify basic needs, but does not address the fundamental goals of increasing choice, maintaining independence and maximising people's potential. Additional skills are

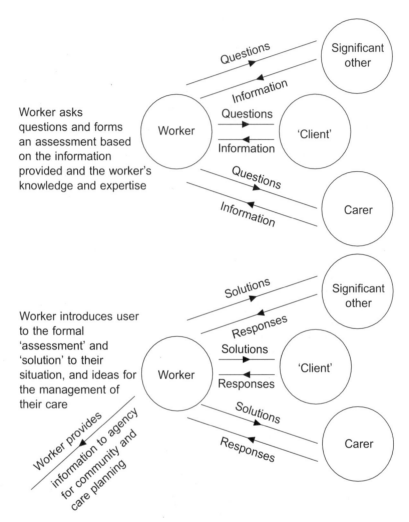

Figure 7.1 The Questioning Model (Smale, Tuson *et al.*, 1992)

needed for work with people that empowers them to have as much control over their lives as possible, and specifically enables them to exercise choice in how their needs are met. In the UK, government policy initiatives in the late 1980s (DoH, 1989) made it clear that assessment should be a needs-led not service-led exercise: that is an assessment of what the people in the situation want and need and not how can they be fitted into existing provision.

The Exchange Model

In the Exchange Model, the worker concentrates on an exchange of information between herself, Mrs Jones, Shirley, Colin and others. The question-and-answer pattern of behaviour is avoided. The kind of information produced by this sort of assessment will be different because the underlying principles of the process are different. Work focuses on engaging with these three people and others where relevant, including other workers. Meetings may be with the whole group, in pairs or individually: participation is negotiable.

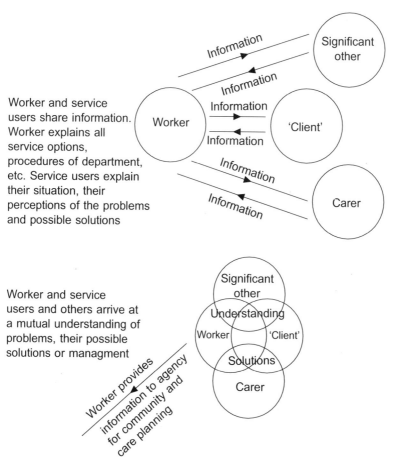

Figure 7.2 The Exchange Model (Smale, Tuson et al., 1992)

The behaviour of the worker here has to establish respect and trust. Perceptions of the situation, its problems, availability of resources and the need for more are shared. A definition of the problems and the options for resolution or management are arrived at as much through the initiative of Mrs Jones, Shirley and Colin, as by the worker. The skills required to engage in this kind of relationship are set out in Chapters 9 and 10. The worker shares information about her organisation and other service providers, and explains her role and any relevant statutory limitations. She does not lead the content of the dialogue because she does not know any more than, if as much as, the other people about the specific situation, its problems or what existing resources could contribute. The worker follows or tracks what the other people say and communicate. To lead is to assume that she knows where to go, usually resulting in a service-led response.

Understanding what people need and want includes exploration of, and takes into account, the different assumptions of the people involved, the different languages they use, think and feel in, and the different levels of communication that exist. Communication across ethnic, racial, age, class, gender, occupational or other cultural boundaries needs particular care if preconceived assumptions and prejudices are not to lead to misunderstanding or worse. Interpreters, for example, should demonstrate the communication skills outlined in Chapters 10 and 11 in both languages used: it is not sufficient to translate only words (Ahmad, 1990).

People have their own ideas, beliefs and knowledge: they are not passive or neutral receivers waiting for messages. In practice communicators enter into dialogues with people who interpret messages in accordance with their own assumptions and beliefs, which may or may not be the same as the communicator's. Those sending communications may be clear about what they intend to say, but they can never prejudge what the other person receives. In their own minds those receiving a message will hear what the message means to the communicator, will understand or not, agree or disagree, and then react, which may or may not be overtly consistent with what they think. For example, consider a young offender who tells his social worker 'I have decided to go straight'. The worker asks 'why?'; at which the young man swears and replies 'don't you want me to go straight?' In his world you are only asked 'why' by a person in authority when you have done something wrong; in the worker's world 'why' is a neutral question implicitly aimed at exploring the impetus for change, how he plans to achieve it, and what role she can contribute.

Using all available expertise

In the Exchange Model new solutions to problems are not disseminated by information passing from an expert or from the policy makers at the top of an organisation to others who are either open to help, information, advice or instruction, or 'resistant' to change. The model does not perceive communication as a linear act in which information is transferred from sender to receiver: mutual understanding, and mutual agreement over the meaning of a situation, is arrived at, or not, through a process of negotiation leading to a convergence of perceptions and expectations. Mrs Jones's doctor initially framed the problem in terms of 'where and how soon can the social worker obtain a residential place for Mrs Jones, but then became drawn into a process of renegotiation out of which different understandings of the problem and possible solutions became agreed.

A recognition of where expertise is located, that is who is expert in what, is central to collaboration and to the way the relationships between people develop, and whether partnerships are formed or only the formal role relationship of worker and service user. No one is enabled to retain and extend whatever control they have over their own lives and decisions by someone else assuming an all-encompassing expert role.

People are, and always will be, the experts on themselves: their situation, their relationships, what they want and need. This is not to argue that people automatically know all there is to know about themselves. All of our perceptions of ourselves, our situations and those of others can be expanded by sharing ideas with other people. Indeed, the essence of much good counselling is to provide an opportunity for people to reflect on their experiences and 'reality test' their perceptions. But still the final arbiter of how a person feels and judges the perceptions of others will be the person him or her self. Even Freud (1948) warned against the dangers of 'wild analysis' where the therapist or helper steamrollers over a person's view of reality with their own pseudo-psychological interpretations of events. People also bring a degree of control over their own behaviour that workers can never have, and so are able to influence the viability of the present and future relationships that underpin a package of care, or that underpin any attempt to change behaviour seen as unacceptable by others.

The Exchange Model recognises that there are many sources of information, only one of which is the product of direct questions by the worker. If she knows the community well the worker may already have a great deal of information about the general circumstances of the service user. She has had no direct contact with the particular person, but may have had some with neighbours or others in the immediate vicinity. If there is no information about the social situation then the worker sets about finding it. In the relationship with Mrs Jones, Shirley and Colin, the worker draws on this information as much as she applies her skills to hear what they say, to make assessments about their situation, of the relationships between them and other key individuals and organisations and negotiate how they might be helped.

All people have expertise in these areas, some more than others. It is essential that the worker recognises that she does not start with a monopoly of this knowledge and that she should share what she has with all the others involved. People who use services are very clear about how important it is for workers to share information which assists them in taking more control over events and procedures, and enables them to assess support (Harding and Beresford, 1996; Beresford and Croft, 1993). An essential part of the worker's responsibility is to contribute to, not take over from, people exercising their own social problem solving skills.

The Questioning and Exchange Models of assessment compared

There is a crucial difference between the assumptions behind the Questioning and Exchange Models of assessment. The first assumes that the worker is the expert in people, or their problems, or both; the second that all people are expert in their own problems and that there is no reason to assume that the worker will or should ever know more about people and their problems than they do themselves, and certainly not before they do.

Both models assume the worker brings expertise in relating to people, knowledge about the welfare system, and skills in problem solving and developing the mix of different people's efforts and other resources. The worker may also have expertise in specific conditions and methods of intervention which may or may not contribute to the resources available in a particular situation.

In the Questioning Model the worker exercises this knowledge and skill to form an assessment, identify people's needs and the resources required to meet them, and, where appropriate, acts as a broker to secure an appropriate response from others. She is responsible for making an accurate assessment of need to determine eligibility and taking the appropriate action.

The Exchange Model emphasises the worker's expertise in the process of problem solving: the ability to reach a mutual understanding of the problem with all the major actors. The process involves working with people to understand their differing perceptions and interests and arrive at a compromise. This means negotiating with a range of people – from the service user, their immediate carers and other people in the community, to service providers from different organisations and fields. Instead of the worker making an assessment and organising care and support for people, thereby implicitly or explicitly remaining central and in control, she negotiates to get agreement about who should do what for whom.

The worker in the Exchange Model is responsible for conducting the negotiations and delivering the organisation's contribution to the situation. Responsibility for arriving at the best possible arrangements for the care of the people involved, or for the best obtainable resolution of the problem within the constraints of available resources, is shared with others, as it is dependent upon the willingness and ability of other participants to contribute. In this sense the worker can never be responsible for the whole package of care. Each participant is responsible for their contribution, or lack of it.

The goal of the Questioning Model is to obtain the best possible package of care to meet the needs of the person assessed as defined by the worker, and it leads to a focus on service delivery. The Questioning Model has advantages for the organisation in framing information which fits its data collection approaches and eligibility criteria which ration scarce resources: it is relatively quick and straightforward. The focus tends to be on the dependency needs of the individual or group, ignoring the resources actually or potentially available in the social situation and underestimating the control that other people have over them.

In contrast, the goal of the Exchange Model is difficult to achieve and relatively complex. Its aim is to obtain the best possible arrangements for care or control as identified by the major parties so that people can continue to have as much control over their lives as possible, and in the process achieve maximum possible independence and have a greater individual say in how they live their lives and the services they need to help them do so: that is, be empowered to exercise choice (DoH, 1989; Beresford and Croft, 1993; Morris, 1996;

Beresford and Turner, 1997). The limitations on resources are taken into account in this process and arrangements made, even if it is acknowledged that more resources could greatly improve the situation for some or all of the participants.

The Exchange Model typically includes more people and takes longer because it is concerned about processes in building a relationship and working towards solutions. It focuses on the support and personal assistance needs of the service user, their carers and others, their various perceptions of the alternative options and the dependability of all the people in the situation. There are advantages for the organisation in establishing partnerships with the providers of the resources usually mobilised to provide care in the community. The advantages for people who use services, their carers and the other people involved are that their contribution is valued, resource deficits are acknowledged and they have greater say in the management of services additional to their own efforts.

The Questioning and Exchange Models compared

The Questioning Model
Assumes the worker:

- is expert in people, their needs
- exercises knowledge and skill to form her own assessment to identify people's needs;
- identifies resources required;
- takes responsibility for making an accurate assessment of need and taking appropriate action.

The Exchange Model
Assumes that people:

- are expert in themselves.

Assumes that the worker:
- has expertise in the process of problem solving with others;
- understands and shares perceptions of problems and their management;
- gets agreement about who will do what to support whom;
- takes responsibility for arriving at the optimum resolution of problems within the constraints of available resources and the willingness of participants to contribute.

The Procedural Model of assessment

The Questioning Model assumes that the assessor's judgements and actions are objective and underestimates the power of the organisation in shaping the questions and deciding what is given weight. Marsh and Fisher's (1992) work on 'partnership in practice' illustrates how easily staff get pulled into an administrative model even where there is no

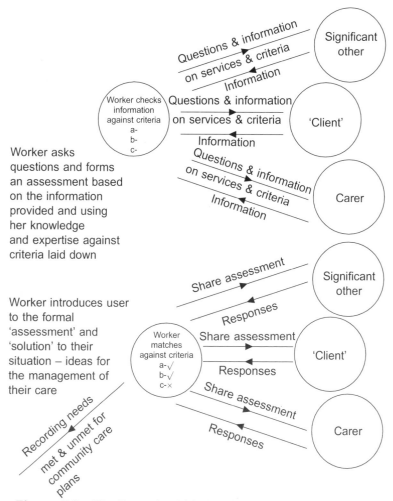

Figure 7.3 The Procedural Model (Smale, Tuson *et al.*, 1992)

organisational demand to do so. The Procedural Model's (Figure 7.3) goal is to gather information to see if the person meets certain criteria that make them eligible for services. Those defining the criteria for eligibility are in effect pre-allocating services for generally identified needs, and have predetermined the judgement as to what sort of person should get which resources. The worker's task is to identify the specific people who match the appropriate degree of need defined within the categories of service available and to exclude those not eligible.

In this model the worker completes a form, with or without the identified service user, carer, parent or other significant persons. Including the citizen in this process does not facilitate empowering them to make choices about the arrangements to be made for their care or that of their relatives, friends or neighbours. Questions are asked and/or information gathered to answer each of the points deemed relevant by those setting the criteria for resource allocation. What is, and is not, a relevant question is judged by those laying down the procedures, and reflects the policy of the organisation. The information typically sought attempts:

- To identify a particular level of dependency, that is to categorise the service user. This is effected without comprehensively mapping who does or could meet these dependency needs, without describing the social situation or thinking through what changes could take place. Any mapping here will be based on the most conventional assumptions about, for example, what can be expected of a daughter or spouse; or stereotyped notions about the caring attitudes of groups such as black and minority ethnic communities; or what can be achieved by older people, disabled people and those with learning difficulties (Butt and Mirza, 1996; Butt and Box, 1997; People First, 1994a, 1994b).
- To define the nature of the user's needs in terms of the services offered, that is whether the person's needs make them eligible for services which are actually or potentially available.

The problems with the Procedural Model are:

Definitions of service and perceptions of problems
The service user's definition of his problems, or that of others, may or may not be included. However, the explicit or implicit agenda of organisation-focused assessments cannot match the infinite variety of ways in which different people from very different backgrounds with

very different expectations see their problems and the potential solutions. Consumer studies and research on services for minority ethnic groups consistently demonstrate that the current definitions of service often do not fit people's own perception of their problems because their definitions do not align with criteria based on Eurocentric assumptions. Community groups are not simply supplementing or filling gaps in mainstream services. They are providing alternatives which operate on different frameworks and assumptions (Butt and Mirza, 1996; Butt and Box, 1997).

The agenda is predetermined and minimises flexibility and responsiveness

The agenda is set not by the worker or service user, but by those who draw up the forms and procedures which the individual worker uses to guide her actions. Where the questions require specific answers about needs related to potential services, the process will be service driven rather than needs driven. For example, a request for help with the garden might be met with an offer of hours of personal assistance. Even if the service user gets what he wants, he does not retain or extend control over decision making by the process. He does not make choices, nor does the worker, beyond interpreting how the information is used. Whether what is provided fits or not is a matter of chance. The service user has to make the best out of what is supplied.

The organisation remains central to the definition of problems and the range of available solutions. Workers see only the organisation or other workers as the primary resources, because that is the way the process is structured and where the signposts to solutions point. The worker has little room to manoeuvre except in her personal style and the way she interprets how to put the questions and record the answers. Her responsibility is to use her delegated authority to make judgements within a fixed agenda. Workers, service users, carers and managers are each clearly allocated responsibilities – users and carers are responsible for providing information and accepting the decisions made, using complaints procedures to challenge them when they are aggrieved, or filling gaps as best they can either individually or collectively.

The 'helpful' worker problem

Two interrelated problems confront the managers of workers operating the Procedural Model:

- the private nature of social work in general, and assessment and intervention in particular;
- the tendency for workers, particularly sensitive, caring ones, to identify with the people who are experiencing problems.

The worker may try to help the service user to meet the criteria. This will enable him to get what people say, and what the worker judges, he needs, even if he does not actually meet the management criteria, or when this means labelling the service user as pathological. An unintended consequence of the Procedural Model, therefore, is a significant increase in the number of people assessed as in need of particular services. For example, people identified as in need of residential care will increase if danger of admission to residential care becomes the criterion for receiving day and domiciliary services.

The Procedural Model is essentially a management-led form of assessment based on the organisation's formulation of eligibility criteria for access to services, effected through the processes described in the Questioning Model. The expertise of the worker is in:

- knowledge of organisation policies and professional theories;
- making decisions about resource allocation;
- the application of policy about who should get what resource;
- defining the criteria that should be applied;
- making judgements about the nature of the problems that people have;
- the use to be made of available resources.

The contribution and limits of the Procedural Model

The Procedural Model's goal is to provide a cost-effective way of identifying the people who are eligible for the services available and to achieve the equitable allocation of scarce resources to individual people meeting specific criteria, or to secure quickly information required in the interest of the service user. The Procedural Model is simple and quick. Staff can be trained to use it without being educated to make judgements. Managers remain in control, and changes in policy about resource allocation can be responded to by changing the criteria without changing the format of interviews or departmental forms.

The Procedural Model may be enough to identify individual need, but:

- It does not increase the choices of the people involved.
- It does not maximise the maintenance of independence and people's potential.
- The focus is on the dependency needs and difficulties of the individual.
- The tendency is to ignore the resources actually or potentially available in the social situation and underestimate the control other people have over them.
- It is less likely to result in establishing the levels of shared understanding and mutual trust required if the worker also needs to intervene.
- It is more likely to lead to standard packages than innovative or tailored solutions.

Which model to choose?

Workers and managers cannot pick and choose from the three models, because in each case specific features of one model exclude application of the others. If the major goal is to allocate certain resources to particular people using briefly trained staff, then the Procedural Model is the most practical, but it will not facilitate the empowerment of all those involved to participate in the complex choices to be made. The Procedural Model can be used when the decision on who should get what rests on the worker's judgement of need, or to circumvent a longer process because of constraints of time or circumstances; but the questions are designed primarily to help the worker carry out her task, understand the situation and come to a conclusion. Going through the process of discussing this conclusion with other participants does not equate with involving all the users in the decisions which affect their lives. The Exchange Model, in contrast, is designed to share decision making between all parties: to negotiate who can do what for whom and to maximise people's choices even when the function is social control.

When the minimisation of risk to the service user and others is a major concern, it is more effective to start with the approach of the Exchange Model: this enables the worker to give a full explanation of their position and that of the organisation, which is often precluded by the Procedural Model's pattern of questions and answers.

Models of assessment and conflicts of interest

Where social problems are the expression of conflicts of interest, or conflicts of perceptions and expectations, between people or organisations, the different models of assessment will reflect the tensions between such conflicts. A social care organisation acting as the gate-keeper of resources on behalf of the state and local communities may have an interest in developing procedural models, which are effective in controlling and limiting access to scarce resources. However, the individual worker has an ethical commitment to professional values and conceptions about the nature of social problems, how they should be solved and how services should be delivered. This runs counter to the procedural mode. Service users, other workers and the public generally will be involved in the tensions inherent in the different approaches, depending on how they understand the nature of the particular problem and its possible solutions. The expectation that somebody else should do something about an individual's behaviour would align with acceptance of a Procedural Model of assessment; the behaviour of a worker who seeks to engage in an exchange relationship would thus appear puzzling. Consequently deciding which model to use in which circumstances itself requires some measure of negotiation.

Assessment of individual need or the social situation?

Models of assessment, like camera lenses, are used for different purposes. The 'telephoto' lens focuses on the assessment of individual need, whether through individual worker judgements, or procedural organisation-led models of assessment. The 'wide angle' lens concentrates on the wider community, the context within which individuals with social problems live. Workers here may be neighbourhood community developers involved in community action at different levels, or participating in the formulation of social policy. Systems theorists (Pincus and Minahan, 1973; Goldstein, 1973) have gone beyond the polarisation that results from using either a wide-angle or telephoto lens by adopting the equivalent of a 'zoom' lens, to switch flexibly from focusing on the individual, to the family, to the community, and so to assess the relationship between them as events change over time.

The objective is to move beyond the outside observer role, that is working with service users as objects of concern, towards recognising that the network of relationships surrounds and includes *us*. Care and control is predominantly being carried out by the community and we need to join with it and add on organisation contributions so that the network of support is more complete and more open. A model of assessment which acts on this perception entails ending a reliance on photography or moving-picture shows with us behind the camera. The Exchange Model's focus is on the whole network of people, emphasising the need to establish wide partnerships and include the worker, her behaviour and the organisation's contribution to the whole social situation being assessed.

The dependability of social networks

We introduced in Chapter 1 the idea of the dependability of social networks as a focus for assessment and intervention. Social work interventions are a response to the nature of a person's social relationships. Intervention is required because somebody defines a situation as one that should not continue as at present: the support needs of a person are inseparable from the dependability of others.

Social networks are diverse and in this lies their strength and relevance. Teams of workers, managers and others engage in work at the local level to identify and develop resources and expand options for help, care and social control in the community, for all age groups and all categories of people. Assessment, planning and intervention in the round is essential to ensure the coherent development of practice, built up from the experience at the front line of workers who aggregate day-to-day local knowledge gained through partnership with local people.

Beyond the purchasing of care

People using services can be given more support and choice by encouraging the involvement of a wider section of the community. Financial incentives are not central to family-based care or parenting. Indeed it costs many people much to fulfil these roles in terms of both their health and income (Levin *et al.*, 1994). People's reliance on others for support and personal assistance is an everyday process, made fragile by the fact that all too often it is shared by too few people. This can make for overwhelming imbalances of power (Oliver, 1990) and loss of control, compounded in many situations by too little access to resources. Identifying or assessing the usual way of meeting people's needs in an area or social network forms the found-ation of the team's direct and indirect work to develop the possibilities for more people to share the burdens of care and control. The capacity of the community to offer care needs to be assessed and extended, with services complementing, not replacing, what is available or can be developed. This is not to suggest that exploited people should be asked to do even more, that public, private and voluntary services and resources should be reduced. The aim is to improve people's support by directing time, expertise and energy at understanding and developing resources in the community and recognising that, at most, formal services can do no more than supplement and complement these. Only on rare occasions are they replaced, particularly for any length of time.

The Exchange Model of assessment and practice

The main areas of the whole social situation that team members need to assess and understand include:

Identifying and engaging with existing resources for care and social control in the community, neighbourhood and social networks
In the Jones family, some indirect work had already taken place for the lunch club to be available as a resource for Mrs Jones and others in similar positions. The team member or manager who undertook this initiative could have proceeded by consulting the community through advertising and holding public meetings, or by commissioning an inde-pendent organisation to do so. However, the evidence (Smale *et al.*, 1994) is that response is poor to such approaches unless coupled with other activity. It is necessary for team members to spend time identify-ing ways in which they are already in touch with members of the community to whom such a development would be most immediately relevant. Once specific people have begun to be identified, a process of negotiation and networking takes place at a range of levels: indi-vidual discussions; formal and semiformal discussions in different local forums; initial low-key conversations between home care staff and social workers, residential workers and care home providers; dis-cussions with staff from other organisations with a stake in the same social issues. These sorts of activities identify the potential for chang-ing relationships between people. The redirection or reformulation

of people's efforts provides a springboard for developing new or different patterns of care from those that exist.

Viable lunch clubs and similar schemes can be developed in other ways, but, by initiating processes of working with people in the community right from the start, other energies and resources will in turn be mobilised because of the nature of the exchange process itself. Different approaches, however sensitively handled, tend to produce the sense of doing things to, or for, people in the community, and the results are not sustainable without a high level of worker input. We as workers cannot empower: we can only facilitate that empowerment.

Identifying, assessing and negotiating boundaries with staff of other organisations

Staff working with individuals and families have experience of negotiating with other organisations about mutual roles and responsibilities. However, in addition to these individualised boundary negotiations, team members need to assess the more underlying structures of inter-organisational power and responsibility – where power lies in practice as well as formally, who influences whom, what is open to negotiation and what is not. These processes of assessment use formal and informal levels of relationships with other organisations, institutions and community groups within the area.

For example, a user-led group of mental health survivors may require little more than the allocation of worker time within the team to negotiate with a parish council for use of a hall. If the parishioners represent nothing more than a potential resource to the group this might be relatively simple, but the group's very existence may be threatened by another parish group which has to change its meeting day. Handling this requires team members to have prior knowledge of the perceptions and expectations of those who hold positions of influence and gatekeep resources, even at this very local level. By contrast, a team seeking to develop joint working with a primary care team with the aim of maintaining older people needing substantial support in the community have to recognise that a great deal of preparation time is required. The aims of the project must be validated by senior managers in both organisations and with local GPs, and this in turn requires team members to know about the likely views and existing priorities of these people. Middle managers will want to be satisfied that routine referral and assessment procedures are effective. Workers and administrative staff in both organisations must be prepared to accept assessments and recommendations from new sources, and so on.

Here team members' actions blur current job demarcations between organisations and thus add up to a renegotiation of boundaries. This is part of using the exchange process in assessing and reassessing the ways current inter-organisational boundaries foster or inhibit the development of solutions to social problems of mutual concern in a locality or community of interest.

Assessing and negotiating boundaries between staff in the workers' own organisation

Whether as a formal organisation-based team or a looser network of staff involved in working together on specific tasks, members of teams recognise the importance of being aware of boundaries. This is not a simple matter of job demarcation: what each team member can expect from others changes over time and needs to form part of a continual exchange process in which responsibility for who does what forms part of the assessment. Such intra-team exchanges also inform and are informed by boundary negotiations over areas of activity controlled by the team, or by others in the wider organisation. These interactive processes are sometimes described as team building. They involve participative management and joint goal setting, contribute to the assessment and clarification of relevant issues facing the team, and the definition of the work to be done. In turn the team as a whole can intervene and interact with other parts of the organisation from a position of strength as a team and from a knowledge base which makes its organisational position difficult to ignore.

Continual processes of exchange between team members and all the others with whom they work enlarge their repertoires of work methods. Consequently job descriptions may need to be rewritten to follow changed practice; administrative systems modified; and levels and areas of autonomy redefined. These processes need to be monitored and assessed together since they form the crucial information through which teams negotiate and communicate with their own management and people in the wider organisation.

Exchange relationships and teamwork

Teams are the smallest units which can undertake the whole of the social work task. The range inherent in the four quadrants of the content map (Chapter 4) is potentially very wide, and frequently broader than the whole range of social services activity currently found in most teams and organisations. A high degree of collaboration is necessary to provide a coherent service, through an effective division of labour both within and outside the specific organisation. If people's needs and the needs of communities and social networks are not to fall between the actions of all those involved, individual activities have to be coordinated in such a way that, as in a relay race, the changeovers are smooth, and the care and change-oriented interventions are continuous where necessary, and consistent where not.

Without a strategic approach, sharing work is a difficult principle to put into practice because the individualisation of social problems is compounded by the individualisation, and so fragmentation, of practice. Obstacles to teamwork are created: where individual caseloads are seen as 'theirs', each worker operates as if contracted to engage in private practice. In contrast a team of workers undertaking exchange-type relationships with people in the community and other organisations fosters a sense of collective responsibility for all requests for work. They develop exchange-type mechanisms for negotiating a sense of reciprocal responsibility and accountability. This opens the way to work being carried out by various combinations of workers according to time available, the nature of the task, the interests, skills and aptitudes of workers, rather than on the basis of formal job descriptions and procedural boundaries.

The Exchange Model and professional expertise

The expertise required by social workers needs redefinition if partnership with people and full participation in choices and decisions is the practice goal. Acquiring knowledge predominantly about certain categories of people, for example 'schizophrenics', 'juvenile offenders' or 'the elderly' implies that in an encounter with an individual with the relevant label, the worker is able to draw upon 'expert' knowledge of these classes of people and problems to generate solutions to the specific problem being tackled; or that this knowledge is codified in routinised procedures. Evidence from research into particular problems and the efforts made to solve them is an essential part of the knowledge on which practice is based, but this is at a high level of generality and only one of several sources of information which the worker brings to her negotiations with others. It can never be assumed that general knowledge necessarily applies to a particular individual and her circumstances. The expertise of workers lies in the way all these other sources of expertise and people are brought into conjunction and successful negotiation with each other.

Summary and implications for practice

Social workers' specific skills are located in the expertise required to undertake the negotiations characteristic of the Exchange Model of assessment and intervention. Citizens are experts on themselves and their relationships because they see them from inside their situation, and *they* have to cope with any negative aspects of change – not the worker. Through processes of communication exchange the worker can contribute the essential third-party perspective common to all forms of conciliation, conflict mediation and negotiation by:

1 *Enabling people to articulate* and so identify their own needs, clarify what they want, and feed into policy, strategic planning and training.
2 *Adding to, but keeping out of the way of, others exercising their own social problem solving skills.* Everyone has expertise in these areas, some more than others. Workers do not start with a monopoly: they share what they have with all the other people involved.
3 *Understanding and responding sensitively to differences* in disability, language, culture, ethnicity, age, race, gender and sexuality and preferences for different forms of communication, in order to work towards an appropriate and relevant solution and identify the necessary resources.
4 *Providing or making accessible information to citizens and sharing expertise* on the workings of the social care, health and other systems, and informing people of possible alternative choices. Workers are in a pivotal position in the transfer of information skills and knowledge between the public and the organisation.
5 *Helping people through major transitions involving loss*: assessment and intervention can take place at times of great stress, brought about by the loss of a partner or some physical capacity, or some other change that has precipitated referral.
6 *Negotiating and conciliating between people* who have different perceptions, values, attitudes, expectations, wants and needs. Situations can be bound up in the conflicting needs of several people whose relationships have formed over many years.
7 *Identifying the relationships between people*: how their behaviour supports current relationships and perpetuates destructive self-fulfilling prophecies, self-defeating strategies and other harmful relationships; how this may be changed to support a different set of behaviours so that the problem can be managed differently, or

resolved in the case of people's behaviour being the reason for referral.

8   *Recognising, understanding and intervening in the patterns of relationships* between individuals and between groups and organisations that precipitate and perpetuate social problems.

9   *Recognising, understanding and intervening in the patterns of relationships that precipitate and perpetuate social problems,* and accessing the expertise required to contribute to the particular option decided upon.

10 *Providing information for strategic social care planning* to their own and other organisations and acting as advocate for the needs of citizens.

In this chapter we have discussed three different models of assessment, and identified their relationship to different assumptions about the nature of the social work task. In particular we discussed the ways in which the Questioning and Procedural Models, while effective in assessing eligibility for predetermined services, are not as effective as the Exchange Model in facilitating collaborative and empowering problem solving within a network of people.

Large amounts of worker attention and time are often taken up with relatively few, particularly intractable, problems which get sustained, perhaps for years at a time, by characteristic patterns of interaction which thus need to be understood in ways which can lead to change. To effect change, workers have to be skilled and effectively supervised, not only because of their accountability to the organisation as gatekeepers of resources, but also to enable them to maintain their third-party position or 'marginality' in complex negotiations, and to support them in work which makes acute emotional demands. In Chapter 8 we discuss some of the common blocks to change, and in particular the way self-fulfilling prophecies help precipitate and perpetuate social problems. In Chapters 9 and 10 we identify the skills required to practise this approach.

8

Overcoming Blocks
to Change

Introduction

There are a number of respected texts setting out the theory and practice of specific social work methods (Coulshed, 1991; Davies, 1991). Others provide a holistic framework for practice (Pincus and Minahan, 1973; Goldstein, 1973). There is also a substantial and well-researched literature on the effects of poverty, unemployment, poor housing, discrimination and oppression, both at the individual and structural levels (Cabinet Office: Social Exclusion Unit, 1998; Davis, 1997). All are essential components of the knowledge base for practice. This chapter does not replace them, but focuses specifically on a theoretical framework directly relevant to change agent activity.

The content map (Chapter 4) shows how through direct or indirect interventions and service delivery social change agents attempt to support people to meet unmet needs in the community, and change or at least manage behaviour which creates difficulties. Change agents achieve this by:

- introducing new resources to social situations, either through providing the services of their organisation, by purchasing services from other providers or by mobilising help from others in the community to meet needs which cannot be met by those in the network containing the problem;
- collecting information at the local level, using research to understand social problems and the means of tacking them;
- involving people who use services and local groups, for example ensuring timely involvement of stakeholder black and minority ethnic groups;

- interventions aimed at changing the patterns of relationships within a social situation that precipitate or perpetuate problems; or
- a combination of the direct and indirect work, the balance changing as problems alter over time and as participating people gain or lose control of their own situations.

The social problems addressed involve relationships based on people's and organisations' perceptions of themselves and others. These perceptions include the ways that:

- the expectation that family members care for each other, or not, is perceived;
- workers and their organisations see their responsibilities to work together and how they define the task;
- individuals perceive themselves and their ability to make a difference to their situation, their relationships and their behaviour;
- young and adult offenders are perceived by others and labelled, and how this can impede constructive change;
- neighbours perceive each other and so receive or give support;
- racism, attitudes to disabled people, gender, older people, those with learning difficulties, and so on, impinge on people's lives and attitudes, including those of the workers.

Understanding the stereotyping of individuals and groups is key to changing the processes of social inclusion or levels of unmet need, through identifying the different ways we need to intervene if we want to influence change. This chapter offers a framework to help understanding of complex interactions, which recognises that:

- the individual brings to each interaction her own perceptions and expectations – her own feelings and ideas about people and behaviour based on her previous experience;
- he or she will also be influenced by the behaviour of others in the situation.

This framework helps analyse how attributes of individuals, including those of the worker, and the policy and practice of the organisation influence interactions and so the perpetuation of, or change in, social problems. It has four dimensions:

- **self-fulfilling prophecies**
- **self-defeating strategies**
- **solutions as problems**
- **mutually defeating interactions.**

These are very common everyday patterns of behaviour at family, group, organisation and community levels. They operate in our own lives as well as those of the people we work with.

Self-fulfilling prophecies

Definitions

The self-fulfilling prophecy is best illustrated by Merton's original example (Merton, 1948). He describes the demise of 'The Last National Bank'. It starts the day as a solvent institution but a rumour spreads round town that the bank will fail. This prophecy leads people to act: they rush to withdraw their deposits. Until then they believed the bank was safe, but once they believed the rumour and acted on their belief, the prophecy became true – the run on the bank drained its resources and the bank failed.

There is a distinction between this process and that of accurate prediction. Any self-fulfilling prophecy has three stages:

- the expectation or prediction is formed;
- action is taken based on this expectation;
- this behaviour then brings about or significantly contributes to the prophesied outcome.

The middle 'behaviour' stage distinguishes a self-fulfilling from an accurate prophecy: it has to be possible for a person's behaviour to influence outcome. Self-fulfilling prophesies are a significant factor in social relationships – in contrast, they have no effect on the weather.

Evidence for the existence of self-fulfilling prophecies in human affairs comes from diverse fields:

- so-called hypnotic states (Barber, 1969);
- pupil performance in schools (Rosenthal and Jacobsen, 1968);
- interviewer bias in a wide range of research situations (Rosenthal, 1979);

- the labelling theory of delinquency (Becker, 1963);
- the behaviour of well people placed in a psychiatric hospital, interpreted in terms of their assigned diagnostic label despite the absence of any real illness (Rosenhan, 1973).

These studies have their critics (Wilkins, 1977) but in at least one area, placebo medicine, the power of expectations in relationships is universally accepted. Shapiro (1977) has pointed out that the history of medicine is 'the history of the placebo effect' and that only in recent times has there been any certainty that medical procedures and cures are more than placebos. The power of the placebo is clearly based on the expectations of those involved and their subsequent behaviour. Its significance is so firmly established that no drug trial is considered adequate without double blind procedures designed to counter the effect of patient's and health worker's expectations of treatment.

More recently, the powerful counterproductive effects of such processes have been acknowledged in the social welfare field: moves to divert juveniles from entering criminal careers, through alternative responses aimed at avoiding the development of a criminal identity, have pushed young people up the tariff system in the juvenile justice system, and inadvertently resulted in reinforcing juvenile offending (Thorpe, 1994).

Self-defeating strategies

The analysis of self-fulfilling prophecies raises a significant question: why are some people's prophecies fulfilled even when they do not want them to be? That is, when behaviour, based on expectations, defeats their goals and results in a self-defeating strategy.

Complicated patterns of interactions are not easy to understand either in our own lives or those of the people who use services, but when we do it helps us understand why we can sometimes find ourselves in positions we do not want to be in and also find hard to get out of. Mrs Brown's story illustrates such a process.

Mrs Brown and her daughter Dinese

Dinese lives near to and supports her mother, who also receives some home care. There are other family members in the area but they live at a distance. Dinese is married to John who works long hours. They have two teenage children. Mrs Brown lives on her own and needs more help about the house than that provided by home care. At her mother's request Dinese often comes round to tidy up in preparation for the home carer's visits.

Dinese begins taking Mrs Brown to do all her shopping when her mobility is restricted following an illness. After some time Dinese begins to think her mother takes her for granted and expects this to continue. Her mother begins to think that Dinese does not 'really' care for her as much as she would like, and expects Dinese will think of her as more and more of a burden.

This situation comes to a head one day when Dinese is tired, having made a special effort to juggle her mother's needs with those of her own children. She does not feel her mother has thanked her properly for her help. She gets extremely angry and upset, but does not openly express it. She all but stops talking to her mother because she is so angry, and frightened of making things worse. She thinks it best to say nothing, which she does, but cannot help doing it rather angrily. This immediately has the effect of precipitating all that it attempts to avoid.

Feeling that she does not get enough support from the rest of the family in the area but afraid she will be alienated from them if they know how angry she is with them and her mother, Dinese virtually cuts off contact with all of them. The other family members are consequently alienated. Afraid of upsetting things further, they avoid talking to Dinese. Dinese's belief that she is becoming alienated is 'proved' correct and encourages her to have even less contact with the family. Which 'proves' to the rest of the family that they were right to expect Dinese to be 'more difficult' and they avoid her even more. Avoiding Dinese is increasingly easy since she is avoiding them, which goes to prove everybody right.

Meanwhile, Mrs Brown reacts to her daughter's initial hostile near-silence with guilt and considerable pain. Guilt because she wants to be independent and feels she should not be a burden to Dinese, but also anger because Dinese could 'have better understood her'. She feels pain and anger because this 'proves' she is a burden and that 'Dinese does not *really want* to help' and so 'does not *really care* for her mother'. After an attempt to say thank you and to explain she does not mean to be a burden, which she thinks is rebuffed, Mrs Brown expresses some of her frustration and anger and accuses her daughter of not really wanting to care for her. (Dinese, remember, is at this stage keeping quiet in case the expression of her feelings 'makes things worse'.)

Mrs Brown's self-fulfilling prophecy is also a self-defeating strategy, because at this point she says she really feels that 'there is nothing to lose' and by her outburst makes losing all far more likely. Her reaction to the further silences and lack of contact is to threaten to have 'nothing more to do with her daughter – if that's the way she is going to be'. This, of course, pushes Dinese in the opposite direction of what the mother wants to happen.

Self-fulfilling prophecies and self-defeating strategies like this are common. Although the cause of frustration does not always escalate into major problems, this often happens when a member of the family is rapidly changing. Mrs Brown's illness has accelerated the ageing processes, reduced her valued independence and increased her unwilling reliance on others. Adolescence is another example. Parents' expectations move from being accurate predictions about how the young person will behave to becoming obsolete. They expect the young person still to behave as a child when the latter feels grown up, but regresses to fit the parental expectation. The opposite then happens as they seesaw around each other: the parents treat the young person as an adult only to find that he or she feels like being a child. This reaction fulfils the stereotype of adolescents as being 'difficult', which can be perpetuated by parents assuming they will get it wrong so ceasing to try to get it right – and thus further increasing the likelihood of getting it wrong, which only proves them right. These interactions also prove 'right' the young person's expectations of parents as overbearing, authoritarian and increasingly indifferent adults.

In the vast majority of families the adolescent will become free of the obsolete parental expectations by persisting with the new behaviour until parental expectations change. Leaving home, in some instances, may be necessary before everyone can adjust to new perceptions and establish new behaviour patterns. In many societies rites of passage are adopted to enable a smooth transition into new role relationships. Going away to college, setting up home with peers or a partner, getting the first pay packet are all social markers of a changed status for young people in our society.

Conflict and self-defeating strategies

Conflict is a usual part of transitions which involve constant adjustments in behaviour as people revise their expectations of each other. It can escalate into problem proportions where a person holds unshakeable expectations, as well as when he or she persists in obsolete behaviour. A person who expects all people to be untrustworthy is unlikely to trust others enough to establish mutual trust in their relationships: feedback from others that they are in fact trustworthy remains suspect. Stereotypes involve entrenched expectations of behaviour. Thus where young people are expected to be hostile and alienated they are avoided; where boys are expected 'to be boys' they may feel compelled to live up to this image, just as young people in care may produce the difficult behaviour they know is expected of them. In all these cases, other options are blocked.

Self-defeating strategies and teams

A team's work can be affected by self-defeating strategies even when the problem appears to be a very simple one. Something as apparently straightforward as organising tea and coffee arrangements in a new office can profoundly influence team functioning.

What are we doing about tea and coffee?

A senior manager wanted to improve the quality and quantity of informal interaction among the staff of several teams for whom she was responsible. When a new building became available she insisted that space be given up for a staff tea/coffee room. Staff were not allowed to take tea cups into their offices, or make tea or coffee in their own or team rooms. She wanted to ensure social contact, which would be jeopardised if staff could remain in their own space throughout the day.

The manager took initiatives consistent with her expectation that in the new building staff would not socialise adequately. The way she put this into practice contributed to the perpetuation and formation of the very barriers and cliques which her initiative was intended to prevent. This happened in a range of ways:

- Someone was employed to make tea and coffee, wash up and clean the staff room. Tea and coffee were to be paid for weekly on a pool basis. Not everyone contributed so conflict developed between the tea maker and those whom she saw as non-payers.
- Some staff members were deviant and took cups of tea to their rooms, which created tension between them, more conformist staff members and the senior manager.
- Some staff members refused to join the pool and insisted on being able to make their own tea and coffee in the staff room. Conflict ensued between some of these staff members, the tea maker and other staff members who supported the tea maker over such issues as priority of access to boiling water, responsibility for washing up and ownership of coffee mugs.
- There was ambiguity about who prepared and paid for tea and coffee for visitors, service users, carers and volunteers, and this too became a source of conflict.

> In time, the staff room became the preserve of a relatively small
> clique, and many hours of acrimonious debate about the tea and coffee
> arrangements took place at staff meetings. The senior manager's
> actions contributed to the very outcome she sought to avoid by them.

Self-defeating strategies operate at a range of levels and have to be
addressed to achieve any solution or open up other options. Emotions,
perceptions and habitual behaviour are components in their operation.

Solutions as problems

Watzlawick and his colleagues (Watzlawick *et al.*, 1967; Watzlawick
et al., 1974) identify three ways in which the solution to a problem can
become the problem:

1 The terrible simplifications:
  A solution is attempted by denying that a problem is a problem:
  action is necessary, but is not taken. (Watzlawick *et al.*, 1974,
  p. 39)

A problem is an 'impasse, a deadlock, a knot'. Acting *as if* a
deadlock must inevitably continue is the same as 'denying there is
a problem'. There are all kinds of reasons why people behave as if they
expect the problem to continue – and many are not conscious, but
habit, routine ignorance of the facts, conventional wisdom and so
forth. Not to take action because of an expectation about the intract-
ability of a situation is the same as denying that there is a problem, and
contributes to a self-defeating strategy (Darvill, 1997).

2 The utopia syndrome:
  Change is attempted regarding a difficulty which for all practical
  purposes is either unchangeable (e.g. the generation gap, or a
  certain percentage of incurable alcoholics in the general
  population) or non-existent: *action is taken when it should not
  be.* (Watzlawick *et al.*, 1974, p. 39)

Watzlawick takes the common example of relatives and friends
trying in commonsense fashion to cheer up a depressed person, who

then, bewilderingly, not only does not get any better, but gets even sadder and gloomier:

> What for the patient might originally only have been a temporary sadness now becomes infused with feelings of failure, badness, and ingratitude toward those who love him so much and are trying so hard to help him. *This* then is the depression – not the original sadness. (Watzlawick *et al.*, 1974, p. 34)

This process can be understood as a specific example of a self-defeating strategy. Others believe that the unhappy person will not recover by continuing to be sad, so attempt to make him feel happy by their cheerful behaviour. He then feels invalidated and guilty at not being happy and so gets even sadder, which is then understood by him and others as 'depression'. People then behave towards him, and he may behave towards himself, as if he were depressed, that is in a relatively permanent 'sick' state of learned helplessness with behav ioural patterns that go with this (Seligman, 1975). Once this is labelled as depression everyone predicts the sadness will continue, and behaves towards it in mutually complementary ways. More attempts at cheering him up in response to increasing sadness simply reinforce expectations and continue the behaviour which drives the self-defeating strategy.

3 *Paradoxes:*

> An error in logical typing is committed and a Game Without End established. This may occur either by attempting a first order change in a situation which can be changed only from the next higher logical level ... or conversely, by attempting second order change when a first order change would be appropriate (e.g. when people demand changes of 'attitude' and are not content with changes of behaviour): *action is taken at the wrong level.* (Watzlawick *et al.*, 1974, p. 39)

Confusions arise when a message is contradicted by the way it is communicated. The classic example is the 'be spontaneous double bind' (Bateson, 1972) which takes the form in many organisations of the 'you must take initiatives' bind (Smale, 1998). This is very different from management responses which encourage innovation (Pottage and Evans, 1994). People cannot be ordered to be spontaneous or to take the initiative: new ideas and actions have to come from them. The person giving the command puts the other in an impossible contradictory position: they can either stop taking orders and respond spontaneously, or take the initiative, or disobey the order and continue to rely on the initiative of others by, for example, waiting for the next instruction. All parties feel confused, frustrated and angry, as they cannot win without also losing (Smale, 1998).

Wanting staff to take decisions for themselves when they had previously relied on instructions is a second-order change. It can only happen if the manager changes the way she relates to her staff, and if she can get them to change the way they behave: a climate is thus produced that encourages them to take the initiative and not wait for instructions. Such patterns are not symptoms of pathological individuals or even always a problem, and exist to some degree in all our lives. But they are sources of misunderstandings in personal and work relationships and can be significant factors in sustaining relationships that need to be changed. Social workers and other change agents have to be alert to them if they are to contribute to finding other options for change.

Mutually defeating interactions: the unambiguously helpful worker

Children and families are referred to improve their chances of a healthy personal and social life. Yet the very process of becoming involved with a social care organisation can stigmatise these children and their families and actually promote additional problems despite the best intentions of all concerned. The thrust of children's legislation and practice guidance in the UK is to prevent children from being accommodated because of the negative effects this can bring. The family preservation movement in the USA is evidence of widespread awareness of the potential harm caused by lack of awareness of the negative effects which can result from interventions. In health care this process is termed **iatrogenic** and well recognised (Illich, 1976).

Understanding how self-fulfilling prophecies, self-defeating strategies and mutually defeating interactions operate can lead to clear analysis of the unintended outcomes of social work, particularly where our attempts to help people further entrench them in their role as 'problem people'. Further discussion of John's story illustrates these processes.

John's story revisited

You will recall (see Chapter 5) that the actors in John's story include: John; his social worker; her manager; the secure accommodation panel; the police; the school; the court.

The organisation's panel filters applications made by social workers for admission of children into the authority's secure accommodation. At one level the system could be seen to be working. The application is made to the panel by the worker, procedures are followed correctly, her applications are appropriately examined by the management panel. Following further events and more information being provided to the panel the social worker finally 'succeeds' in getting the service she feels is best for her client.

The consequences of the mechanism of the panel

This summary conceals a social process through which a young person is increasingly labelled as deviant, and results in the loss of his liberty. Was this the intended outcome of professional intervention or an unintended outcome of good intentions? Much effort is expended on managing the panel while little time is available to work with the young person or his family on what they think the problems they face are, or on ways to tackle the relationship problems which precipitated the young person's initial removal from home. Research into the impact of children's services has shown that over-concentration on child protection procedures and single incidents can have a lasting, undermining impact on the child and the family's support systems (DoH, 1995; Platt and Shemmings, 1996; Amplett, Katz and Worthing, 1997).

Beyond the obvious

In John's case the department's policy guide describes the secure accommodation panel's purpose as being 'to decide whether the department approves of the appropriateness of the application'. This could be read as an assumption that the person making the application is not part of the department, which, as we will see, is to some degree how the worker begins to behave. A senior manager's views reinforce this, stating that 'the panel exists to protect the social worker from the pressures of other systems, such as the courts and police'. Again this is not unusual – many organisations have such gate-keeping, filtering, rationing mechanisms in respect of many client groups. However, commonsense principles can be self-defeating when implemented: solutions may seem obvious, but they may fail or even make the situation worse.

The *overt* communications of the department and the secure accommodation panel were that the panel existed *only* to filter out inappropriate applications. But the existence of the panel and its behaviour, as perceived by the worker and her manager, communicated a lack of trust in their judgements and actions and an assumption that all applications were *expected* to be inappropriate, including hers. On the first application she was told by a panel member, 'we will make this difficult'. A senior manager had already said that the panel should be treated like a court, where very high standards of proof are required.

The panel had a reputation for being challenging and demanding of workers seeking access to the residential resources it controlled, rather than as acting as an additional resource for the worker to check judgements, or to balance the needs of one young person against another. The image was one of a quasi-court that began with the assumption of the worker as guilty of trying to spend resources unnecessarily on an expensive placement. This also made the worker feel punitive, while the panel members looked like benign protectors of young people. This interpretation was implicit in the penal-judicial language and in the panel behaving as if they were conducting a trial by jury, a misleading picture of what was intended to take place. Although many people want to lock up youngsters who behave like John, for the protection of the public, many workers, including John's, believe it is right to use secure accommodation as little as possible. They and their managers resort to such care when they have exhausted other options.

Here, although generally very cautious about using secure accommodation, and initially ambivalent about using it for John, the worker increasingly became an advocate of it in response to her experience of the panel's expectation that she would be guilty of presenting an inappropriate application. Her judgement was implicitly assumed to be flawed and the only way it could be validated would be by ensuring the panel accepted her request for John's admission to secure accommodation. The task of making the best available decision for John, or for the public, became lost in a battle about whose assessment and recommendation should be implemented.

The paradox is that the worker wishes to communicate that her particular application is appropriate, but she is doing so in a context which is already defining it as, in principle, *inappropriate*. She expects to do the right thing for John, but has to present her plans to a panel which to her and her colleagues appears to be operating on the assumption that she will make an inappropriate application. She strengthens her application by building a more pathological picture of

John, thus engaging in the behaviour the panel expects, but this is a self-defeating attempt at control. As within paradoxical situations generally, her efforts to 'prove' appropriateness easily serve as evidence to confirm the opposite. In the end she behaved inappropriately to achieve what she thought was appropriate.

John's story, stage 2: covert criteria and 'working the system'

The worker presented her application to the secure accommodation panel on three occasions over the space of a few weeks. Instead of operating in a way that opened up options for John's future, the worker's response to the first panel refusal was to begin to build a stronger case, or 'manipulate the system'. She believed that John met the overt criteria for admission to secure accommodation and concluded that the initial refusal of the panel was due to their having *covert* criteria: that is, criteria which were implicit in the assumption that all applications would be treated as inappropriate. She added evidence to meet the possible covert criteria, sought out more precise information about John's offending behaviour and other problems in his social situation so that she could develop a stronger case, and inevitably presented a more pathological picture of John. She began to use rhetoric and innuendo. She tacitly conveyed to the court the nature of the conflict between herself and the secure accommodation panel, expecting them to take action on her behalf, which they did, by direct communication to the director of social services and by pointedly informing the local press. She actively sought out the help of senior police officials and encouraged them to contact her department about John's behaviour.

She responded with what Bateson (1972) has called 'complementary reciprocity'. Such manipulative behaviour will be seen by some as unprofessional, but by others it will be seen as regrettable but realistic: a legitimate 'working of the system' which was within the tradition of social work. In addition to doing more of the same, she then began to 'put pressure on' departmental personnel through using the opinions of people and organisations outside their system. Far from protecting the worker and John from the pressures of other systems such as the courts and the police, the panel provoked the worker to mobilise them to put on pressure.

What is success?

The worker finally 'succeeded' in getting John admitted to secure accommodation, and did so by effective use of traditional skills and strategies of social work. The panel 'succeeded' in challenging and testing the application before letting it through. The magistrates 'succeeded' in getting the disposal they wanted. But were these successful, or even legitimate, interventions? The questions raised here include:

- What happened to the young person through these processes and what are the long-term consequences likely to be?
- Do the adversarial relationships within the organisation promote long-term collaboration and partnerships between the worker and service users and the other organisations and workers involved?
- Could the difficulty the worker had in meeting the young person's needs have been managed through effective, routine management supervision?
- If the worker is managed appropriately by her line manager, why should such decisions be vetted by another group of managers?
- If the answer to the last two questions is 'yes', then shouldn't management resources be directed at ensuring appropriate line management and consultation for staff and service development to provide further options for working with young people like John?

Intervention and service delivery easily let John slip from the centre of attention. Had John stopped behaving in deviant ways it would have been more difficult to escalate the response to him, but this is not likely to happen without more attention to resolving the problems as *he* sees them and finding solutions that *he* is going to cooperate with. We have to be as sure as possible that our interventions and social problem solving systems check rather than perpetuate and exacerbate such patterns of behaviour.

If managers behave as if their staff will manipulate them to get children admitted inappropriately into secure accommodation, or to overcome the rationing of scarce resources, there will be unintended consequences. In John's case attention was diverted away from his needs and all the options open to him, and on to managing the system. No one person in this network is to blame. Each person's expectation and behaviour is 'reasonable' and even 'correct', given their understanding of the situation, yet the outcome is to stigmatise a young person and increase the probability of further offending behaviour.

Dominant actors, dominant perceivers and the role of perception

The **dominant actor** is the person whose expectations and actions dominate the content of any one social situation. Typically a person seen as 'mad' or 'bad' like John is the 'dominant' person. His perception of reality and behaviour dictates many of the relationships concerned, in as much as it is his offending behaviour that the relationships focus upon and are dominated by. This happens even if other people, such as the worker involved or members of the secure accommodation panel, have more formal power and their definition of 'reality' has more authority – that is their definition of the other as 'mad' or 'bad' wins general acceptance. The person whose definition of others and their behaviour is accepted is the **dominant perceiver**.

The worker's and the court's definitions of John are likely to dominate because of their authority. This comes from common law and statutes which define in broad terms society's expectations of its citizens and its social control agents. At the individual level of John's behaviour and problems, there is considerable room for disagreement about the nature of the problem and what should be done to control, help and change him and those circumstances that support his antisocial behaviour. The same debates persist at local and national policy levels. In personal relationships the basis of the authority to define what is right and wrong, what is really happening and who is responsible, is even more complex.

In contrast to the worker's authority, which can be backed up by powers exercised through the court, John's power comes from his persistence in behaving in a deviant way despite sanctions used by those in authority, or because of his own inability to behave differently. In John's story the worker became the dominant actor in the interaction with the secure accommodation panel and its context. Her repeated applications and the way she managed them determined the quality and nature of the overall process. Her ultimate 'success' leaves the system unaffected and even reinforced. The same pattern will recur over other applications, but panel members will expect them and be on guard. Future workers may have to be even better at '*making* their case'.

Deviancy

The process employed reinforced John's deviant identity and possibly his deviant behaviour. More and more of his personal and family circumstances were brought into the public domain (although still subject to the system's definition of confidentiality) and given negative labels as they were used as evidence of the need for secure accommodation. The actions of the worker and the various people in her department were consistent with his continuing to behave in a deviant way. The escalating behaviour of the worker, however, cannot be understood just in terms of a response to the escalating deviant behaviour of John, as indeed the worker and others understand it. John's behaviour did not *have* to change at all: simply more evidence found to back the original perceptions of the worker. At the same time it could be assumed that with all this going on around him, John's behaviour would also be affected.

The worker and the organisation managers shared the same objective, of seeking to reintegrate John into his family and the community, an aim which John may also have had. The preoccupation with overcoming the panel, and the worker's and the panel's behaviours, defeated this common long-term aim. The consequences for children and other people caught up in systems set up to help them can be disastrous. The parties contribute to the escalation of problems and in so doing prove their expectations right, but get further away from achieving their own goals. These processes constitute mutually defeating interactions.

Behaving as if *predictions are true: contingency planning, openness and trust*

How could the organisation have operated to avoid these potentially harmful self-defeating strategies and frustrating and expensive mutually defeating interactions? The short answer is that if the senior management of the organisation had acted *as if* staff and line managers were competent and trustworthy, they would have acted on the assumption that the recommendation would be fully considered by the worker and reviewed by a competent line manager. These staff would be held accountable for their decisions. Resources would still have to be rationed, but this is a separate issue from making an assessment of need. Monitoring decisions and getting feedback from front-line workers, managers and people who use services provides information for improving worker and organisational performance and outcomes for young people themselves.

Evidence of the severity of John's behaviour and problems remain on file and will influence all subsequent decisions made about his situation. The use of similar mechanisms can be widely identified, for example when teachers feel they have to build up a case to get a child into special education, which can result in unintended exclusion.

Significant numbers of people are affected by such perverse attempts to protect them. These mechanisms act like drugs given to counteract the unwanted side effects of other drugs: the resulting cocktail can be lethal. Effort is more productively channelled into improving practice and its management than into acting prematurely: that is slipping from thinking about *what if* it happens, to behaving *as if* it is happening.

Contingency plans and the impact of negative 'as if' behaviour

---

The Brown family

In the Brown family, Dinese at one point stops talking to her mother and other members of her family because she is 'fearful of making things worse'. Her withdrawal of contact is a form of contingency plan against their possible responses to her being open with them about how angry she is, and her mistrust of their predicted responses. Dinese behaves *as if* the expected unpleasant responses from her mother and other family members have already occurred, and withdraws as a self-protective measure against their responses – even though when she does this they have not actually happened, although subsequently they do in ways which confirm for her that she was 'right' to assume the need for her own withdrawal. In Dinese's family this pattern was broken by a friend who acted as a mediator. She was trusted by all involved and her timing was perfect – Mrs Brown's forthcoming birthday.

In some cases these responses have built up over many years and, without skilled intervention and a willingness, or urgency, to change, they are hard to modify. In others they are the result of a crisis or event which profoundly affects the pattern of relationships and the expectations that people have of each other: Mrs Brown moved from being independent, and a resource for the family, to facing a growing need for assistance with daily living from the very people whom she used to help. These changes are part of life for everyone. In the main, we all make adjustments over time, unless a crisis such as a fall accelerates the need for change. Then the degree and suddenness of the change can be overwhelming: participants can assume that the situation is beyond them and the demand for an external solution and outside help is highlighted.

Trust and mistrust

Entrenched mutually defeating interactions typically involve trust and mistrust. The role of workers and others in third-party positions includes reframing expectations and trying out new behaviour. Explanation is given of the possible alternative expectations and these are tested out, instead of participants assuming what they fear is inevitable. Alternative behaviour is modelled and the possibilities of trust rebuilt. The aim is to create an environment in which more open communication allows testing of assumptions and expectations, and experimentation with new behaviour.

Practice implications

Managing multiple perspectives to avoid self-defeating strategies

Becker (1963) points out that a watershed in a young offender's career is reached when others stop seeing him as a person who steals and begin to see him – we will call him Jack – as a thief. This change in a person's identity leads to a different level of expectations. Someone who has not been caught stealing may be expected to be honest, but by definition a thief steals. The naming of the person as indistinguishable from some of his actions can turn expectations into certainties. Behaving towards a thief *as if* they will continue to steal may seem like the only prudent course. To avoid self-defeating strategies a worker has to behave *as if* Jack will not steal. Others who have identified Jack as a thief will see him differently, and are likely to behave towards him as if he will go on stealing. Inasmuch as Jack is influenced by others, this is likely to confirm any definition he may have of himself as deviant. It will be easier for the worker to behave towards Jack *as if* he is going to be honest if she believes that it is possible and even expects him to stop stealing. The worker's beliefs, expectations and behaviour towards Jack will be out of step with those who see him as a thief, and with Jack's view of himself. Workers in the juvenile justice and probation fields are very familiar with this uncomfortable position, as is anyone who works to include groups of people who are socially excluded. A simplified view of this position is that either the worker is stupid, has been conned, ignores the feelings of Jack's victims or condones illegal and irresponsible behaviour.

Change agents have to work with different people's perceptions of the problem and the solution, with different people's conflicting interests. The self-fulfilling prophecies of others are not *the cause* of offending or other behaviour that leads to people being seen as a social problem or excluded, but social processes such as these play a significant part in perpetuating the problem. Understanding them and learning how to develop benign alternatives is an essential dimension of social problem solving.

The behaviour of workers and change: eight principles

The worker's expectations and behaviour are but one variable among several which influence the course and outcome of any attempt to bring about change, and even if expectations are at optimum level, other variables may intervene to alter the course of events. However, expectations themselves are very important in affecting the outcome, for better or worse. Shaping ways of working together to achieve positive outcomes depends on eight principles which are basic to the practice of social work and its management:

1 Begin with hope
2 Know our own expectations
3 Search for positive qualities
4 Identify realistic expectations
5 Establish trust
6 Manage and supervise with realistic hope
7 Improve and clarify public expectations
8 Move beyond past 'pathology'.

1 Begin with hope

Workers who see a problem as insoluble make no significant contribution to others seeking a solution. One of the first steps is to redefine the given situation as a problem to be solved (Alinsky, 1972). An open mind bespeaks optimism and hope.

The change agent's expectations provide a model for people needing to bring about change in their situations: workers need to be able to demonstrate at least a minimum level of personal optimism and hope, an ability to tackle and solve problems personally and go on learning how to promote and cope with change. This has implications for the selection, education and training of workers, the selection of educators, trainers and managers, and argues strongly for the involvement of service users and carers in training workers. Optimism and hope need to be modelled, not just discussed.

2 Know our own expectations

The potential power of expectations to fulfil themselves through behaviour makes it imperative for agents of change to be aware of what their own prophecies and expectations are. The action of self-fulfilling prophecies and self-defeating strategies can be covert, implicit, subtle and easily disguised from worker, service user and manager alike. Often called self-awareness, this is the capacity to identify, understand and challenge our own implicit negative assumptions, expectations and stereotypes.

3 Search for positive qualities

Workers are optimistic and able to identify the strengths, abilities and grounds for change in people they like, and when working with people who like them (E. Rogers, 1996; Carkhuff, 1987; Bergin and Garfield, 1994). Ideally, service users would be matched to workers who like them, perceive them positively, and firmly believe that they can help develop their potential and bring about change. This rarely happens, and requests for a change of worker are frequently denied.

Part of professionalism is that workers are able to extend the range of people they can work with and who can work with them, through being self-aware about their own preferences and limitations and working to broaden their understanding. Some differences, such as ethnicity and gender, and some disabilities, are visible at first meeting; others are based on culture, religion, social class, sexual preference, personal style and interests. For example:

> We have consistently made the point that it is not the case that only Black workers can provide services to Black children . . . all spoke of the value for them of having a Black worker, not because they are any better, but because they could better understand these experiences [of racism]. Having a worker validate a young person's pain in this way is a powerful therapeutic tool and is key to helping young people deal with abuse, but also the development of an integrated, positive identity as a Black person. (Jones and Butt, 1995, p. 122)

Working through relationships based on respect is given high priority by the people who use services (Harding and Beresford, 1996), and is no less significant in networking professionally. One dimension of consistent performance is the worker's ability to form relationships with, and work in partnership with, people whom many would find it difficult to relate to; to hold positive expectations of individuals who are seen through negative stereotypes and in consequence as not contributing as citizens. The negotiation of strengths, the identification of what users are contributing as citizens, is one of the key themes in feedback from people who use services (Beresford and Turner, 1997).

4   Identify realistic expectations

An appropriate level of expectations has to be negotiated with the service user and others at the beginning and during the processes of assessment, intervention and change. Expectations that are too high or too low have a null or even a perverse effect (Smale, 1977; Goldstein, 1962). If someone does not expect to be helped or does not expect change to be possible, intervention will be of no advantage until hope is aroused. The change agent walks a tightrope in negotiating with others a realistic level of expectation, but veering on the side of expecting too much is more beneficial than risking the stunting and paralysing effects of expecting too little or nothing at all.

5   Establish trust

A central feature of mutually-defeating interactions is that a 'solution' is applied to a problem which itself then becomes 'the problem'. This happens because of inadequate negotiation about the nature of the problem being addressed, and its possible solutions. An Exchange Model of assessment and intervention (Chapter 7) avoids this outcome, through an exchange set of relationships, open discussion of the problem and negotiation of possible solutions.

6   Manage and supervise with realistic hope

The role of management and supervision is crucial if the change agent is to have confidence and faith in his own abilities and potential. To achieve this the worker needs to operate in a team and organisation culture where there is commitment to achieving high standards of practice and supporting its development.

The depression or frustration caused by apparently intractable situations is not alleviated by a manager or supervisor who 'reassures' the worker that 'nobody could reasonably be expected to help such a person or family'. Officially approved and accepted impotence is no easier to bear than a private sense of failure, without some strategy for making progress. The worker has to battle on regardless: success may lie in maintaining the situation or slowing its deterioration. These goals are recognised in health and medical care, but more rarely identified in social work. In turn, positive feedback from the worker can promote a subsequent more fundamental change in the situation as people begin to reconstruct the possibilities open to them – that is to say, begin making positive self-fulfilling prophecies about their own futures.

7   *Improve and clarify public expectations*
Public perceptions are part of the context for practice. The actions of workers and their employers need skilful and effective presentation to optimise the image of social work to the public and the media. These are skills that can be learned and improved with practice. Making information available to the public is key in achieving greater openness about rights, provision and understanding of the worker's tasks (National Commission of Inquiry into the Prevention of Child Abuse, 1996; Beresford and Turner, 1997). Information may be well presented and plentiful, but it has to be in a form that is appropriate for the outcome sought and be found in places frequented by the people who need it (Audit Commission and SSI, 1997).

Part of the reason for negative perceptions of social work lies in the inevitable public disillusionment of expectations that workers should provide ready solutions to any problem. The worker's role lies rather in negotiating between conflicting perspectives. There can be no certain outcome, yet coping with uncertainty is not exclusive to social work. In medicine, for example, there is public acceptance that outcomes are uncertain. If we go to the doctor we do not expect to be provided with a cure that will ensure we never have to go again. It is recognised that the body is a complex organism, vulnerable to a variety of conditions. We expect, and normally get, help with a specific problem, but neither doctor nor patient anticipates that this is the last time they will see each other. Our emotional, social and psychological lives are just as complex as the physical organism we inhabit and just as vulnerable to a variety of conditions and to interaction with our environment. The worker's openness about her limitations and refusal to play the role of omnipotent expert leads to a clarification of public expectations so that the worker's achievements are valued rather than perceived as failures.

8   Move beyond past 'pathology'

As we move from understanding to action, there is a shift in the focus of intervention from the past to the future. How workers see the user's future is crucial to contributing to that future. A focus on the user's past, on the symptoms of present distress, on under-standing previous traumas, deprivations and problems is central to building an explanation of the present situation. But the process of moving on involves looking at strengths, healthy attributes and adap-tive skills. Drawing up a plan of intervention based on pathologi-cal information is analogous to trying to rebuild a house out of the rotting timbers that caused it to collapse.

By understanding the strengths, expertise and experience and positive personality characteristics of individuals, families and wider social groupings we come to expect growth and positive change. Action based on the past – we do this because of yesterday – is in danger of perpetrating a self-defeating strategy. The past is of great significance but it cannot be corrected: the future meanwhile has yet to be determined.

Conclusion: towards the positively marginal worker

In this chapter we have discussed some of the characteristic patterns of interaction that help create and perpetuate the seemingly intractable problems workers are expected to deal with. Having a capacity to be involved with people in often complex and emotionally loaded situa-tions, while at the same time retaining some measure of neutrality, is often crucial to the worker's effectiveness.

It is essential for good practice that workers neither completely agree with the perceptions of those who would exclude some people from the community, nor identify completely with those who are excluded. This is an uncomfortable situation. Like any mediator, the change agent can only contribute towards the reconciliation of differ-ences between others by being accepted to some degree by both sides. This is unlikely if the mediator is wholly identified with one side or the other: the worker has to display a degree of neutrality, or margin-ality. This position is frequently described by workers themselves as 'juggling' (Levin *et al.*, 1998). Social work can accordingly expect a bad press when it does its job well and confronts the expectations of the status quo.

If the discomfort goes away this suggests one of three things. The worker has:

- been successful in resolving the conflict;
- slipped from his neutral position and taken sides;
- become numb from conflict fatigue.

We call the successful occupation of this uncomfortable and ever-shifting position of neutrality the capacity for 'marginality', and, as it is so crucial to the role of the worker in facilitating change, we devote the next chapter to a full discussion of what is implied.

9

Independence and Marginality

Marginality

Throughout the previous chapters, we have developed a view of
the worker as a facilitator of change, as someone who is employed to
'do something' about particular social problems in the community
in partnership with others. At the conclusion of the previous chapter
we identified that the worker, while engaged with others, must retain a
certain neutrality. We have called this **marginality**, defined as: **the
worker's ability to operate effectively as a participant and as an observer
in any circumstance, to neither become a part of problem-perpetuating
interactions, nor slip unintentionally into being a permanent part of the
solution, nor remain impotently on the outside of the networks of people
with whom he or she is involved.** This chapter discusses and illustrates
the concept of 'marginality'.

Marginality and marginalisation

The term 'marginal' is often used in a negative way. Someone 'on the
margin' is seen as having been pushed there, excluded from action; as
so insignificant that they can be discounted. However, being 'marginalised' in this sense is not what we are proposing. The distinction
between maintaining a position of marginality, and merely being
marginalised, is crucial, if subtle. The ability to work at the margins
of organisations, families, groups, social networks and other sets of
human relationships is essential for change agents. Maintaining this
position so as to influence change within a set of relationships or an
organisation is quite different from *being marginalised* by the people
being worked with. To be marginalised is to be ignored by being

pushed out on to the fringes of the organisation or social network, or to behave in such a way as to actively take up this position: to be stuck in a relatively permanent 'sidelined' role. Marginalised or sidelined workers have no impact on the mainstream, and may even be a part of the pattern of relationships that maintains the status quo. In contrast, workers displaying marginality are on the move, still displaying freedom of action. Typically their goal is one of redundancy – they leave once change has been achieved. They use specific skills in negotiation, working with conflicts and understanding the processes of change and how to manage it, in addition to having the capacity to acquire information about the different perspectives and experience of people.

A position of marginality will often be uncomfortable for the worker. This has long been recognised. For example, the worker has been characterised as being 'caught in the middle' (Clarke, 1993, p. 19), but, whereas this is often seen as essentially a problem which the worker should seek to overcome, in our view it is actually essential to the task. The 'problem', if there is one, is how to maintain this position, not how to get out of it.

We have deliberately chosen not to use the term 'neutrality' as it is not our view that the worker can ever be 'neutral' in the conventional sense. The worker has to engage and be involved with others and cannot take a neutral position in relation to legislation, for example. At the same time, however, the worker cannot just be partisan, or advocate on behalf of only one person or one point of view in the social networks involved. Hence we coined the term 'marginality' as an attempt to capture the particular quality of 'engaged independence' which seems so crucial to the agent of change in social situations. The position is that of the honest broker negotiating with people and between social groups to seek good enough compromises, rather than that of the final arbiter or 'objective' assessor.

Marginality and the Jones Family

To return to the Jones family: at the point in time where the worker first became involved there were conflicting perceptions about the nature of the problem and possible solutions, although these were not all explicit to everyone. The worker did not 'take sides' or promote a particular interest in the conflict. This is difficult to achieve since people tend to provoke different responses in workers, and overtly or covertly promote certain alliances (Parker, 1996). The worker heard, for example:

- Mrs Jones's sadness and loss and her desire to return home;
- Shirley's feelings of being trapped by the responsibility, but also her guilt at seeming to reject her mother;
- Colin's protectiveness towards Shirley and his own interests;
- the hospital doctor's concern to make a bed available for another patient as soon as possible.

Consequently the worker had to negotiate a balance between the differing rights and responsibilities of everyone involved. He could do this only by maintaining the dynamic independence which we call 'marginality'. This gives an overview from which he can support the people involved to decide who should do what next, and renegotiate the division of labour if necessary, especially where there are conflicts of interest and perception. Because the position is dynamic it changes as the participants and their situation change.

Balancing expectations, needs and responsibilities

Workers are not employed simply to meet the needs of identified service users. The job involves constantly balancing the expectations and demands placed on them by different people: parents, children, health workers, teachers, the police, the magistrates, neighbours, senior managers, trustees, directors of private care companies and local politicians. Workers do not start with their assessment alone. People coming for help and support and those referring others can begin by expecting the worker to implement a particular solution such as 'this child needs to be taken into care' or 'find this person a residential home'. Each person expects the worker to respond in different ways to the same set of circumstances. In addition, the worker may be crossing cultural and religious boundaries and working with people from different ethnic and social class backgrounds from her own, or of a different gender or sexual orientation. Identifiable and often visible diversities can militate against the worker being perceived as able to function independently because workers are seen as representing a powerful and dominant group (Ahmad, 1990; Dominelli and McLeod, 1989; Morris, 1996; Sternfeld, 1993). Workers themselves can feel out of their depth and this too can affect their ability to maintain a marginal position.

Members of the personal and professional network do not ask the worker to help them as individuals to change, as they would if approaching a counsellor or psychotherapist. Referrers are resistant to seeing themselves as part of the problem. More often a relative, neighbour, or someone from another organisation tries to get the worker to 'do something' about a person they think needs support or some form of personal assistance, or to bring about change in the behaviour of someone transgressing social norms. This referrer can be seen by the worker as part of the problem, and potentially part of the solution. Hence we see these people as a target for change equally as much as the identified 'client'; just as the police inspector in Chapter 5 recognises that he is addressing part of the problem every time he speaks to the public who are demanding that something must be done about speeding traffic. In order to facilitate negotiations about who should do what to tackle the problem someone has to be able to develop a perspective outside that of the network of people involved. This does not mean that the worker submerges her own views or abdicates responsibility, but that she creates and retains sufficient trust and credibility to work with people whose views and behaviours may be in conflict. Where this is not possible because of perceived profound differences, it becomes a social work issue, not one personal to the worker or the people involved. Similarly the issue is neither about control nor authority, but about establishing an effective relationship. Hanmer and Statham (1999) set these diversities out in relation to men and women, black and white people, and Morris (1996) in relation to disabled and non-disabled people. The intervention of the worker can be necessary to balance the rights and responsibilities of everyone involved, including the wider community.

Workers who do not hear what is said rarely produce positive change in people's circumstances. Providing a service without taking into account people's social networks, and their own strengths and resources, fails to carry out the balancing act integral to social work, because the whole task is not addressed. A marginal position is key to avoiding inappropriate absorption and becoming an inbuilt part of the network, either because the worker has been swamped by feelings or recruited by one set of vested interests.

The key elements of marginality

The worker's behaviour

The most significant resource over which individual workers have maximum control is themselves, their own person. The importance of providing concrete resources and services to people, and using skills in specific areas of knowledge and expertise, is not disputed, but the worker herself is a key resource. Her style and behaviour can be the crucial factor in mediating the complex problem solving negotiations central to collaborative practice (Harding and Beresford, 1996; Kearney, 1995).

Most assessments and follow-up referrals are a response to a problem arising from change or loss. Workers have to respond to the contradictory feelings these situations provoke. They can respond appropriately, acknowledging and carrying out their work aware of these feelings, or compound people's problems by ignoring them. However, workers also recognise the essential and crucial significance of practical help at these times, since more sophisticated forms of help are only acceptable when married to tangible immediate assistance (Newburn, 1993). An effective framework for practice provides a means of understanding how specific areas of knowledge and skill fit within the worker's use of her own personal and organisation resources in contributing to social problem solving with others. The ability to avoid becoming a central player results from a synthesis *in* the person of the worker of the whole range of skills, knowledge and values. Without this synthesis, separate skills or items of knowledge have little meaning or value.

What the worker needs to demonstrate

An effective agent of change in social situations needs a minimum level of:

1   **Cognitive complexity** – the ability to:
    - analyse complex social situations and different perceptions of problems and their solutions;
    - examine ideas critically and develop effective planned responses;
    - understand and plan interventions into behavioural patterns such as self-defeating strategies that perpetuate social problems

and complicate their management. This knowledge and skill is often associated with specialist areas of practice such as family therapy and organisation development.

2 **Emotional flexibility**: the ability to identify and work with a wide range of emotional responses in oneself and others, particularly the ability to engage with feelings of pain and anxiety which are usually avoided, and to relate to people whom others find difficult to communicate with.

3 **Behavioural fluency**: the ability to develop and use an extended range of practice skills and strategies.

All three capacities are equally necessary. A sound technical understanding of a particular social problem, and an ingenious strategy for tackling it, come to nothing if the emotional quality of the relationships has not been properly understood by the worker, or appropriately used. How people feel about things, how such feelings are understood and responded to at an emotional level by the worker and others, can constitute the core of the problem the worker is trying to resolve. A worker can develop a high level of rapport and shared understanding with the people involved, but not have the behavioural repertoire to model the changes in behaviour which one or more people need to make. Other strategic abilities depend upon the existence and continuing development of these underlying cognitive, emotional and behavioural resources.

The capacity to ask key questions

Complex scenarios like Carol and Gary's in Chapter 1, or John's in Chapter 8, often involving staff of many different organisations, illustrate the need for the worker to be able to sustain a position of marginality, and some of the difficulties in achieving this. The worker has to ask herself a number of questions:

- Who has what problems?
- How do these people normally relate to each other and how can the participants jointly work towards change?
- Whose story is being told? That is, whose perspective is the information coming from?
- Who are being seen as the service users, and why?
- Whose overview or interpretation of events is being presented?

Identifying perspectives on social problems

Marginality means recognising the different definitions of problems held by all the different actors, and the different expectations about who has responsibility for what in tackling them. Some of the possibilities with which the worker is confronted can be illustrated from a consideration of Patrick and his family's involvement with social care organisations.

Patrick and his family

Patrick is the four-year-old son of Hilary and Wayne, who are divorced. Patrick has been fostered with April for nearly two years, following neighbours' allegations of neglect because of Hilary's alcohol abuse. This was originally meant to be for a very short period, to supplement care from Patrick's father and new partner, but for a range of reasons has continued longer than intended. April is now very attached to Patrick, but has become worried about continuing to foster him as her own husband has recently left her, and this is of concern to the worker who has responsibility for April and other foster carers. Wayne is now living with Gloria and her three children from a previous relationship, together with his own daughter of seven, that is, Patrick's sister.

It is intended that Patrick be placed for adoption and much of the necessary work has been undertaken, but it has not been possible to find adoptive parents, and Patrick's worker has not been able to move Patrick to a short-term, pre-adoption placement, although that has been the intention. Patrick continues to have regular contact with his mother and especially with his paternal grandparents, who have offered to look after him but have been assessed as unsuitable. There have been, and continue to be, many different organisations and staff involved in this complex family situation, and consequently different 'assessments' made and different perspectives on 'who' is the problem, and 'who should do what'.

These have included:

1 **The 'they–you' perspective**: '*They*' have the problem. '*You*' should do X or Y or *something*. The neighbours who make allegations of neglect and Hilary's unsuitability for parenting both define who is the problem and behave as if they expect the social care organisations should solve it.

2 **The 'I–they' perspective**: '*I*' have the problem. '*They*' must *change*. If Patrick were old enough to articulate his perception of the problem he might say 'I, Patrick, have the problem of parents not

looking after me adequately, and 'they', my parents, must change.' This could also be the position of Hilary. ' I Patrick's mother, have the problem of being unable to look after him on my own at present, and so 'they', his father and the new partner, should change so as to be able to parent him adequately until I can take him back.'

3 **The 'I–you' perspective**: '*I*' have this problem. '*You*' should do X or Y or Z or *something*. This could be the situation of April's worker who experiences herself as having the problem: that April, the foster parent, is showing stress. She tackles this by explicitly or implicitly saying to Patrick's worker that *she* should do something, or more specifically, should move him home or to a new foster situation.

4 **The 'I–we' perspective**: '*I*' have this problem. '*We*' need to do *something*. For example, the worker may experience the situation as one in which the main issue is *her* problem: what to do about meeting her responsibilities to ensure the proper parenting of Patrick. On this basis she makes various attempts to include a range of others in solving 'her' problem. For example, she could move Patrick quickly to an alternative foster placement, ignoring the problems created for children by multiple placements (DoH, 1998a, 1998b); or make demands on the grandparents to take over care, even though this had been considered previously and rejected as a long-term solution.

5 **The 'they–we' perspective**: '*They*' have this problem. '*We*' need to do *something*. This may happen in multidisciplinary teams. A great deal of work may have gone into the formation of good working relationships and team cohesion across an interdisciplinary network, but this can reinforce a 'them and us' perspective between the family members and the staff network, in which the latter are seen as attempting to foist a particular solution on 'us'.

6 **The 'we–us' perspective**: '*We*' have this problem. It is up to '*us*' do *something*. This is an 'opt in' position taken by the worker and one she should assume is operating. It is consistent with the Exchange Model because the premise is that:

- the social situation is the primary unit of assessment and intervention;
- the worker and the worker's team are included in the definition of the problem and possible solutions;
- the service user and others are as fully involved as possible in defining the nature of the problem and possible solutions.

Different actors, often implicitly, assume the 'situation' fits one or other of the above possibilities. The worker has to be able to stand back and take an overview, while engaging with as many people as necessary to move everyone towards involvement in a 'we–us' scenario.

The capacity to ask the question, 'who is the service user?'

When there are conflicting perspectives about who has responsibility for what, the question of who is seen as the service user needs to be asked. A major feature of child abuse inquiries is that the workers involved have been sidetracked from a focus on the paramount needs of the child and drawn into activities with the parents, other carers, their own organisations; and so have failed to notice significant factors about the child or children for whom they have primary responsibility (DoH, 1998; Clyde, 1992). In England and Wales the Children Act 1989 makes it clear that where there are conflicts of interest between children and parents or carers, the child's interests are paramount. This has at times been implemented in an unthinking way which ignores the importance of families in the lives of children, and the fact that most children return to them in a relatively short period of time even when they are in the public care (DoH, 1991b; Platt and Shemmings, 1996). In spite of growing policy emphasis on family support, workers find it difficult to view the *whole* – to notice, listen to, reach out for all the other people in the situation and their different perspectives on the problem and possible solutions. In all our examples it is almost impossible for any one worker to be in touch sufficiently with all the players in an extended and complex family. Yet failure to achieve this has high risks. The consequences can be inability to bring about good enough collaboration; inability to identify and develop the resources in the whole network; or inability to be confident that the care or support necessary is 'good enough'.

Marginality, partnership and deviance

The partnership role of the worker is that of a broker or third party who plays a significant role when:

- an exchange of resources is taking place;
- there is conflict between individuals, in families, groups, communities or organisations;

- people are stuck in patterns of behaviour but cannot see their way out of them.

Where someone is behaving unacceptably the worker has to understand both the deviant and those who stand for the status quo: the perspectives of both the young offender and the local people who have suffered from his or her behaviour. Marginality is essential for carrying out the task of effecting change in both, so that reconciliation can be achieved. This implies an equal responsibility to change. A young person, for example, is expected to change his or her behaviour; however, the public and the magistrates who represent them may have to change their perception of the person from that of an offender to ex-offender and fellow citizen for this to come about.

The skills of the change agent are not exclusive to social work: for example, they are also essential in arbitration in business, industry and politics. In social work, sustaining a position of marginality contributes to the partnerships needed to resolve social problems. Models of partnership can be based on extremes: for example, the blurring of roles and boundaries between partners, or the strengthening of roles and boundaries in precisely defined and maintained divisions of labour. Partnerships to tackle social problems are more diverse and typically involve at least three parties, for example:

- the person needing support – a carer – the worker;
- service users – health and housing, employment, education workers – social services staff;
- purchasers – providers – service users; and so on.

The relationships between these parties change with circumstances. Consequently the worker needs to be able to analyse the nature and change the quality of her partnership relationships at any time.

Competence in practising marginality

Competence in marginality means:

- demonstrating understanding of the different demands placed by others on the worker;

- the ability to make judgements about who to work with and who to confront;
- the capacity to be participant, observer and actor, and retain a marginal position despite all the pushes and pulls which could lead to the worker becoming a permanent part of the network and a part of the problem;
- the ability to cope with being isolated, or to stand apart, in a partnership;
- the ability to understand and change patterns of behaviour such as self-defeating strategies and mutually defeating interactions which help perpetuate problems.

Although the concept was not used, the timing and balance required to remain marginal was recognised, for example, by the Cleveland Inquiry:

> It is a delicate and difficult line to draw between taking action too soon and not taking it soon enough. Social services, whilst puting the needs of the child first, must respect the rights of the parents; they also must work, if possible, with the parents for the benefit of the children. These parents are often in need of help. Inevitably a degree of conflict develops between these objectives. (DoH, 1988, p. 244)

What knowledge contributes to marginality

Knowledge enables the worker to stand back from the immediacy of situations. At the same time it has to take into account, and be tested against, the immediate experience of the people involved and other workers' evidence. The worker who can remain on the boundaries of different and at times competing definitions of the problem, and is able to change position rapidly according to what the situation demands, has to underpin practice with knowledge. In Patrick's story this includes knowing:

- that couples at a certain stage may have particular kinds of developmental issues to face;
- what children's developmental needs are at Patrick's age;
- the impact that alcohol abuse can have on people's health and their ability to look after a young child;

- the impact of separation and loss for Patrick and his family;
- the effects of multiple moves on Patrick's emotional, educational and social development;
- child care legislation which requires certain behaviours of parents and of workers;
- that people in organisations tend to behave in certain ways because they have a culture of their own, with procedures and policies to follow which shape the opportunities and limitations placed on the worker's own actions.

The dynamic participant–observer–actor role requires that the worker never just applies knowledge but is always part of a convergence towards, and exchange with, the immediate and wider understandings which the particular people involved have of their social situation. Recent perspectives on the nature of professional knowledge and competence endorse this dimension of marginality (Eraut, 1994; Schorr, 1992). The complexity of knowledge to be applied to a particular situation can seem overwhelming but the concept of marginality assists the worker in patterning and structuring information. It facilitates the process by focusing on understanding of the worker's own situation, that of other people and organisations, what change is required and how it can be achieved.

Marginality and respect

An actively marginal position in relation to groups, families and communities requires acceptance of all the individuals involved. If the worker is drawn into judgmental attitudes towards particular people, thereby offering acceptance to some, conditional acceptance to others, and rejection to yet others, this reduces her ability to create a convergence of ideas about who should do what and bring about compromises in behaviour. The worker becomes a partisan, unable to facilitate negotiation across networks and organisations. People in vulnerable or powerless positions are ever alert to non-verbal clues and attitudes which demean or express prejudice towards them, to views or behaviour that discriminate against groups of people on the grounds of their ethnicity, age, gender, disability or sexuality. Strategies have to be devised which enable respect for the person to be demonstrated without condoning behaviour which is damaging to others, and applied in specific contexts to negotiate shared understandings and change.

Marginality, worker stress and independence of mind

Being in a marginal position is a major cause of stress for workers, just as it is for first-line managers who occupy a marginal position in the organisation hierarchy and face the differing perspectives and responsibilities of both senior managers and workers: 'caught betwixt and between' is how they sometimes describe this position (Levin *et al.*, 1998). Managing conflict and contradictions (Darvill, 1997) is an essential part of social work for both workers and managers. Stress arises when workers experience the 'betwixt and between' position as being out of control. This is managed by appropriate staff support and development within the organisation (Pottage and Evans, 1994), not by futile attempts to remove the conflicts and contradictions which are inherent in social situations. Workers are called upon to represent their organisations, the wider community and their 'clientele' in work at all levels, and these needs are often in conflict. Ignoring potential conflict is in itself a source of stress because there are no easy answers to questions like:

• In the family, whose needs should the worker meet: the mother's or the child's; the older person's or the carer's?
• What is the balance between the demands of the organisation, other relatives and the wider community?
• What resolution is possible when there is a clash between 'disruptive' families and 'respectable' neighbouring families?
• How can the worker maintain an appropriate independence in the clash between the interests of taxpayers and those of the 'needy'?

Workers with a sufficiently strong personal and professional identity can, with support from colleagues and managers, withstand and use the many different kinds of pressures and lobbying which occur in social and communication networks, while not drifting into defensive rigidity. The ability to create an environment which maintains marginality and independence of thought is part of the necessary underpinning for practice. Without it, the balancing or 'juggling' will be too costly to the worker, and her effectiveness and personal well-being compromised.

Creative use of expertise

To be able to lead or participate in team work, continually reinventing definitions of social problems and possible solutions, the individual worker has to be able to use her skills creatively. Like the improvising jazz player described earlier, she responds in many different ways to the other players, to both the basic underlying pattern and the specific nuances. Detailed practice guidance and specialist knowledge can be understood as the notes making up the tunes which individual practitioners need to learn to play. But workers also have to be able to improvise, or reinvent, because of the uniqueness of each individual, family, group and social network.

Knowing from within

Marginality requires particular knowledge about the unique configurations of specific situations, a 'knowing from within' (Shotter, 1993). While always remaining open to the perceptions and evaluations of others in the situation, the worker requires the ability to challenge and to intervene, to find out more. To be marginal is not just to accept existing definitions: it is to seek to affect and influence them in order to construct jointly different realities. Courage and confidence are necessary to stand out against dominant perceptions of situations, combined with the humility to hear and accept viewpoints different from our own.

The expertise required for this kind of social improvisation, the ability to create new, yet patterned and purposeful ways of relating in partnership with others, cannot be reduced to simple discrete items of formal knowledge, lists of what must be known or done. 'Knowing from within' is the kind of knowledge:

> ... one has *only from within a social situation*, a group, or an institution, and which thus takes into account (and is accountable to) the *others* in the social situation within which it is known. (Shotter, 1993, p. 7)

Shotter is describing the often implicit underlying personal qualities, behaviour and 'know-how' which workers need to possess and continually develop throughout their working lives. The implicitness of such know-how makes it difficult to present it in the form of codified knowledge. But it is crucial that this tacit practice knowledge becomes more fully explicit and thus more capable of being disseminated, criticised, codified and developed (Eraut, 1994).

Conclusion

If all problems had a single cause they could be removed by the delivery of a simple service, or a straightforward intervention. In practice most social problems ranging from who can provide support to somebody whose needs are not currently met, through to child protection issues and substance abuse by young people, are not so simple. They require workers to work in often complex partnerships in which the people involved may have different perceptions and expectations of the problem and possible solutions.

To achieve effective partnerships, a changed view of what constitutes leadership and professional expertise is required. Several dimensions of orthodox 'professionalism' militate against partnership, including:

- when social problem solving is seen as being achieved through workers using and retaining exclusive knowledge and skills;
- the maintenance of barriers between organisations and service users;
- workers and managers defining their own success as being in control.

The service and the worker are visibly at the centre of this analysis.

Our framework is based on a different conception, where the measures are skills in networking and negotiation, the ability to work with competing perceptions of social problems, combining different skills and resources in tackling them. Workers should support and develop existing social support systems rather than displace them or replace them, whether operating in the community, in residential or day care, or as change agents; or whether providing direct nurturing care or personal assistance. Such workers are part of a system of social support and control and not the centre of it.

The term 'marginality' is intended to remind us that:

- The contribution of most workers is made primarily through existing support and control networks, supplementing or filling gaps rather than taking a central position.
- The contribution of workers can make a significant impact on social problem solving, but most often the aim should be to withdraw from the situation and move on.

- Long-term involvement requiring extensive care by workers alone is relatively rare, although this may occur when children are in public care, or when learning difficulties or physical and mental health issues necessitate involvement in lifetime planning.
- The nature of the task and the knowledge and skills required by the worker as agent of change are distinct from those involved in long-term direct care.
- It is necessary to shift the paradigm of practice and provision from one that pathologises and individualises to one where people and their social networks are seen as a source of, and resource for, solving problems, and to counter centralised decision making which excludes the involvement of service users, carers and others.

This approach provides a framework within which everyone involved can refocus on the practice of social problem solving, and workers can begin to develop new and better codified understandings of exactly what is required in the way of knowledge, know-how and skills by those initiating deliberate and planned change in complex social situations. In the following chapters we identify the kinds of skilled behaviours required of workers approaching this task.

10

Core Skills:
The Joining Skills

In this and the following chapter, we identify the core skills required by the worker using the approach outlined in the previous chapters. We make a broad distinction between:

- **Joining skills**: getting alongside people effectively enough for the formation of a problem solving partnership; and
- **Intervention skills**: directly bringing about change with other people.

First we give a brief introduction to our approach to thinking about skills.

Skills and tasks

The catalogue of tasks carried out by people in organisations is as long as that of the legislation, statutory responsibilities and procedural guidelines which govern them. Added to these is the way that organisations compartmentalise and categorise people according to their needs or problems. Relatively simple, though lengthy, 'shopping lists' of the knowledge, skills and values required by the individual worker can be produced, compiled on the basis of the different weight given to the function and responsibilities of a particular employer, the expertise and needs of a service user or carer group; by political agendas and local community and user- or carer-led groups. Further lists can result from negotiations with the wide range of different interests and stakeholders in social care. These lists often cover the same ground and have similar content: this is not always obvious as they are conceptualised differently. For example, some authors identify 'assessment' as a separate skill (Pincus and Minahan, 1973; Davies, 1991; Thompson, 1995), whereas we see assessment as a recurring task in which certain skills are used. Our approach has been to identify the most general and transferable skill areas which are consistent with our view of the social work task, and consequently some more specific areas may seem to have been neglected. For example 'self-management' skills are identified by Thompson (1995, p. 97), but not separately identified here. Our assumption is that the specific task of managing our own resources of time, energy and know-how in particular situations is a task towards which all the skills we identify make an essential contribution.

Inevitably lists involve compromises. In the UK the practice framework for qualification is set in terms of competencies in line with the government's policy of establishing a national system of vocational qualifications and occupational standards for the workforce as a whole (CCETSW, 1995; Occupational Standards Council, 1997). In each case, irrespective of the status and origin of the list, the worker, manager and educator are faced with making judgements about priorities, the level or depth of skill, and how different skills and knowledge relate to each other.

Core skills as the foundation

We identify here the core skills on which individual workers and teams can then build their own detailed repertoires of more specific skills, knowledge and behaviours. These skills are not new. They are part of a reinvention, a reframing of knowledge, skills and values which draws on evidence of the effectiveness of practice approaches and also provides a basis for working on social problems. Core skills can be grouped into two main categories:

The **joining skills** of:

- empathy
- authenticity.

The **intervention skills** of:

- social entrepreneurship
- reflection
- challenging
- reframing.

The joining skills

This chapter concentrates on the joining skills, the foundations of good practice, which workers need to enter into and sustain effective relationships. These do not stand alone. Together with the intervention skills described in Chapter 11, they are part of the necessary conditions for positive change and effective service delivery.

Community-based practice means collaborative problem solving. Workers join with people and groups to create teams or active networks where isolated individuals or groups exist, where there are gaps in resources or they are inappropriate, or where there is persistent problematic behaviour. The 'know-how' to manage or lead collaborative problem solving is essentially derived from interpersonal skills because the task requires working with, and helping to coordinate, the knowledge, skills and other personal resources of all the people involved. At the same time, to avoid getting 'sucked into' the problematic situation the worker will have to use his own behaviour, knowledge and skills to facilitate all the necessary negotiations from a marginal position.

Empathy

Empathy is the worker's ability to communicate understanding: to stand alongside what the other person is thinking and feeling, their position, their perception of the situation and what they want. To empathise is to communicate understanding of the other person's world.

Empathy refers to the hard work of listening, hearing, comprehending and communicating understanding of what other people say, the thoughts and feelings they express and the way they make sense of the world. The worker checks that he has heard what the other person intended to say in words and through the expression of feelings or use of metaphor and analogy. When a person empathises with others there is a convergence of their perceptions of the situation, the problems that have to be resolved, the potential resources available and the possible solutions.

Collaborative interpersonal problem solving and conflict negotiation requires that the worker has the ability to understand the experience of all the people in the network with whom he is working, to successfully communicate that understanding to them and, where appropriate, to others. It includes being able to extend this capacity to people who differ from ourselves because of their gender, ethnicity, disability, age, culture, religion, social class or sexuality. In such situations we cannot always draw on knowledge from within our own personal experience and culture. Here we have to make imaginative leaps into the experience of others, using a knowledge of history and the experience of excluded groups (Ahmad, 1990; Morris, 1996; Lindow, 1994; Cambell and Oliver, 1996). Categorising people as 'other' than us will close down our capacity for empathy (hooks, 1991).

The skills of empathy have been seen as crucial since the empirical work of Carl Rogers and his colleagues used film to look at the behaviour of helpers and relate their actions to the outcomes of intervention (C. Rogers, 1961; C. Rogers *et al.*, 1967; Carkhuff, 1987; Egan, 1994; Gurman *et al.*, 1986). Research in the completely different and usually unrelated field of the diffusion of innovations has also demonstrated that empathy is a key skill for change agents who aim to introduce a new way of solving problems to others (E. Rogers, 1996; E. Rogers and Kincaid, 1981).

Empathy is:

- The ability to communicate to people that we understand how they think and feel. It is more than an intuitive understanding of another person or other people. It is neither a near-telepathic power, nor a 'natural sympathy', nor simply an understanding of a person and an ability to communicate this only to a third person. All these may be involved in an empathic understanding of another person, but they are not sufficient in themselves.
- Achieved when people think they are understood because they know and agree with the other person's understanding of them.
- A technical skill that needs to be developed. Like language or any other form of communication, it is a complex process in need of constant practice and refinement. Individuals and groups inevitably start with different perceptions, attitudes and beliefs formed by their cultural and religious backgrounds, ethnic origins and gender, social situations and personal experience. Even in the same language, words can have different meanings and different forms of communication may be preferred. As with any skills, being at ease with empathy develops over time and with practice but has to be relearned on entering a new culture or working with different social problems, service user, carer and professional groups.
- Optimistic and hopeful. The worker has to believe that positive change is possible even in the darkest and most despairing situations and, more importantly, convey that hope and optimism.

For example, if someone is depressed, having the experience of another person communicating an understanding of these feelings and perceptions, and not just sympathising or trying to argue the despair away, can, paradoxically, communicate hope. The despairing person's perception is that 'If someone understands me that well, and is even bothering to try to understand me, then perhaps I am not alone. Perhaps things could be better.

- Facing up to pain and distress. This aspect highlights the need for the worker to act in a 'counter-intuitive' way: not avoiding confrontation with the experience of pain and anxiety but going forward to spell out the problem being communicated; staying with the problem being expressed and not rushing in with premature reassurance or solutions. Premature reassurance runs the risk of communicating that the problem is so bad that the worker cannot stay with it. Empathy involves going at the other person's pace and demonstrating tact, timing and sensitivity, as well as the ability to listen, hear and communicate in the preferred language.

Empathy and the Jones family

In the example of the Jones family, Shirley and Colin feel unable rather than unwilling to support Mrs Jones. The worker recognises the need Shirley and Colin express to have Mrs Jones out of Shirley's way for part of the day. It is easy to misinterpret Shirley and Colin's initial view that they cannot have Mrs Jones home from hospital as an unwillingness to continue caring for Mrs Jones, rather than understand this as an expression of their need for respite time for Shirley and their own relationship. The worker is able to encourage Shirley and Colin to explore their own feelings and perceptions sufficiently to make this distinction explicit, by hearing what people are saying and checking on his own understanding.

Empathy and negotiation

Entering into meaningful negotiations with all the people involved in a social problem requires empathising with and accepting each person's initial perceptions of the problem. Some of these may have to be challenged: this will not be successful unless those people hear the worker communicating an understanding of their starting point. For many people using services, not being heard is both their expectation and their experience. Their definition of what is happening goes unheard: they are used to workers imposing a false consensus which negates the user's perception (Harding and Beresford, 1996; Beresford and Turner, 1997).

The Exchange Model of communication and assessment discussed in Chapter 7 stresses the way the worker tracks and follows rather than leads the person's description of the situation. The worker's agenda, his role and responsibilities, are not lost or forgotten. These are relocated in the context of working in partnership. To track rather than lead is to empathise. Empathy is crucial to developing mutual understanding of the way different people construe their worlds, what they see as social problems, and whether the solution lies in altering certain kinds of behaviour or providing for unmet needs.

Empathy and Patrick's family

The worker involved with Patrick and his family, discussed in Chapter 9, has to develop many levels of mutual understanding. She has to have enough shared understanding of the perceptions and feelings of all the people involved to be able to lead negotiations about the ongoing care of Patrick, and to do this while remaining sensitive to many of the other needs of the individuals and groups involved. This may well involve her in reconstruing or reinventing her own assessment as she develops better understanding of all the different starting points of the different actors. This is not to say that the worker has to develop a full, 'deep' rapport with everyone in the network; but she does have to ensure that there is sufficient common understanding to inform negotiations and encourage decisions based on a good exchange of information about people's needs, wants, feelings, rights and responsibilities. Family conferences are an example of a formal way of constructing negotiations about how the care of vulnerable children and adults can be achieved within a social network (Morris and Tunnard, 1996).

Empathy and the worker's desire for information: the Questioning Model

Assessment should 'strike a balance between invading privacy and obtaining sufficient information to gain an understanding of need' (DoH, 1989b). To empower others, that is to work with them so that they analyse and act on their problems during an assessment, and not just use them as sources of information, *it is necessary to recognise that the worker arrives at his understanding with the other people assessed, and not ahead of them.*

The analysis of the Exchange versus the Questioning Model of assessment came about through many hours of looking at video tapes made during interactional skills training. It became clear that many staff felt they *should* come up with a solution to the problem being presented very quickly, often ahead of anything like a full description of the problem, and always ahead of the user. There was a recognition that they felt this urgency, even when it was unnecessary or even counterproductive, in order to set themselves up as 'the expert' (Smale *et al.*, 1992).

Within a relationship designed to help others and achieve constructive change, the gatekeepers of privacy are the people who hold the relevant 'secrets': they reveal these when they decide they are relevant and that the recipient is trustworthy. How the worker responds to hints or clues about these secrets either facilitates their sharing or delays or blocks this completely. This holds even where statutory powers are involved, where the person may deliberately conceal, keep private, what has happened because of shame or fear of the consequences; or the person may even block out memories of what happened because they cannot face or think about it. We have argued in Chapter 7 that interrogative approaches or the Questioning and Procedural Models of assessment implicitly assume that the worker can arrive at an understanding of the other person and their situation first, through asking the 'right' questions. No matter how tactfully carried out, the approach inevitably moves into private areas at the pace of the worker, not that of the person or group involved. While this is appropriate when there is serious risk to life and liberty, it is more difficult to then move back to a more Exchange type of relationship.

Interrogation, or the use of a Questioning mode, no matter how benignly conducted, sometimes drives the answers further away. This is true for even fairly ordinary memories, let alone 'secrets' or very painful areas of experience. Merton (1948) suggests that more information will be forthcoming from an invitation to describe an event, like a person's first day at school, rather than from a point-blank question about the experience such as, 'How did you get on when you started school?' A sense of being understood produces a more open response than being interrogated, especially if the source of the questions is not trusted. This is an issue which workers have to address in cases of abuse, in the criminal justice system and in mental health work. Specific skills are needed to overcome the anger and hostility that can result (Thoburn *et al.*, 1995) and to recognise when another worker is required because there is too great a difference between the worker and the service user to establish trust (Jones and Butt, 1995). Workers have to have the capacity to cope with their own feelings and to help others express theirs, as essential ingredients of the job.

Empathising assumes the other person is the expert in their perception of their problem and their situation, even if they are at a loss to know what to do. The task is to help the person develop their own understanding in ways that encourage remaining in control as far as possible of their goals and options, in both the care and control functions of social work.

Empathy and questioning

Questioning and probing without prior establishment of rapport may be experienced by the service user as:

- the worker already having decided and prejudged the situation;
- patronising;
- not being heard, misunderstanding or missing the point;
- ignoring the experience, history and culture of a person or group;
- confrontational;
- being given premature, useless advice;
- being too risky to respond to openly, because there has been no time to establish trust. This may be the result of a past history of being let down or the situation not being critical enough, as in a crisis, to take this leap of faith.

Because of the worker's position of power and in deference to social convention, reasonably cooperative and polite service users may answer even the most irrelevant and impertinent questions. They tolerate misguided questions, assuming that the worker knows best, needs to know the answers, or feeling that it is less trouble to answer than to challenge or remain silent. But questions from the worker's agenda will not always increase understanding of the situation nor support service users or carers in coming to terms with it and changing it.

Consistent empathy: an 'unsocial' behaviour

Consistent and effective communication with and comprehension of another person, especially a person in difficulty, is not usual social behaviour. There is a natural tendency to avoid pain and discomfort, and social conventions reinforce this behaviour. Empathy requires suspending these codes and looking constructively at pain, loss and what is really going wrong within a relationship. The tendency to avoid other people's pain and loss has to be countered. Avoidance of facing up to losses and rejections is most likely to occur where there is little professional support available for the worker (DoH, 1985).

The suspension of such codes of behaviour has implications for service users and what they expect. Typically they initially give a clue – 'I have been feeling tired recently' – without actually saying they have a problem – 'I cannot sleep at night' or 'I feel depressed'. Most will test out what is safe and what is unsafe to talk about. If the worker responds in a way acceptable to the other person it gives permission to move to the next stage, if the person is ready.

A further social convention is that the person with the most power is expected to determine the priority given to particular topics, and speak the most and longest. While power itself is complex and fluid, these codes are well understood by people who are discriminated against or disadvantaged, such as black and minority ethnic groups, women, disabled people (Spender, 1980; Morris, 1996). Those who see themselves as powerless or in disadvantaged positions are often very sensitive to quite small cues from people who are seen to be in positions of power or authority. In general, the opposite holds for those who are seen to have power. The worker is usually in a position of some authority, although the degree of perceived power difference varies according to their personal and social characteristics and those of the service user (Hanmer and Statham, 1999). Starting with the user's agenda requires the worker to overcome the difficult problem of confronting these attitudes and expectations: in many Exchange interactions the worker avoids beginning with specific questions and after sharing information about her role starts with a short statement of her understanding of the referral, and a pause for a response. Although the precise words vary with the situation, the message the words have to communicate is:

Worker: 'I want to understand your situation. Where shall we start?' – then waiting for the user to describe the problem as he or she sees it: to, in effect, set the agenda.
Service user: 'Silence' – as if saying to him or herself: 'Do you really want to hear my agenda?' or 'Am I really supposed to define the problem? Experts and people in authority normally do that'.

Overcoming embarrassment or confusion means learning new social rules for practice. No one can keep up empathic practice all the time. Supervision and other ways of supporting and developing practice are needed to enable the worker to cope with the trauma and intense feelings, such as grief and loss, routinely experienced in the work; and to help keep the focus of intervention on another person's or group's needs and the resolution of their problems. Support is also necessary to enable the worker to sustain the psychological and emotional stamina necessary to maintain awareness of different people's conflicting perceptions, without giving up under the strain and simplifying the problem by ignoring some of the information.

Empathy and socio-cultural difference

Empathy includes developing the capacity to understand the experience of people from backgrounds and cultures different from our own. Bandana Ahmad, discussing how workers can develop their skills of confrontation without being racist, argues that:

> An essential requisite of an ongoing programme of self-evaluation is self-confrontation, i.e. confronting one's own approach and incentive for expressing warmth, concern and empathy that may be insensitive to the Black client's dignity and pride (e.g. patronising), or may not relate to the real problems of the Black client (e.g. concentrating on those aspects of the problem that least require expression of warmth, concern and empathy). (Ahmad, 1990, p. 35)

Similarly,

> Disabled people have to work continually against destructive forces which see us as powerless, passive and unattractive ... Being defined by others in ways you don't choose to define yourself is not, of course, a problem exclusive to disabled people. Women have for many years been writing about our need to reject being defined exclusively by our bodies and the way we look, but it is different for disabled people because some of us deviate so significantly from what is considered to be within the range of 'normal' appearance. (Keith, 1996, pp. 70–1)

The special risk of false, and thus patronising and irrelevant, understanding exists whenever the worker is faced with a person, family or group who have significantly different life experiences, histories, cultures or religions from themselves. Whether the reason is applying generalised information or local or personal prejudice, if we bypass the learning required, the difficult and time-consuming task of establishing common ground and struggling to reinvent a common 'language' together, and assume that we know how a person thinks and feels – this is the foundation of stereotyping. Not stopping to check that we accurately understand the communications of the particular person is the beginning of discriminatory behaviour. No matter how much generalised knowledge a worker may have of 'the kind of person' or the particular group or community, the individuality and the uniqueness of each set of relationships has to be recognised. The worker's perceptions and practice are constantly reinvented to match each set and reinvented again to keep up with them as they change. Sophisticated stereotypes based on years of study are still stereotypes.

Authenticity and genuineness

Authenticity is the congruence between what the person says, what he feels and what he does: the worker's ability to relate to others with personal integrity; to be able to engage with others, 'person to person', while at the same time being aware of and using his own feelings and values, as well as the resources of his organisational role and the other roles he occupies.

The communication of empathic understanding is not demonstrated through mechanistic technique, nor by just stating a value position, nor through a mysterious and private intuitive state. Authenticity is a cluster of behaviours, attitudes and knowledge, the synthesis of which becomes a genuine part of the person of the worker – something within the person. The capacity for genuineness, or authenticity – the capacity for using a wide range of role behaviours and attitudes and yet making them one's own, or in other ways remaining a real person within the relationships – is a tenet of good practice.

Real support, care or assistance cannot be prescribed or guaranteed by job descriptions, procedures or organisational role expectations, or by being able to write eloquently about them; it depends heavily on the personal attributes, style and behaviour of the individuals concerned. The key components of a quality service are defined by service users and carers from Wiltshire Users Network as follows:

So often it is the style or the way services are delivered rather than the service itself which produces a quality service. This makes it quite difficult to separate out quality of services from quality of relationships: the home carer who gets you up in the morning can do this in an empowering way which enables you to face the effort of the day positively or in a way which means that you are dressed and ready, but not psychologically ready. (Harding and Beresford, 1996, p. 5)

Authenticity and trust

Trust cannot be prescribed – people do not trust others just because they are told they can or should. Similarly, trustworthiness cannot be prescribed by an organisation or any other role relationship. Good experiences of other people lead to investing trust in others, but many service users have had bad experiences in their personal relationships, in their contact with those in positions of authority, and have negative stereotypes of workers. When these people come into relationships with workers they may be suspicious and apprehensive and reserve their trust until the workers have at least demonstrated that they can be of some practical help. Even then, they may feel they have just been lucky to get an atypical worker (Newburn, 1993).

Many of the individuals, groups and communities using services are excluded, rejected and stigmatised by society. The very fact of entering into a role relationship with a worker is seen as deviant. Although the number of people using social care organisations has grown over the past twenty years, social work is still seen as being for a minority. Part of the worker's task is to reduce to a minimum the negative effects consequent on entering such role relationships (Hardiker *et al.*, 1996; Smale, 1995). Central to achieving this goal is to move beyond the role of an 'expert' who solves an individual problem and to work through reciprocal roles in families and communities to relationships which include rather than exclude them from their social networks and the wider community.

A capacity for authenticity, in the sense of congruence between what is thought or felt and what is expressed, informs all the actions and communications of the worker. There are two main levels.

1   For the individual worker:
    • the straightforward demand that workers are honest with people about themselves, their organisation, powers, responsibilities and resources even when the news may be bad;

- the worker's self-awareness and how he uses himself in facilitating complex processes of change;
- the need for congruence between different levels of communication: between what is said and what is meant and the integrity of subsequent actions. The worker may need to voice directly his anxiety about somebody's hostile behaviour, rather than carrying on behaving as if in control while covertly communicating fear. Non-verbal messages are powerful forms of communication and are both attended to and believed.

2   The organisation can provide a context which ensures:
- there is congruence between the espoused values and purposes of an organisation, and how these are conveyed through information, office opening hours, the environment or reception area;
- information from people who use services and front-line workers informs policies and the development of provision;
- support for the worker for learning from and developing his own practice and for keeping up to date.

Authenticity and the Jones family

When the worker involved with the Jones family makes his initial contact he is not immediately committed to either service delivery work or change agent work. He has been careful to explain that he is not necessarily there to help but to find out what people want and to see if anything can be organised. The worker's behaviour demonstrates that he is sufficiently self-aware to realise the importance of being open. He does not pretend that he will always know what to do or unrealistically imply that a service is actually available before he has negotiated some shared understanding of the issues, of who might offer help and who might be eligible for certain services. When the contact is based on control functions, the first encounter also sets the tone for the future (Thoburn *et al.*, 1995; Platt and Shemmings, 1996).

Authenticity, marginality and change

A major part of the worker's task is to build bridges between people, create and maintain links, and help negotiations and renegotiations (Harding and Beresford, 1996; Morris, 1996; Hanmer and Statham, 1999). This can be difficult when the multiplicity of conflicting interests, perceptions, hopes, demands and other pressures jeopardises maintenance of an appropriate position within the network. The worker is not always able to get respite from these pressures by recourse to organisational and institutional structures. Ambiguities, gaps in, or lack of, resources, vagueness in policies and procedures and in other people's expectations, and inconsistencies in different social policies and organisational priorities become exposed during practice and have to be dealt with at the front line.

In the context of such deep-rooted ambiguities and uncertainties, authenticity is the test. It is founded on the worker's capacity to remain in touch with his own feelings, thoughts, values and experiences, and to resist taking on the perceptions, emotions and behaviours towards which others may be leading him. Colleagues, managers, service users and their family members, and inter-organisation groups influence the worker in particular directions and express or imply views on the worker's appropriate role in general and in this particular instance. Without a capacity for authenticity, the worker risks being drawn into accepting one person's definition of the problem and what action should be taken. Powerful interpersonal influences or organisational forces may indeed impose a particular definition, but a minimal level of authenticity and recognition of moral autonomy will enable the worker to continue to operate with marginality in particular situations. The authentic worker is constantly asking what he can do to contribute to a solution of the problems he confronts. Such workers do not seek detailed directions about what to do. This is the road to role-playing at being, rather than the way to becoming, a genuinely helpful worker.

Authenticity and modelling

Workers need to be able to practise what is preached and be aware of the ways in which their own behaviours may contradict espoused values. It is false to challenge the father to listen better to his son, while simultaneously failing to hear and validate the father's own concerns. As people are inclined to do what others do as much as what they are told to do, the manager who gets tough on procedures, ignoring the content of the work and the feelings this engenders in the worker, can expect staff to do the same with service users. The worker who says 'you can trust me' will in the end be mistrusted if his words are subsequently contradicted – however legitimate the reason might be – by the discharge of statutory responsibilities and the use of authority when the user's definition of what is needed conflicts with that of the

worker, his organisation or the court. The trustworthy worker points
out that he cannot be relied on in all situations to act in what the
service user or the carer sees as his interests, and that there are limits to
the confidentiality of the information he obtains. Paradoxically these
workers are more likely to be trusted as a result.

Workers exercise authority on behalf of society and its institutions.
They gatekeep access to the organisation's resources. Knowledge of
the law and its requirements, and willingness to be frank and open
with people, is necessary for the effective use of authority for workers
in all settings, but most obviously so where they carry statutory
responsibilities. People who experience the control functions value
information, openness and sensitivity in difficult situations (Platt and
Shemmings, 1996).

Authenticity and Patrick's family

A capacity for authenticity is demonstrated in Patrick's story,
especially in relation to all the different pushes and pulls from the
different people and organisations involved. There can be considerable incongruence between the worker's view of the problem and
possible solutions, and that of some of the family members and other
workers involved. Irrespective of who is 'right' or which is the 'best'
assessment, the worker allows herself to be aware of these differences
even though they may present her with extra demands to negotiate
towards a more common perspective. This is necessary as the basis for
a strategy for dealing with and using such differences rather than,
perhaps implicitly, communicating an overconfident 'right' viewpoint.
One of the key factors which drive self-defeating strategies and
mutually defeating interactions is precisely people behaving in ways
which conform to what they think others expect of them, that is,
playing a role. For change to happen, someone in the system has to
model the possibility of stepping outside the role boundaries, however
defined by others. This in turn requires a capacity for authenticity.

Authenticity and difference

Social and cultural differences between the worker and those he is
working with create additional demands on the worker. In relation to
black and minority ethnic groups, Bandana Ahmad writes:

> Feeling warmth, concern, empathy etc. are nothing new in social
> work practice. Acquisition and application of these skills are

fundamental to the social work encounter. However, the social work encounter with Black clients often has difficulties in applying these fundamental skills. These difficulties may vary from personal prejudice against Black people in general to dislike or disapproval of the behaviour or values of Black people or simple paranoia and mental block in dealing with Black clients. It is imperative that these difficulties are acknowledged by social workers. (Ahmad, 1990, p. 34)

These points are equally applicable to working with other differences. The worker, while recognising difference in people, must also be able to relate to each as a person without any particular social label, and vice versa. One of the complaints of black disabled young people is that workers see only their disability, and not the fact that they have a black identity which is just as important for them as for a non-disabled black person (Macdonald, 1991).

Authenticity and partnership

Partnership relationships cannot be created by a faceless representative of the organisation but by a genuine human being, a fellow citizen willing to share in tackling a problem with others. Operating only on the Questioning or Procedural Model of assessment and intervention encourages the worker to remain in an essentially organisational role relationship, an approach which undermines the development of partnership. For example, research into routine assessments for adult residential care concluded that they were:

> ... sometimes approached as if they were primarily an administrative task, simply a question of filling in forms. Unlike the admission of children to residential care this transition was not always viewed by professionals as a major life event which could be very stressful for the individual involved. (Neill and Williams, 1992).

Workers can think they have achieved partnership while the user experiences the same interaction as doing what the worker wanted. A defensive or unthinking position is adopted which blocks learning. The attitude is that 'we do it already', without checking what service users and carers think (Marsh and Fisher, 1992).

The worker has to be open, straightforward and go beyond playing a formal organisational role to enter negotiations on a more equal level, and see people as citizens rather than as clients (Smale,

1995). Equally it is unhelpful, dishonest and ultimately disempowering merely to simulate understanding of the situation or person, or pretend to a level of interest or care which is not actually experienced. Incongruent communication can be picked up even if it is not overtly commented on by the other person, and affects his judgement of the worker and his behaviour in response.

Authenticity and respect

It is a well-established value that workers should demonstrate a genuine acceptance and valuation of people irrespective of their personal qualities, behaviour, social position or occupation. Respect is communicated by the way all the other skills and knowledge involved in the task are deployed in the relationship. Working consistently at communicating understanding of the other person's experience; reaching out to develop partnerships with a wide range of people; carefully and tactfully challenging people's self-defeating behaviours and helping them risk making changes; ensuring a good detailed knowledge of local resources and local issues: these are all ways in which respect is enacted in practice. But all of this has to be conducted within the framework of relationships characterised by authenticity – in which the worker reaches out from his formal role towards genuine person-to-person encounters. Fundamental values about respect for and acceptance of others have to be enacted rather than just espoused.

Authenticity and self-awareness

Genuine respect does not imply an acceptance of all the acts of other people. The individual worker will at times experience considerable repugnance or indifference to the attitudes, thoughts and behaviours of some of those with whom he works. Self-awareness has to be developed in relation to his own values, behaviours and feelings. Training for practice can emphasise the differences between the worker and the people using services, rather than the commonalties between them. Workers can find themselves alongside service users and carers who, like themselves, are having difficulties with parenting children and young people, who have experienced severe losses, violence in relationships, been abused as children, or cared for an older relative. Without self-awareness these commonalties can impede authenticity; with it they are a powerful force (Hanmer and Statham, 1999). The communication of empathy involves the hard work of struggling to understand the often painful or bewildering experience of others, and its impact on ourselves and our behaviour. The communication of respect requires the hard work of struggling to find the common humanity and so value the strengths and experience of people who may be seen both by themselves and others as of little worth. This cannot be done through following a procedural guide or other people's role expectations – it is either a genuine personal response or it is nothing.

In this chapter we have discussed the behaviours required by workers seeking to be genuinely empathic towards those with whom they are working, the relationship between these skills and the need to communicate respect, and the importance of developing self-awareness. These skills are crucial for workers seeking to develop problem solving partnerships with anyone, whether with an individual, a family, community groups, or other workers and colleagues. In the following chapter we build on this by identifying the skills required for intervention.

11

Core Skills:
The Intervention Skills

The worker needs to join with others in order to understand their situation as they see it, and to be experienced by them as genuine, and not just someone hiding behind a professional or official mask. However this, while necessary, may not be sufficient to bring about change in the situation, for which other skills are additionally required. We call these the **intervention skills**. They are:

1 Social entrepreneurship
2 Reflection
3 Challenging
4 Reframing.

Social entrepreneurship

Social entrepreneurship is the ability to initiate, lead and carry through problem-solving strategies in collaboration with other people in all kinds of social networks.

Social workers and managers are initiators and leaders in the collaborative design of solutions to social problems. Effective solutions to complex problems utilise diverse organisational and human resources and involve long-term development as well as immediate work. A care plan for shared parenting of a child with learning difficulties may involve many people with different skills and experience in working with children, families and learning difficulties. The plan responds to the changing developmental, social and emotional needs of the child and looks to the future so that attention will be given to what support is required for independent living. These plans are not 'off the shelf' solutions. Different people make up the team and at times difficult and highly charged circumstances have to be faced. The worker initiates and takes a lead in following through all the collaboration and negotiations. None of the people in the team substitutes for the parent, even though in residential and day care they may be carrying out some of the parenting and nurturing tasks. Later on, no one can substitute for the young person grown to adulthood, whose rights to be actively involved in what happens in his or her life are then promoted.

Successful leadership in social and interpersonal change is not necessarily grounded in the authority of a particular role, position or organisation, but stems from the capacity to initiate and carry through credible collaboration, and to coach, model and show the way to others through sometimes difficult and painful experiences and decisions. This definition differs from one which sees leadership as taking charge and trying to impose, whether wittingly or not, the worker's own or the organisation's views on everyone else. Social entrepreneurship, like entrepreneurship in other fields is the capacity and willingness to take responsibility for initiating change and, directly or indirectly, to lead others through a collaborative process of designing and implementing solutions to problems. It is **entrepreneurial** because workers are active in developing resources, and see the locus of control of their own actions as lying as much within themselves as within the rules and guidelines of the organisation in which they are located and the legitimate demands and patterns of accountability of which they are a part.

The worker who is a social entrepreneur is a pro-active change agent who mediates and acts as a gatekeeper to scarce resources. These roles and tasks can be described as care management. Usually a specialist in a particular area of work or method, her aim always is to ensure that services are tailored to the specific situation and all the different contributors and organisations are in place. She has a significant role in ensuring a holistic approach through taking an entrepreneurial lead in negotiating and mediating across the networks of people and organisations involved in particular social problems.

The individual worker, the team and the whole task

Social entrepreneurship is not about individualistic practice. Each worker makes an identifiable contribution to the network of people tackling social problems in all the quadrants of the content map (Chapter 4) through participation in two main forms of teamwork.

In Chapter 4 we said that the team is the smallest unit that can undertake the whole task and comprises whoever is required to accomplish the task. This can be an organisation-based or a multiple-organisation team involving service users, carers and other significant people. A package of care is not like a basket of goods and services. It is a fluid set of human relationships and arrangements where the service user, carer, other family relations, friends and neighbours as well as other providers establish an infrastructure of social support in a specific social network.

Creating partnerships

The systems and structures of local responses to social problems are built from the bottom up by pro-actively bringing together knowledge developed through partnerships with local people, community groups, voluntary, private, religious organisations, and other statutory organisations. These resources are combined with those of individual workers and their teams through their direct work. The premise is that the work of individual organisation teams, their locality plans and analyses of the resources and needs of their areas, are the building blocks for strategic community care and children's services plans. Separation of the management role from the practice of front-line staff undermines a community-based approach, which is founded on front-line information. Dividing purchasing from providing makes it especially important that managers and workers take a lead in bringing people together across these functional divisions, in order to clarify who can best do what, or which specialist provider can best tackle the whole of a particular social problem in a community. Individual workers and teams actively inform and influence the processes by which local social policies and social interventions are developed in their areas, and do this in partnership with service users, carers and local citizens generally, as well as the different provider organisations.

Community-based policy and practice at the departmental level is the product of genuine partnership with citizens, be they direct users of services, carers, providers, volunteers or others. The kinds of local information which the individual worker and her team colleagues acquire can be brought together into a coherent picture. The entrepreneurial indirect work necessary to develop resources in the community which do not already exist, and to change the way resources are currently deployed, both requires and helps create the kind of local knowledge crucial to the process. The individual worker's contribution to this wider planning process itself creates the resources for some of the direct work involved in problem solving with individuals, and individual families.

All staff and each area team have a pivotal, entrepreneurial role in actively contributing to the communication networks necessary to link these different planning and development levels.

Social entrepreneurship and the Jones family

In the case of the Jones family (Chapter 4), the nature of the social problems at the individual and family level, and the kinds of direct problem solving activity engaged in by the worker, are fairly clear. However, the team's indirect contributions may be less obvious.

We have established that the very existence of a lunch club which Mrs Jones can attend, run by a local voluntary organisation and financially supported by the local authority, is a product of a local social care planning process. In order to underpin the initiative and demonstrate that this service represented best value, to influence the social services committee to commit funding, a team member prepared a report jointly with local members of the voluntary organisation, users and potential users. That report used local census and health statistical information costings, area profiles and small-scale research which provided an analysis of case examples drawn from the team's direct work, including the work of local groups.

Such planning is a continuous process. For example, if efforts were being made to improve services to members of a minority ethnic group this would require changes in the lunch club. The aim would be broader than simply changing menus (Ahmad, 1990). It would include encouraging wider recognition of cultural and religious needs. Throughout the lunch club, staff, volunteers and users would be clear about how racial harassment and abuse would be handled if it occurred and efforts would be made to recruit staff and volunteers from the minority ethnic community. Implementing this plan is likely to set in train a renegotiation of other relationships with local groups and organisations about what is required and how it could be supported.

Social entrepreneurship and Patrick's family: entrepreneurial flexibility in the division of labour

Professional groups and networks tend to divide up their responsibilities in ways which make sense to them, and which suit their own organisation. These divisions may neither reflect people's actual skills and resources, nor the ways which fit best with the service user's own network's understanding. Key people in the community can have a greater awareness of what should be done to support them and what would make a difference in their lives than specialist workers working within a specific area of expertise, or within the separate compartments of their organisation.

In Patrick's case the social care organisation had three different teams working with the family:

- the initial referral and investigation team, which passed the family on to:
- the long-term area team, once it was clear there would be no quick resolution to Patrick's care; and
- the adoption and fostering team, which became involved because Patrick was fostered and adoption was being considered.

Family members may not see any distinction between these different workers and teams and if they knew about them they would not necessarily understand or agree with them. Consequently the different service users do not necessarily behave in ways which ensure a good fit with the workers' division of labour. Hilary, Patrick's mother, shares her difficulties with Jane, Patrick's worker, even though officially she is not supposed to; and Jane responds, even though she is not *sure* whether she is supposed to. The decision by the worker to respond in this way may be acting against the norms and the culture of her own organisation. The power of 'the way it is done here' over practice is very strong, even though there may be solid research evidence and experience which demonstrates that this is ineffective or even harmful. The worker may be seen as deviant, as an uncontrollable and unaccountable employee. Equally she can be seen as exercising a necessary entrepreneurial, and moral, autonomy and demonstrating a capacity to initiate and follow through an informed and considered problem solving strategy in partnership with others. She can still exercise accountability to her organisation through her line manager or supervisor.

Entrepreneurial problem solving

Initiating a new solution to a problem – innovating – is a key dimension of the worker's skill, and the focus of the collective input of the organisation team, and indeed the organisation within the community (Smale, 1998). The worker takes the initiative to become involved in the foster mother's difficulties not just for April's sake, but because maintaining her in the role of carer for Patrick is in his best interests, and Jane is responsible for Patrick. Actively seeking out opportunities to build on and use existing relationships in order to tackle different dimensions of the whole problem is a central part of the entrepreneurial spirit necessary for social problem solving. The effective worker, and the effective team, cannot always wait for problems to be addressed by another part of the organisation which is allocated responsibility for a particular role, any more than an entrepreneur in business can wait for a supplier to start producing components for the goods he makes, or markets to just appear or be created by others. This again illustrates how counterproductive it is to organise services as if the fundamental unit of intervention is an individual service user with specific personal attributes. The social worker is centrally engaged with patterns of relationships between people, not just the individuals that make up the pattern.

Entrepreneurial reframing of the problem

The immediate problem as perceived by Jane's organisation and first-line manager was maintaining continuity of care for Patrick, given the uncertainty about the current foster placement and the unavailability at this time of adoptive parents. However, after a period of time getting to know some of the key people involved, Jane began to move beyond this narrow and incomplete definition of the task. She began to recognise that the problem of continuity of care only arose because of the way the problem was being presented. Providing an alternative way of caring for Patrick was seen as the only or best solution to a different problem in the family functioning. To initiate and follow through a revision of the basic definition of the problem, in the face of well-established perceptions, decisions and stereotypes across a multidisciplinary network, requires a tenacious entrepreneurial flair, channelled into a well-thought-out and strategic plan of action which has been checked out against research and experience.

Social entrepreneurship and the enabling manager

Participative, creative and empowering styles of management are necessary for individuals and teams of workers to initiate, develop and build on partnerships with service users and carers, community groups and others at the local level (Brown, 1996). The manager has to be able:

- to understand the expertise available within the organisation team and outside it in order to have the confidence to operate in this way;
- to be a skilled worker himself in order to have credibility with other workers and managers;
- to provide support to workers, to learn from and develop their practice;
- to be committed to shared views about standards of practice, and the approach to the work;
- to delegate responsibility for workers, to be able to take the initiative in identifying and forming all the partnerships required for all levels of the work;
- to expect that workers take responsibility for problem solving and partnership in team decision making and the utilisation of scarce resources, without constantly passing these problems up to middle or senior management;
- to have the capacity to learn from front-line workers, service users and carers and to communicate this to senior managers so that it informs the organisation's practice and its strategic planning.

The Exchange Model on which the community-based approach is founded is unworkable if the individual is tied down by narrowly prescriptive procedures, or if too many decisions are referred to a manager. Workers cannot make decisions in partnership with service users and at the same time do only what they are told to do by their managers (Smale, 1998). Joint planning at the organisational level has to be translated into working partnerships at the local level if it is to be more than a policy statement. To be effective, agreements have to be made about the framework within which a team will approach the work of supporting and developing the local infrastructure for social care. The entrepreneurial development of local partnerships is a major task in its own right, and one in which the individual worker and the organisation team as a whole has a major role.

Competition and collaboration

The way some aspects of social care are structured, with an emphasis on separating purchaser from provider, is increasingly out of step with trends in business and industry, where the pattern is more likely to be what is fit for the purpose than adherence to a single solution. Petroleum companies and some fast food chains successfully combine ownership of the natural resources, production and distribution. Increasingly in industry the relationship between a producer and customer is one of partnership in order to arrive at the best solution to a shared problem (Handy, 1994). We also see increasing collaboration between competing producers where research and development costs are high, such as in the motor car, aerospace and drugs industries. Alliances often cross international frontiers as well as the boundaries between separate companies. There are sound economic advantages to be gained through economies of scale and the benefits of greater vertical and horizontal integration. They are part of making the complex connections necessary for businesses to remain competitive in a global market. The patterns industry and business are developing can contribute to our knowledge of the limitations of adhering strictly to a particular model, unless there is evidence that it is fit for the purpose (Kearney, 1996).

Three-way partnerships

Partnership practice (Marsh and Fisher, 1992) involves three-way relationships:

- service users (key members of their networks);
- the commissioner making resources available from her organisation; and
- the provider.

In many situations the commissioner and the provider will have more power over their resources than the service user and will be able to construct a partnership in their own interests which excludes the user. But the sources of power are complex and power is not static. Like other key participants, users have power over their behaviour and their own resources. They may have chosen not to use this power, be unaware of it or can use other resources to support their own power. User- and carer-led organisations and advocacy schemes are ways in which users and carers can share and analyse their experiences and the outcomes they want, and be a means of altering the power balance.

The worker with Patrick, for example, needs to be able to use her own judgement in partnership with her colleagues, members of the family and people in the wider social context, about what changes may be possible, what direct services might be made available, and what the next steps might be. Effective problem solving requires and is encouraged by devolution of decision making as close to the team of people actually tackling the problem as possible. This in turn models the devolution of decision making which the worker herself encourages through her partnerships with service users, carers and others in the community. Where this does not take place, the involvement of citizens in planning and managing their services can lead to conflict and dis-illusionment (Smale and Bennett, 1989).

Reflection

Reflection is the worker's ability to pattern or make sense of information, in whatever form, including the impact of her own behaviour and that of her organisation on others.

If the social problems which workers are employed to tackle could be resolved by standardised responses contained in procedures and guidelines, then the capacity for independent thought, reflection and judgement would be relatively unimportant. All the significant thinking would already have been undertaken in the formulation of the procedure or guidelines which the worker could then apply as a routine in typical situations. However the individual worker has to be capable of pro-active, independent, reflective thought and action to contribute to problem solving and meet appropriate standards of performance. This is essential because of:

- the often complex conflicts of interest involved in the nature of social problems;
- the unique mix of skills, resources, experience, strengths, weak-nesses and gaps involved, particularly where some people's behav-iour is defined as 'the problem';
- the need to understand and unravel the complexities of relation-ships that perpetuate social problems through self-defeating strategies and mutually defeating interactions: the need for main-tenance of the marginal position of the worker;

- the frequent necessity for an Exchange Model of relationship to achieve effective and lasting change;
- the risk that procedures, guidelines, the worker's own behaviour and that of their organisation can contribute to and perpetuate the problems which the worker is intending to resolve;
- the need to identify and respond to unintended and unforeseen consequences of social interventions.

Organisational procedures and legislative frameworks set the boundaries and minimum requirements of the organisation's interventions: the powers and duties of workers. Standards of services and performance targets reflect the aspirations and strategic direction of the organisation. But they can only ever represent one source of the knowledge and information which the worker has to hold in balance, make sense of and operate within. Procedures, for example, define how the worker should implement the department's policy: that a visit or appointment will be made within 48 hours of referral; or that the worker is permitted to spend up to a given amount of time per week on a particular category of service user without the consent of a senior manager. In themselves these mechanisms are not intended for solving social problems. But implementing the procedure can substitute for using initiative and lateral thinking to seek solutions to seemingly intransigent, unsolvable and emotionally charged problems.

The combination of the ability to stand back and reflect, at the same time as remaining involved, enables the worker to avoid either being swamped by raw experience or distancing herself from the problem to ensure personal, emotional and cognitive safety. Through effective partnerships and adequate negotiations, planning and decision making become possible.

Studies in child care and child protection point to the failures of simplified procedural, service-led responses (DoH, 1995). A holistic model of practice clarifies assessment and links outcomes with processes and methods of intervention – that is, a practice theory allows systematic reflection on professional intervention (DoH, 1985, p. 21). The conclusion of a substantial body of research is that:

It is no longer enough to look narrowly at the needs of an individual child, for the child's welfare has to be understood in the context of a web of relationships. It is not enough to offer a service. The way in which it is offered and the attitudes of the service providers are also crucial. (DoH, 1991, p. 77)

And:

> A more balanced service for vulnerable children would encourage professionals to take a wider view. There would be efforts to work alongside families rather than disempower them, to raise their self-esteem rather than reproach families, to promote family relationships where children have needs met, rather than leave untreated families with an unsatisfactory parenting style. The focus would be on the overall needs of children rather than a narrow concentration on the alleged incident. (DoH, 1995, p. 55)

The recurring themes throughout are the need for workers:

- to confront the full extent of the problem, particularly when individuals are at risk of harm;
- to develop a wider and more complex view which identifies and brings together all the different aspects of the particular problem.

These themes apply equally to work with other groups of service users and with carers. Central to both dimensions of good practice is the capacity of the worker, and of members of the team, to identify and build upon the strengths of people and communities with whom they are involved. The development of family support (DoH, 1995) and the implementation of the original intentions of the community care reforms to promote user-centred services and support for carers in the community can only be achieved through developing and supplementing, but not by taking over from, people's own resources. In the USA the development of family preservation policies and the 'strengths' perspectives parallel this development in the UK (Adams and Nelson, 1995).

In Chapter 8 we argued that self-defeating strategies and mutually defeating interactions are often driven by people's expectations that undesired behaviours will continue. The labelling of certain service users by their problems is an integral part of this process. Conversely, we described how more responses can be initiated and driven by identifying people's resources and reinforcing more optimistic expectations that may contribute to behaviour change. These responses also build upon identification and support for the problem solving strengths which people and communities already have.

A community-based approach requires reflective practitioners and managers because:

- provision of a service is seen also as a way of bringing about change;
- 'upstream' preventative work is a part of the whole task and not just a luxury to be undertaken when there is time or extra money;
- the development of resources in individuals and families, just as in communities, is the most appropriate way to confront problems, not an alternative.

Commonsense and practice

The stuff of social problems dealt with by social worker staff is grounded in ordinary social experience. Personal loss, violence or the fear of it, poverty or financial worries, disability, illness, learning difficulties, are experiences faced by most of us or those close to us to some degree at some time or another. A growing number of people experience unemployment, financial problems through income fluctuations, job losses, contracts ending and so on. But the very pervasiveness of these problems does not mean that there is no radical distinction between ordinary day-to-day social problem solving and the interventions which workers make. Social work can easily seem so commonsensical that demands for sophisticated reflection and conceptualisation are thought to be superfluous. Paradoxically, it is equally easy for workers to be swamped by the amount of theoretical material available in the form of research, guidelines and practice handbooks. Neither of these options is useful for workers who only become involved either when commonsense solutions have already failed or through social development activities which aim to prevent harm and crises arising in the first place.

Accountability of practice

The capacity for reflection is part of appropriate accountability. The worker is able to explain her practice and to say:

- *why* a particular action was taken and give the evidence for taking it;
- *why* alternative explanations were rejected or thought to be less feasible;
- *what* range of options for action were available;
- *who* was involved in making the assessment and planning the action;

- *what* outcomes are being sought and how the intervention will be monitored.

Explanations go beyond commonsense assumptions about the 'right' way to behave, the 'normal' way of thinking about a social problem, particularly where this involves stereotyping people. The worker is able to communicate the answers to these questions and the knowledge on which they are based to service users and carers, to other workers as well as managers, to team members, elected members, trustees or company directors. Accountability is demonstrated by being able to explain and justify a particular use of a procedure or interpretation of legislation, and the relationship to an understanding or assessment of complex social situations. The exercise of accountability is backed by the worker's and the manager's critical use of existing research, experience including that which originates from service users' and carers' experience and research, and all the tacit knowledge contained in everyday social interaction and social expectations. Support from first-line managers who are well informed about research into practice, local conditions and resources is an essential component for effective practice.

Reflection and partnership

The complexity of assessing social situations increases as service user and carer involvement becomes more of a reality. An Exchange approach will often be complex because:

- negotiations need to take place across often large and fluid networks of people;
- the experiences and history of the people involved will vary;
- collaboration occurs between different organisations, across sectors, and at different levels within organisations;
- the range of information from which useful patterns are created through reflective practice is very varied. There will be disputes from time to time, and some information may remain contested. Information includes:
  - hard facts, for example the names, ages, addresses of the people involved, the relevant agencies and the legislation, policies and procedures covering their activities;
  - the expression of personal feeling within the networks;

- the emotional response of the worker;
- knowledge about a particular kind of social problem or condition;
- insight into recurring patterns of relationships between people, groups and organisations;
- research on models of how to bring about positive change;
- information obtained from another organisation.

The sense which the worker makes of all this disparate information is the product of reflecting in partnership with others. The worker's understanding of 'the problem' is a dynamic product of a process of reflective understanding achieved through partnership with family members and others. Less obviously the individual worker's interpretation and use of particular legislation or local procedural guides is the product of reflective negotiation between the worker, organisation practices, the law and the people, such as court officials, senior managers, policy makers and employers, who are accountable for enforcement of law and procedure.

How reflection was used in Patrick's family

The agency and the worker as part of the problem. In Patrick's story, the worker's own understanding has to include insight into the ways in which both earlier and current behaviours of workers, including her own, are parts of the problematic patterns of interaction. Not because there is 'bad' practice, although this might also be true, but because by definition the workers involved are a part of the social construction of the problem, possible solutions and their consequences, intended or otherwise. Jane, the social worker, demonstrated her ability to observe her own behaviour and its impact, and make sense of it in some systematic way while also remaining part of the action.

We have seen how self-defeating strategies and mutually defeating interactions in the behaviour of the worker may actually help resolve or exacerbate an initial problem. Consequently the worker's own expectations and behaviour, and that of other staff in the organisation, become part of the information that is reflected upon. The capacity to stand back and think about one's own attitudes and behaviour and their impact on others cannot be just a private activity – it requires the assistance of professional learning mechanisms such as:

- live supervision
- systems of user feedback
- peer review of practice
- audio and video taping of interactions
- explicit conceptual analysis of social problems
- local practice research projects, and so on.

Reflective understanding is an active social process – part of the work itself – not a private cognitive exercise or one-off research project.

Assessment of the quality of parenting relationships. Jane, among other things, had the task of assessing the quality of relationship between Patrick and the various relatives who have access to him. This is partly to do with her statutory responsibility to monitor his care, but also with her role in assessing the nature of possible continuing contact between Patrick and his relatives after adoption. Should contact with his mother, half-siblings and grandparents be allowed, prohibited, encouraged, discouraged? The worker required an answer to the fundamental question, 'On what basis do I judge the quality and suitability of Patrick's ongoing relationships with his relatives?' When she asked this question of herself, she realised she could easily just fall back on 'gut reaction and experience'. Although practice experience should not be dismissed, it is not sufficient in itself and can be used as an excuse to persist in current patterns and not learn from the service user's and carer's experiences or the research evidence.

Understanding gross distortions of human relationships is relatively easy. A mother who refuses to hold her baby from birth, fails to feed him or regularly assaults him, is exhibiting behaviour very inappropriate for any parent and harmful to the baby. But most relationship assessments are less obvious and require understanding of human relationships grounded in research-based knowledge (Stevenson, 1996).

Challenging

Challenging refers here to the ability of staff to confront people effectively with their responsibilities, their problem-perpetuating or -creating behaviours and their conflicting interests.

We use the term 'challenging' in a particular way. Common usage is often about taking on another in conflict, scoring points and winning over or defeating another person. These connotations carry with them the implication for the worker of losing the game herself if she takes on too powerful interests. Our use of the term implies being able to see and say the unsayable in ways which are timed to contribute to the reconstruction of a social problem. Strengths are used to build new patterns of behaviour and relationships, and not to add to the existing chaos by creating more conflict. The worker is acutely aware of her own personal and professional power, and actively seeks to reduce the distortions these can create. The aim is not to use power to impose a view, but to negotiate between competing definitions and solutions.

Elements of challenging

People who use services often have different perceptions of problems and their possible solutions and the conflicting interests influencing their choices. The worker is able to challenge and confront these differences and negotiate a path through them to arrive at a suitable agreement about who will, and can, do what to support whom. The worker draws on the core joining skills of empathy and authenticity. We will review briefly their contribution to the capacity to challenge.

Empathy, for example, can itself be challenging. Just to experience another person fully understanding the core issues and communicating this, rather than avoiding them, offering redundant advice, or merely sympathising, can itself challenge a person's assumptions and perceptions. Empathising with one person in front of another can be even more confronting: simply making explicit different understandings, based on hearing several different points of view across a network, and drawing on sources of information which participants may not have 'heard' or had access to. Reflecting what each person says may well be challenging to people's interests and expectations.

The authenticity of the worker – behaving consistently more as a rounded human being in encounters with others, rather than hiding behind a mask or role – may challenge people to re-examine their own assumptions about what can be expected of the worker, and thus what they can expect of themselves in tackling the problems with which they are faced. The behavioural, cognitive and emotional tools which can be drawn upon by the worker to challenge people, are essentially the same as those which she is challenging others to use, or use differently, in tackling their problems of living, and in this way the worker can be a significant model.

Negotiation, the mediation of conflicting interests, expectations and perceptions, the development of relationships of exchange and the facilitation of change in behaviour: all imply challenges to the status quo for one or more people involved in the formation and resolution of social problems, including policy makers. Some, including the worker, will face the message that the problem cannot be solved or ameliorated unless an attitude changes, additional resources are available, or this behaviour or emotional response is modified; or that an expectation, service or policy needs to change.

The inevitability of unpopularity: challenging is rarely a simple process. Workers need to be able to challenge on many different kinds of issues, ranging from the effects of particular social policies to challenging the sexually abusing father about his behaviour. A worker's challenge:

- articulates different perspectives and 'open secrets' in ways which engage people in the process of change rather than alienate them from it, or enable them to escape the consequences of their behaviour;
- confronts what everyone else may be finding too painful, frightening or uncomfortable to face;
- confronts the feelings aroused by different people's needs and choices.

People are often not able to have what they want, through lack of resources or because their needs conflict with others, through irretrievable loss of a person or personal capacity, or some combination of all of these. Universal popularity is not one of the attributes of the effective and empowering worker.

Openness to use support and to go on learning: the worker who challenges others is open to and indeed seeks out opportunities to have her own perceptions, assumptions, interests and values challenged by others. It is a feature of an Exchange Model that the give and take of negotiation includes the worker's own behaviours and preconceptions being challenged. This happens within the process of negotiation and is reinforced through supervision and keeping up to date with research, practice developments and users' and carers' experience.

Timing: in each situation the worker and her manager make judgements about when to challenge and what support is available.

For many reasons workers may not challenge in situations where it would be helpful. They may not think it necessary and be happy to offer 'covert' counselling. Alternatively, the worker may not be skilled or aware enough of the need to involve other people in the network, or simply feel that she has not yet developed enough trust and rapport to enable a challenge to be accepted and used. However, waiting for enough trust may itself be patronising and part of a chicken-and-egg problem. Can trust be developed while important issues are known about but avoided by the worker and others involved? The capacity of workers to challenge others skilfully is linked to the extent to which they challenge themselves, and their ability to work in an environment in which managers and others can model and support effective and skilled challenging.

Advocacy: social workers act as advocates. They and their managers may have to challenge those who control resources to change their behaviour and decisions. A community-based approach involves passing these skills on to other citizens. In doing so, workers are challenging assumptions about who should have control over information and expertise. Service users and carers who participate in decisions about what provision should be planned and what outcomes are sought challenge those who have traditionally controlled resources, often managers within organisations, whose value systems may have a different basis from those of the worker or service users and carers.

Reframing

Reframing is the worker's ability to help redefine circumstances in ways which lead towards problem resolution.

Reframing: an illustration

A worker came to a consultation session for some help with what he described as 'a really difficult situation'. The initial story was of a young teenager, Tom, who was refusing to go school, being abusive and aggressive towards his mother and uncooperative with the worker. Whenever the worker called, Tom would climb out of the window or just not be available. The worker said he, like the teachers at his school, found the boy obnoxious. In the discussion between the worker and his supervisor several facts emerged. Tom's behaviour started being a problem not long after his father died suddenly. The

family had to sell their house and move to a different area, and Tom had
to change school. The worker was aware of these events and realised
they might have a bearing on the boy's behaviour but they had been
lost sight of in the pressures to 'do something' about what was increasingly framed as an 'out-of-control teenager'.

The consultation discussion allowed the worker to reframe the
situation. The problem could be as much a grieving teenager successfully avoiding the way that others were managing the loss of his father,
as that of an adolescent failing to make a socially acceptable adjust-
ment. The alternative frame allowed the worker to see more courses
of action, involving staff at the school and the boy's mother and
other relatives in rebuilding a more constructive set of relationships.
Both framings of Tom and his behaviour are true, but neither should
be ignored.

Reframing and the nature of social problems

Problem solving within networks of people is central to social work.
Hence workers need the qualities of creativity and lateral thinking
necessary to help people redefine or find a different perspective on their
situation.

People who approach social care organisations with the expectation
that something can be done about their problem are by definition
implicitly communicating that the problem, as they see it, is unresolvable by themselves and their own networks. In Tom's story the
school's and the mother's requests for help implicitly communicate
that the problem of the boy's behaviour, as they are defining it, cannot
be resolved by themselves alone. A magistrate making a supervision
order on a young offender, a daughter asking for her mother to be
admitted to a care home, or a neighbour reporting abuse of a child: all
are defining the problem as unresolvable by their efforts and as
requiring the involvement of the social care organisation.

At times an alliance between the service user and the worker can
provide an answer. At other times the problem requires some new
resource which the organisation controls being added to the existing
social network. However, in many situations, the glue which holds the
problem together is the way people in the network are defining the
problem. They are acting upon their definition or pursuing their self-
interest or what they think is 'right'. Consequently, resolution requires
the worker to be able to reframe people's understanding of what is
going on so that they can retain responsibility for dealing with it and
call on different behaviours in the future. Reframing is a core skill,

because assessments about provision are always made in the context of judgements about whether the referring network can or cannot retain responsibility for the problem. Unless the worker is able to help the network explore the potential of its own resources through reframing the problem definition, the ability to make necessary provision only temporarily delays a crisis.

It is only when the worker, staff at the school and Tom's mother begin to see that the problem is one of loss and grief as much as behaviour which is likely to lead him into trouble at school, in the community and at home, that they can begin to explore what personal and other resources they may already have to address the whole problem. This reframing may mean that, rather than widening the network, no other formal organisation needs to be involved to solve the problem for them.

Elements of reframing

The elements used in reframing are:

- recognising alternative perspectives and presenting them in a way which others can understand;
- behaving in a way which is consistent with the new framing:
  - thinking laterally and creatively;
  - being able to think and act within a network of competing perceptions about what is going on;
  - hearing all these different perceptions and facilitating inter-change between them;
  - challenging people in ways which are constructive to achieving change.

Reframing is not some kind of simple semantic trick which can magically transform a difficult situation, nor is it a means of explaining away Tom's behaviour or a person's need for personal support. It is not enough to say a bottle is half full rather than half empty: we have to act as if we have resources rather than as if there are few left. Reframing is about being able to help others see things from a differ-ent perspective: perhaps to see how a weakness can be a strength; or that a mother with children on her own and caring for a relative with-out support is trying to do the impossible, and that without some assistance she will collapse in spite of her heroic efforts to cope. These examples emphasise the fundamental reframing of a social problem:

from seeing an individual with unmet needs to looking at the dependability of the social situation; and exploring the energy and resources available which can be built on or redirected.

Reframing is not only a cognitive or linguistic act: people can alter their sense of the possible by experiencing changes in their own and others' behaviours. It is the first step to facilitating the empowerment of the people who are seen as deviant to take control of important aspects of their own lives which they currently assume to be in the hands of other people, despite the fact that their efforts have demonstrably failed to bring about change. For others, it is a recognition of hope in what appears to be a hopeless situation, which expands the choices available to them.

Reframing and patterns of problem definition

Social care organisations can get drawn into situations where the problem is being defined in ways which preclude any resolution of it. Most people are supported and controlled or socialised by themselves and others in their own social and family networks without being defined as a 'social problem'. When they are referred it is often at a point of crisis and when people feel that they 'cannot cope any more' – at the point when they feel the bottle is almost empty or altogether broken. In these circumstances, the process of assessment, the negotiations between members of the person's network, the worker and others, can require reframing of perceptions of the problem so that it becomes perceived as more solvable. Reframing is a first step in unlocking a rigid pattern of expectations and behaviours: it is not the advocacy of certain ways of describing social problems.

In the Jones family the problem is framed as the mother's need for increased support. But it is a problem for at least three other people: her daughter, her son-in-law and other people in the family. The problem can be 'workload pressures' on the team, but it can also be the relatively unskilled supervision and consultancy offered by the manager; the problem may not just be the offending behaviour of the teenager, but also the labelling by the family, school and social worker. Both of these problems can be presented in two ways: as one person's problem, or the problem of several others. A first step is for the worker to help those people to reframe 'the problem' so that they can use their existing resources to resolve it, or develop new resources without assuming that the worker or her organisation will become a permanent part of the network through the provision of some service.

Conclusion

At the beginning of this book we referred to our approach as 'holistic': that is, it is crucial to understand the whole of a situation, so that the different elements that make it up can be understood coherently. It is not possible to understand the meaning of a move in chess without understanding the rules of the game as a whole. Similarly we have had to present our approach in the conventional linear way that a text demands, but a sense has to be retained of the ways the skills described are integral to the framework as a whole. The Exchange Model would not make sense, and would be inoperable, without the worker having these skills. Equally the skills are essential not in themselves but because they are the basis of a holistic approach: the position of 'marginality' is only necessary if the worker's task is to bring about change in social situations. In turn there is the need for team work, because the holistic approach also implies teams have the skills in bringing about change at more than one level, by undertaking upstream 'development' work as well as responding to the needs of individuals and families. The skills presented here are not another 'shopping list' which can just be added to or subtracted from in an atheoretical, incremental way. They are integral to the approach as a whole.

12

Epilogue

Overview

This book began by describing how a social worker responding to a typical problem reinvents her practice in each idiosyncratic situation she encounters. We stress reinvention throughout because social work is a problem solving process, not a matter of applying ready-made 'solutions'. The response to a problem may be to introduce a simple, practical service, but the nature of such a service should not determine practice. Social work should always go beyond service delivery to look at the consequences and the change dimensions of tackling social problems.

We have used the term 'social problem' in a particular way, because the problems of the wider society are the aggregate of individual concerns and crises, and the necessary downstream work of aiding individuals and families is not separable from the upstream work of developing more dependable communities.

Chapter 7 discussed different approaches to assessment and intervention, the main forms of 'aid' activity, and their different outcomes. An Exchange approach to working with people is more likely to facilitate their empowerment, that is expand their choices and involvement in decision making – so that they have as much control over their lives as possible. A Questioning or Procedural approach, treating people as objects of concern, will not achieve this. In the short term they may get the services they need but there is a price: they are not full partners in the problem solving process, and their own expertise and that of members of their network is lost. Everyone can contribute resources both to their own situation and to the community. The task for social work, for the whole social care enterprise, is to work with these resources, taking a marginal problem solving position (Chapter 9) rather than sliding into becoming a permanent part of the problem and its management.

Managing change and innovation using the Innovation Trinity underpins the management of those processes (Chapter 6). Perspectives such as self-fulfilling prophecies and self-defeating strategies (Chapter 8) contribute to understanding the complex interactions that bind people, including us, into a particular way of relating to each other. This analysis can be used whether we are trying to release untapped resources in the community, or unlock someone from a pathological or delinquent role that perpetuates their antisocial behaviour and social exclusion.

The social work task: key assumptions

The task is to constantly reinvent practice through forming partnerships with all the people involved in particular social problems. This necessitates recognition of six key characteristics of change agent activity:

- Workers move in an environment of different definitions and perceptions of the reality of social situations: of what is a problem for whom, what the solutions are, and what is expected of them to help or change the situation.
- The formulation of a problem is always a joint enterprise between the key people involved, workers and other staff.
- Assessment, intervention and service delivery are essentially the same enterprise.
- To achieve change it is often necessary to reframe the problem as perceived by some or all of the participants.
- Alternative behaviour, alternative ways of tackling problems or responding to difficult behaviour, has to be demonstrated.
- Resources often have to be reallocated.

The assumptions underpinning this approach to practice and management can be summarised as follows:

- The people we work with are, like ourselves, citizens who have a right to be treated with respect, to have their expertise and skills valued in working to agreed outcomes.
- Social workers and other change agents tackling social problems actively engage with a wide range of people and organisations to define their goals and objectives while remaining accountable

to the people they serve, acknowledging their rights and responsibilities and those of others, including their organisations.

- Policies and the economic and social position of individuals and communities shape the options available to people using services and to workers. These include factors which lead to social exclusion such as discrimination, poverty, poor health, unemployment, transport and lack of community resources. Understanding how these impact on the range of options and available solutions cannot be achieved by outsiders alone.

- Change agents work with others in teams by making alliances or partnerships with individuals, families, groups and organisations within the different communities they work in.

- The malfunctioning of a network of people, which can include the worker and his organisation, perpetuates social problems. Even if the behaviour of people who are the target of intervention is not caused by the social situation, the way that people respond is crucial for the resolution or management of that problem. If social workers and others respond inappropriately they can perpetuate or exacerbate problems, including their own.

- Combining with existing resources and relationships and using them in different ways can bring about change in social situations and in social networks.

- To understand and promote change in the patterns of relationships that create and perpetuate social problems, workers need to act from a marginal, honest broker position.

- A strong value base is essential, to operate from a marginal position and balance conflicting needs and priorities. These values are not the property of social workers alone, but embedded within the statutory framework which reflects society's values, and in particular those to be implemented in respect of children in need and adults needing more support than their own social networks can provide.

Increasingly the social well-being of communities, and the individuals and families that are part of them, is seen as a political issue in the UK, in Europe and internationally. Public policies promoting healthier and safer communities, for regenerating the local economy and developing its resources, and promoting social inclusion, create new expectations of social work practice and the skills and abilities of social workers. To meet these changing expectations social work has to address two major issues:

- the crucial importance of development, and moving beyond simply providing aid in response to crisis;
- the expectation that service users and carers will participate fully in the whole range of activities, from policy making through to outcomes and standard-setting.

Social work should be a development activity: designed not only to meet the needs of those requiring immediate support, but also to contribute to making the social situation, the families and communities that we live in, more dependable. It is essentially a teamwork task, and field social work has much to learn from best practice in day care and residential settings and multidisciplinary teams. Teams and their managers should map out how all the dimensions of the task are being tackled in their area and work in partnership with, develop teamwork with, service users and carers, other organisations and workers to achieve more dependable communities. Unless the way we work with others is explicit there is always a danger that we unintentionally work against them. Working at cross-purposes means that the action of one organisation feeds referrals to another and undermines the expertise and resources of people using services and those in their networks.

This is neither an over-ambitious claim nor an attempt to expand the domain of social work. To act as an aid agency without attempting to bring about change in the circumstances that require aid runs the risk of perpetuating the problem. The solution itself becomes part of the problem: in social welfare terms this is seen as perpetuating dependency and maintaining people in their 'client' status, rather than working towards sustainable solutions and their social inclusion.

The move towards full partnership with others in both development and aid activities is not a disavowal of the uniqueness of the individual, but of individualism. The emphasis is on people as citizens who have rights and responsibilities, their own expertise and skills. The role of the paid worker in a range of occupations has changed, from that of an expert finding solutions to other people's problems to working in partnership with the people who use services. The focus on social networks and communities is not romanticism, based on deluded assumptions about the resources of the people who live in them. It is based on an assessment of how little social workers can achieve without them and recognises that we are all part of the solution and of the problem.

Most care and control in the community is provided by citizens through their normal relationships, but the needs of some go unmet and some are socially excluded by the prejudice of others or as a consequence of their own behaviour. Social work will need to innovate, to reinvent its practice to contribute to resolving these problems. It will work with partners, citizens expert in their own situation and other organisations and staff engaged in social and economic regeneration and the development of more sustainable communities. It will continue to draw on traditional values and skills such as the importance of the quality of relationship and the ability to demonstrate empathy and authenticity. These will be applied in an ever-changing context, in new teams and new organisations both formally arranged and through networks focusing on shared concerns. Increasingly user- and carer-led organisations are providing and researching services as well as campaigning. Service users, carers and members of the wider public will hold key positions in the institutions governing, regulating and setting standards for practice, and multidisciplinary working is likely to become the norm. The agenda for tackling social problems is enormous. Social work has the potential to make a significant contribution, but it can never act alone.

Bibliography

Adams, P., Alten, C., Krauth, K., Andre, M. St. and Tracy, M. (1995) *Strengthening Families and Neighbourhoods: A Community-Centered Approach. Final Report at the Iowa Patch Project*, Iowa: University of Iowa.

Adams, P. and Nelson, K. (eds) (1995) *Reinventing Human Services: Community and Family Centered Practice*, New York: Aldine De Gruyter.

Ahmad, B. (1990) *Black Perspectives in Social Work*, London: Ventura Press/National Institute for Social Work.

Aiers, A. with Kettle, J. (1998) *When Things Go Wrong: Young People's Experience of Getting Access to the Complaints Procedure in Residential Care*, London: National Institute for Social Work/Selly Oak Colleges.

Alinsky, S. (1972) *Rules For Radicals: A Practical Primer for Realistic Radicals*, New York: Vintage.

Amphlett, S., Katz, I. and Worthing, D. (1997) *Enquiries into Alleged Child Abuse: Promoting Partnership with Families*, London: PAIN/NISW/NSPCC.

Angle, H.L. and Van de Ven, A.H. (1989) 'Suggestions for managing the innovation journey,' in A.H. Van de Ven, H.L. Angle, and M.S. Poole (eds) *Research on the Management of Innovation: The Minnesota Studies*, Grand Rapids: Ballinger/Harper and Row for the University of Minnesota.

Archer, L. and Whitaker, D. (1991) *Improving and Maintaining the Quality of Life in Homes for Elderly People*, York: Social Work and Resources Unit, University of York.

Audit Commission and Social Services Inspectorate (1997) *Reviewing Social Services: Annual Report 1997*, London: Audit Commission and Social Services Inspectorate.

Balloch, S., McLean, J. and Fisher, M. (eds) (1999) *Social Services: Working Under Pressure*, Bristol: Policy Press.

Barber, T.X. (1969) *Hypnosis*, New York: Van Nostrand Reinhold.

Barclay Report (1982) *Social Workers: Their Role and Tasks*, London: Bedford Square Press.

BASW (British Association of Social Workers) (1996) *The Code of Ethics for Social Work*, Birmingham: British Association of Social Workers.

Bateson, G. (1972) *Steps Towards an Ecology of Mind*, New York: Balantine.

Bebbington, A. and Tong, M. (1986) 'Trends and changes in old people's homes: provision over twenty years', in K. Judge and I. Sinclair (eds) *Residential Care for Elderly People*, London: HMSO.

Becker, H.S., (1973) [1st edn, 1963] *Outsiders: Studies in the Sociology of Deviance*, London and New York: Free Press.

Beckhard, R. and Pritchard, W. (1992) *Changing the Essence: The Art of Leading Fundamental Change in Organisations*, San Francisco: Jossey-Bass.

Begum, N., Hill, M. and Stevens, A. (eds) (1994) *Reflections: Views of Black Disabled People on their Lives and Community Care*, London: Central Council for Education and Training in Social Work.

Beresford, P. and Croft, S. (1993) *Citizen Involvement: A Practical Guide for Change*, Birmingham/Basingstoke: British Association of Social Workers/ Macmillan.

Beresford, P. and Harding T. (eds) (1993) *A Challenge to Change: Practical Experiences of Building User-Led Services*, London: National Institute for Social Work.

Beresford, P. and Trevillion, S. (1995) *Developing Skills for Community Care: A Collaborative Approach*, Aldershot: Arena.

Beresford, P. and Turner, M. (1997) *It's Our Welfare: Report of the Citizens' Commission on the Future of Welfare*, London: National Institute for Social Work.

Bergin, A.E. and Garfield, S.L. (eds) (1971) *Handbook of Psychotherapy and Behaviour Change*, New York: John Wiley.

Bergin, A.E. and Garfield, S.L. (eds) (1994) *Handbook of Psychotherapy and Behaviour Change*, 4th edn, New York: John Wiley.

Bernard, C. (1994) 'The research process: dynamics of race, gender and class', *Research Policy and Planning*, 12 (2), pp. 20–2.

Bernard, C. (1997) 'Black mothers' emotional and behavioural responses to the sexual abuse of their children', in G. Kaufman Kantor and J. Jasinski (eds) *Out of Darkness: Contemporary Research Perspectives on Family Violence*, London: Sage.

Berridge, D. (1985) *Children's Homes*, Oxford: Blackwell.

Booth, T. *et al.* (1983) 'A follow up study of trends in dependency in local authority homes for the elderly, 1980–2', *Research Policy and Planning*, 1 (2) pp. 1–9.

Bowling, A. and Bleathman, C. (1982) *The Need for Nursing and other Skilled Care in Local Authority Residential Homes for the Elderly: Overall Findings and Recommendations*, London: Hounslow Social Services Department.

Brown, J. (1996) *Chance Favours the Prepared Mind*, HMSO: London.

Bullock, R., Little, M. and Millham, S. (1994) *The Care Careers of Young People in Youth Treatment Centres*, Social Services Research, no. 2.

Butler, I., Davies, M. and Noyes, P. (1995) *Planning for Children: The Effects of Local Government Reorganisation*, London: National Society for the Prevention of Cruelty to Children.

Butt, J. and Box, L. (1997) *Supportive Services, Effective Strategies: The Views of Black-Led Organisations and Social Care Agencies*, London: Race Equality Unit.

Butt, J. and Mirza, K. (1996) *Social Care and Black Communities*, London: HMSO.

Bynoe, I. (1997) *Rights to Fair Treatment: A Practical Study to Developing New Rights for People Seeking Health and Social Care*, London: Institute of Public Policy.

Cabinet Office: Social Exclusion Unit (1998) *Bringing Britain Together.*
A National Strategy for Neighbourhood Renewal, London: TSO.

Caldock, K. and Nolan, M. (1994) 'Assessment and community care: are
the reforms working?' *Generations Review: Journal of British Society of
Gerontology*, 4 (4), December.

Cambell, J. and Oliver, M. (1996) *Disability Politics: Understanding our Past,
Changing our Futures*, London: Routledge.

Cambell, P. and Lindow, V. (1997) *Changing Practice: Mental Health, Nursing
and User Empowerment*, London: Routledge.

Cannan, C., Berry, L. and Lyons, K. (1992) *Social Work and Europe*,
Birmingham/Basingstoke: BASW/Macmillan.

Capra, F. (1997*) The Web of Life: A New Understanding of Living Systems*,
London: Anchor.

Carers National Association (1992) *Speak Up, Speak Out: Research Amongst
Members of Carers National Association*, London: Carers National
Association.

Carkhuff, R. (1967) *Towards Effective Counselling and Psychotherapy: Training
and Practice*, New York: Holt, Rinehart & Winston.

Carkhuff, R. (1987) *The Art of Helping*, 6th edn, Amherst, MA: Human
Resources Development.

CCETSW (Central Council for Education and Training in Social Work)
(1995) *Assuring Quality in the Diploma in Social Work – 1: Rules and
Requirements for the DipSW*, London: CCETSW.

Cheetham, J., Fuller, R., McIvor, G. and Petch, A. (1992*) Evaluating Social
Work Effectiveness*, Milton Keynes: Open University Press.

Children's Society (1989) *Young People under Pressure. Juvenile Justice:
Diversion from Custody*, London: Children's Society.

Clarke, J. (1993) 'The comfort of strangers: social work in context', in
J. Clarke (ed) *A Crisis in Care: Challenges to Social Work*, London: Sage.

Clyde, J. (1992) *The Report of the Inquiry into the Removal of Children from
Orkney in February 1991*, London: HMSO.

Collins, W. (1985) *The New Concise Dictionary of the English Language*,
London: Guild.

Connelly, N. and Stubbs, P. (1997) *Trends in Social Work and Social Work
Education across Europe*, London: Central Council for Education and
Training in Social Work and National Institute for Social Work.

Cosis Brown, H. (1992) 'Lesbians, the state and social work practice', in
M. Langan, and M. Day (eds) *Women, Oppression and Social Work: Issues
in Anti-Discriminatory Practice*, London: Routledge.

Coulshed, V. (1991) *Social Work Practice: An Introduction*, 2nd edn,
Basingstoke: Macmillan.

Creighton, S. and Noyes, P. (1989) *Child Abuse Trends in England and Wales,
1983–87*. London: National Society for the Prevention of Cruelty to Children.

Crosbie, D. and Vickery, A. (1989) *Community Based Schemes in Area Offices*,
Report to the Department of Health, London: NISW.

Cross, M., Brar, H. and McLeod, M. (1991) *Race Equality and the Local
State: An Evaluation of Policy Implementation in the London Borough of
Brent*, Coventry: University of Warwick Centre for Research in Ethnic
Relations.

Cross, M., Johnson, M. and Cox, B. (1988) *Black Welfare and Local Government: Section 11 and Social Services Departments*, Coventry: University of Warwick Centre for Research in Ethnic Relations.

Crowley, A. (1998) *A Criminal Waste: A Study of Child Offenders Eligible for Secure Training Centres*, London: Children's Society.

Darvill, G. (ed.) (1997) *Managing Contradiction and Avoidance*, London: Association of Directors of Social Services and National Institute for Social Work.

Darvill, G. and Smale, G. (eds) (1990) *Partners in Empowerment: Networks of Innovation in Social Work*, London: NISW.

Davies, M. (1991) *The Sociology of Social Work*, London: Routledge.

Davies, M. (1994) *The Essential Social Worker*, 3rd edn, Aldershot: Ashgate.

Davis, N. (1997) *Dark Heart*, London: Chatto and Windus.

Dobson, B., Beardsworth, A. and Walker, R. (1995) *Diet, Choice and Poverty*, London: Policy Studies Institute.

Doel, M. and Marsh, P. (1992) *Task-Centred Social Work*, Aldershot: Ashgate.

DoH (Department of Health) (1985) *Social Work Decisions in Child Care: Recent Research Findings and their Implications*, London: HMSO.

DoH (1988) *Report of the Inquiry into Child Abuse in Cleveland*, London: HMSO.

DoH (1989a) *The Children Act*, London: HMSO.

DoH (1989b) *Caring for People*, London: HMSO.

DoH (1991a) *Someone Else's Children*, London: Social Services Inspectorate.

DoH (1991b) *Patterns and Outcomes in Child Placement: Messages from Current Research and their Implications*, London: HMSO.

DoH (1991c) *Child Abuse: A Study of Inquiry Reports, 1980–1989*, London: HMSO.

DoH (1995) *Child Protection: Messages from Research*, London: HMSO.

DoH (1998a) *Quality Protects: Framework for Action*, London: Department of Health.

DoH (1998b) *Objectives for Social Services for Children*, London: Department of Health.

Dominelli, L. and McLeod, E. (1989) *Feminist Social Work*, Basingstoke: Macmillan.

Eastham, D. (1990) 'Plan it or suck it and see?' in G. Darvill and G. Smale (eds) *Partners in Empowerment: Networks of Innovation in Social Work*, London: National Institute for Social Work.

Egan, G. (1994) *The Skilled Helper: A Systematic Approach to Effective Helping*, 5th edn, Pacific Grove, California: Brooks/Cole.

Eraut, M. (1994) *Developing Professional Knowledge and Competence*, London: Falmer.

Evans, C. (1995) 'Service users: empower the people', *Community Care*, 24 August 1995, inside supplement.

Evans, C. and Hughes, M. (eds) (1993) *Tall Oaks from Little Acorns: The Wiltshire Experience of Involving Users in Training Professionals in Care Management*, Cherhill, Wiltshire: Wiltshire Community Care Users Involvement Network.

Everitt, A. and Hardiker, P. (1996) *Evaluating for Good Practice*, Basingstoke: Macmillan.

Falshaw, L. and Browne, K.(1997) 'Adverse childhood experiences and violent acts of young people in secure accommodation', *Journal of Mental Health*, 6 (5), October, pp. 443–55.

Family Division, *Law Reports* (1987).

Freire, P. (1972) *Pedagogy of the Oppressed*, Harmondsworth: Penguin.

Freud, S. (1963) [1st edn, 1948] 'The dangers of wild analysis', in *Therapy and Technique*, London: Hogarth.

Garfield, S.L. and Bergin, A.E. (1986) *Handbook of Psychotherapy and Behavior Change*, 3rd edn, New York, Wiley.

Gibbons, J. (1981) 'An evaluation of the effectiveness of social work intervention using task-centred methods after deliberate self poisoning', in E. Goldberg and N. Connelly (eds) *Evaluative Research in Social Care*, London: Heinemann.

Glendinning, C. and Millar, J. (eds) (1987) *Women and Poverty in Britain*, Brighton: Wheatsheaf.

Goldstein, A.P. (1962) *Therapist – Patient Expectancies in Psychotherapy*, London: Pergamon.

Goldstein, H. (1973) *Social Work Practice*, Columbia, SC: University of South Carolina Press.

Graham, H. (1984) *Women, Health and the Family*, Brighton: Wheatsheaf.

Green, H. (1988) *Informal Carers: General Household Survey, 1985*, London: HMSO.

Griffiths, R. (1988) *Community Care: Agenda for Action*, London: HMSO.

Gulbenkian Foundation (1995) *Children and Violence*, London: Gulbenkian Foundation.

Gurman, A.S., Kniskern, D.P. and Pinsol, W.M. (1986) 'Research on the process and outcome of marital and family therapy', in G.L. Garfield and A.E. Bergin (eds) *Handbook of Psychotherapy and Behaviour Change*, 3rd edn, New York: Wiley.

Handy, C. (1990) *Inside Organisation: 21 Ideas for Managers*, London: BBC Books.

Handy, C. (1994) *The Empty Raincoat: Making Sense of the Future*, London: Hutchinson.

Hanmer, J. and Statham, D. (1999) *Women and Social Work: Towards Women Centred Practice*, Basingstoke: Macmillan.

Hardiker, P., Exton, K. and Barker M. (1991a) 'The social policy contexts of prevention in child care', *British Journal of Social Work*, 21 (4), August, pp. 341–59.

Hardiker, P. Exton, K. and Barker, M. (1991b) *Policies and Practices in Preventive Child Care*, Aldershot: Avebury.

Harding, T. and Beresford, P. (1996) *The Standards We Expect: What Service Users Want from Social Services Workers*, London: National Institute for Social Work.

Hemmings, S. and Morris, J. (1997) *Community Care and Disabled People's Rights: A Training Project*, NISW Briefing Paper no. 22, London: National Institute for Social Work.

Hoffman, A. (1992) *Seventh Heaven*, London: Virago Press.

hooks, b. (1991) *Yearning: Race, Gender and Cultural Politics*, London: Turnaround.

Hunter, S., Brace, S. and Buckley, G. (1994) 'The inter-disciplinary assessment of older people at entry into long-term institutional care: lessons for the new community care arrangements,' *Research, Policy and Planning*, 11 (1/2), pp. 2–9.

Illich, I. (1976) *Limits to Medicine*, London: Marion Boyars.

Jones, A., Phillips, M. and Maynard, C. (1992) *A Home from Home*, London: Wagner Development Group, National Institute for Social Work.

Jones, A. and Butt, J. (1995) *Taking the Initiative: The Report on a National Study Assessing Service Provision for Black Children*, London: NSPCC/NISW/REU.

Kearney, P. (1995) *Management and Practice: Complements or Alternatives*, London: NISW.

Kearney, P. *(1996) The Great Divide: Managing Practice or Managing the Department*, London: National Institute for Social Work.

Keith, L. (1996) 'Encounters with strangers: the public's response to disabled women and how this affects our sense of self', in J. Morris, *Encounters with Strangers: Feminism and Disability*, London: Women's Press, pp. 69–88.

Kempson, E. (1996) *Life on a Low Income*, York: Joseph Rowntree Foundation.

Kent, R. (1997) *Children's Safeguards Review*, Edinburgh: Stationery Office.

Kilbrandon Report (Scottish Education Department and Scottish Home and Health Department) (1966) *Social Work and the Community: Proposals for the Re-organisation of Local Authority Personal Social Services*, Cmnd3065, London: HMSO.

Kolb, D. (1984) *Experiential Learning: Experience on the Role of Learning and Development*, Englewood Cliffs, NJ: Prentice Hall.

Langan, M. and Day, M. (eds) (1992) *Women, Oppression and Social Work: Issues in Anti-Discriminatory Practice*, London: Routledge.

Law, J. (1989) 'The Barlanark Project', Ch. 2 in G.G. Smale and W. Bennett (eds) (1989*) Community Social Work in Scotland: Pictures of Practice, Vol. 1*, London: National Institute for Social Work.

Lawrence, S., Walker, A. and Willcocks, D. (1986) *She's Leaving Home: Local Authority Policy and Practice Concerning Admissions to Residential Homes for Old People*, London: Polytechnic of North London.

Levin, E., Sinclair, I. and Gorbach, P. (1989) *Families, Services and Confusion in Old Age*, Aldershot: Avebury.

Levin, E., Moriarty, J., Pahl, J. and Webb, S. (1994) *Social Work and Community Care: An Exploratory Study of the Impact of the Recent Policy Changes on Practitioners and Managers*, London: National Institute for Social Work Research Unit.

Levin, E., Webb, S. and Moriarty, J. (1998) *Research on Community Care: Social Work and Community Care Arrangements for Older People with Dementia*, London: National Institute for Social Work.

Lindow, V. (1994*) Purchasing Mental Health Services: Self-Help Alternatives*, London: Mind.

Lindow, V. and Morris, J. (1995) *Service User Involvement: Synthesis of Findings and Experience in the Field of Community Care*, York: Joseph Rowntree Foundation.

Little, M., Leitch, H. and Bullock, R. (1995) 'The care careers of long-stay children: the contribution of new theoretical approaches', *Children and Youth Services Review*, 17.

Lobstein, T. (1997) *It's Their Own Fault! Myths about Food and Low Income*, London: National Food Alliance.

Local Government Management Board and Central Council for Education and Training in Social Work (LGA and CCETSW) (1997) *Human Resources for Personal Social Services*, London: Local Government Management Board.

Macdonald, S. (1991) *All Equal Under the Act?*, London: Race Equality Unit.

Macleod, M. (1996) *Talking with Children about Child Abuse*, London: Childline.

Marsh, P. and Fisher, M. (1992) *Good Intentions: Developing Partnership in Social Services*, York: Joseph Rowntree Foundation.

Marsh, P. and Triseliotis, J. (1996) *Ready to Practise: Social Workers and Probation Officers, their Training and First Year in Work*, Aldershot: Avebury.

Mencken, H.L. (1958) *Prejudices: A Selection Made by James T. Farrell*, New York: Vintage Books.

Merton, R.K. (1948) 'The self fulfilling prophecy', *Antioch Review*, 8, pp. 193–210.

Minuchin, S. and Fishman, C.H. (1981) *Family Therapy Techniques*, Harvard, USA: Harvard University Press.

Moriarty, J., Levin, E. and Gorbach, P. (1997) *Respite Services for the Carers of Confused Elderly People*, London: National Institute for Social Work.

Morris, J. (1993) *Disabled Lives: Many Voices, One Message*, York: Joseph Rowntree Foundation.

Morris, J. (ed) (1996) *Encounters with Strangers: Feminism and Disability*, London: Women's Press.

Morris, J. and Lois, K. (1995) 'Easy targets: a disability rights perspective on the children as carers debate', *Critical Social Policy*, 44/45, Autumn.

Morris, K. and Tunnard, J. (eds) (1996) *Family Group Conferences: Messages From UK Practice And Research*, London: Family Rights Group.

National Commission of Inquiry into the Prevention of Child Abuse (1996) *Childhood Matters*, London: HMSO.

Neill, J. (1989) *Assessing Elderly People for Residential Care: A Practical Guide*, London: National Institute for Social Work, Research Unit.

Neill, J. and Williams, J. (1992) *Leaving Hospital: Elderly People and their Discharge to Community Care*, London: HMSO/National Institute for Social Work.

Newburn, T. (1993) *Disaster and After: Social Work in the Aftermath of Disaster*, London: Jessica Kingsley.

Nord, W.R. and Tucker, S. (1987) *Implementing Routine and Radical Innovations*, Lexington, MA: Lexington Press.

Occupational Standards Council (1997) *NVQs and SVQs in Social Care*, London and Scotland: Care Sector Consortium and the Scottish Council for Vocational Qualifications.

Oliver, M. (1990) *The Politics of Disablement*, Basingstoke: Macmillan.

Oliver, M. (1993) *Disability, Citizenship and Empowerment*, Workbook K665, Disabling Society, Milton Keynes: Open University Press.

Parker, R. (1981) 'Tending and social policy', in E.M. Goldberg and S. Hatch (eds) *A New Look at the Personal Social Services*, Discussion Paper no.4, London: Policy Studies Institute.

Parker, R. (1995) 'An overview of messages from the research,' in *Messages from the Research, Report of Conference Proceedings*, London: Sieff Foundation.

Parker, R. (1996) 'Child protection: research into practice: who takes the risks? An overview of the research', in *Report of the Sieff Foundation Conference on Messages from the Research*, London: Sieff Foundation.

Payne, M. (1996) *What is a Professional Social Worker?* Birmingham: Ventura.

People First (1994a) *Helping You Get the Services You Want: A Guide for People with Learning Difficulties to Help Them Through Their Assessment and Get the Services They Want*. London: People First.

People First (1994b) *Oi! It's My First Assessment: Everything You Ever Want to Know about Community Care, Your Assessment and Your Care Manager, But Nobody Bothered to Tell You*, London: People First.

People First (1994c) *Outside But Not Inside Yet: Leaving Hospital and Living in the Community: An Evaluation by People With Learning Difficulties*, London: People First.

Perlman, H.H. (1957) *Social Casework: A Problem-Solving Process*, Chicago: University of Chicago Press.

Pincus, A. and Minahan, A. (1973) *Social Work Practice: Model and Method*, Ithaca: Peacock.

Pitkeathley, J. (1995) 'Who Does Care?', *Journal of Royal Society of Arts*, December.

Platt, D. (1995) 'Centenary of health related social work', British Association of Social Work's Centenary Lecture, November (unpublished).

Platt, D. (1996) 'Developing eligibility criteria for continuing care', paper given at a Capita seminar, May (unpublished).

Platt, D. and Shemmings, D. (1996). *Making Enquiries into Alleged Child Abuse and Neglect: Partnership with Families*, London: Wiley.

Pottage, D. and Evans M. (1994) *The Competent Workplace: The View from Within*, London: National Institute for Social Work.

Reid, W. and Shyne, A. (1969) *Brief and Extended Casework*, New York: Columbia University Press.

Reisler, R. (1995) 'The history of disabling imagery', in R. Reiser (ed.) *Invisible Children*, Report of a Joint Conference on Children, Images and Disability, London: Children and the Integration Alliance.

Rogers, C. (1961) *On Becoming a Person*, Boston: Houghton Mifflin.

Rogers, C., Gendlin, E.T., Keisler, D. and Truax, C.B. (1967) 'The therapeutic relationship and its impact', Madison: University of Wisconsin.

Rogers, E. (1996) *Diffusion of Innovations*, New York: Free Press.

Rogers, E. and Kincaid, D. (1981) *Communication Networks: Towards a New Paradigm for Research*, New York: Free Press.

Rosenhan, D. L. (1973) 'On being sane in insane places', *Science*, 179, pp. 250–8.

Rosenthal, R. (1979) 'Interpersonal expectations: effects of the experimenter's hypothesis', Ch. 6 in R. Rosenthal and R.L. Rosnow (eds) *Artifact in Behavioral Research*, New York: Academic Press.

Rosenthal, R. and Jacobsen, E. (1968) *Pygmalion in the Classroom*, New York: Holt, Reinhart and Winston.

Rowlands, O. (1998) *Informal Carers: An Independent Study Carried Out by the Office for National Statistics on Behalf of the Department of Health as Part of the 1995 General Household Survey*, London: TSO.

Rowlings, C. (1995) 'Managing practice: post qualifying education and training: the academic perspective', in T. Kearney (ed.) *The Great Divide: Managing Practice or Managing the Department*, London: National Institute for Social Work.

Rutherford, A., (1992) *Growing Out of Crime: The New Era*, Hampshire: Waterside.

Schon, D. (1983) *The Reflective Practitioner: How Professionals Think in Action*, New York: Basic Books.

Schon, D. (1987) *Educating Reflective Practitioner: Towards a New Design for Teaching and Learning in the Professions*, San Francisco: Josey Bass.

Schorr, A. (1992) *The Personal Social Services: An Outsider's View*, York: Joseph Rowntree Foundation.

Seden, J., Hardiker, P. and Barker, M., (1996) 'Child protection revisited: balancing state intervention and family autonomy through social work processes', *Child and Family Social Work*, 1 (1), January, pp. 57–66.

Seebohm Report (1968) *Committee on Local Authority and Allied Personal Social Services*, Cmnd 3703, London: HMSO.

Seligman, M.E.P. (1975) *Helplessness: On Depression, Development and Death*, San Fransisco, California: W.H.Freeman.

Shapiro, A.K. (1971) 'Placebo effects in medicine, psychotherapy and psychoanalysis', Ch. 12 in A.E. Bergin and S.L. Garfield (eds) *Handbook of Psychotherapy and Behaviour Change*, New York: John Wiley.

Shaw, I. and Walton, R. (1979) 'Transition to residence in homes for the elderly', in D. Harris and J. Hyland (eds) *Rights in Residence*, London: Residential Care Association.

Shorter Oxford English Dictionary (1980) Oxford: Oxford University Press.

Shotter, J. (1993) *Cultural Politics of Everyday Life*, Buckingham: Open University Press.

Simmel, G. (1955) *Conflict and the Web of Group Affiliations*, London: Free Press of Glencoe.

Sinclair, I., Crosbie, D., O'Conner, P., Stanforth, L. and Vickery, A. (1988) *Bridging Two Worlds: Social Work and the Elderly Living Alone*, Aldershot: Gower.

Sinclair, I., Parker, R., Leat, D. and Williams, J. (1990) *The Kaleidescope of Care: A Review of the Research on Welfare Provision for Elderly People*, London: HMSO.

Sinclair, I., Crosbie, D. and Vickery, A. (1990) 'Organisational influences on professional behaviour: factors affecting social work involvement in schemes', *Journal of Social Policy*, 19 (3), July, pp. 361–74.

Smale, G. (1977) *Prophecy, Behaviour and Change*, London: Routledge and Kegan Paul.

Smale, G. (1983) 'Can we afford not to develop social work practice?' *British Journal of Social Work*, pp. 251–64.

Smale, G. (1984) 'Self-fulfilling prophecies, self-defeating strategies and change', *British Journal of Social Work*, 14, pp. 419–33.

Smale, G. (1995) 'Integrating community and individual practice: a new paradigm for practice', in P. Adams and K. Nelson (eds) *Reinventing Human Services: Community and Family Centred Practice*, Chicago: Aldine.

Smale, G. (1996) *Mapping Change and Innovation*, London: TSO.

Smale,G. (1998) *Managing Change Through Innovation*, London: TSO.

Smale, G., and Bennett, W. (eds) (1989) *Community Social Work in Scotland: Pictures of Practice, Vol. 1*, London: National Institute for Social Work.

Smale, G. and Tuson, G. (1988) *Learning for Change*, London: National Institute for Social Work.

Smale, G. and Tuson, G. with Biehal, N. and Marsh, P. (1992) *Empowerment, Assessment, Care Management and the Skilled Worker*, London: HMSO for National Institute for Social Work, Practice and Development Exchange.

Smale, G., Tuson, G., Cooper, M., Wardle, M. and Crosbie, D. (1988) *Community Social Work: A Paradigm for Change*, NISW: London.

Smale, G., Tuson, G., Ahmad, B., Darvil, G., Domoney, L. and Sainsbury, E. (1994) *Negotiating Care in the Community*, London: HMSO.

Smart, C. (1976) *Women, Crime and Criminology: A Feminist Critique*, London: Routledge and Kegan Paul.

Social Care Association (1989) *Code of Practice for Social Care*, Surbiton: Social Care Association.

Specht, H. and Vickery, A. (1977) *Integrating Social Work Methods*, London: Allen and Unwin.

Spender, D. (1980) *Man Made Language*, London: Routledge and Kegan Paul.

Staite, C. and Martin, N. (1993) 'What else can we do? New initiatives in diversion from custody', *Justice of the Peace*, 1 May, pp. 280–1.

Stapleton, B. (1976) 'A survey of the waiting list for places in Newham's Hostel for the Elderly', London: London Borough of Newham Applied Research Section.

Statham, D. (1996) *The Future of Social and Personal Care: The Role of Social Services Organisations in the Public, Private and Voluntary Sectors*, London: National Institute for Social Work.

Sternfield, S.L. (1993) '"Learning the Hard Way": Women Labeled with Mental Retardation Describe Their Way of Knowing', unpublished doctoral thesis, Boston University.

Stevenson, O. (1996) 'Emotional abuse and neglect: a time for reappraisal', *Child and Family Social Work*, 1 (1), January, pp. 13–8.

Stocking, B. (1985) *Initiative and Inertia: Case Studies in the National Health Service*, London: Nuffield Provincial Hospital Trust.

Sutton, C. (1994) *Social Work, Community Work and Psychology*, Leicester: British Psychological Association.

Thoburn, J., Lewis, A. and Shemmings, D. (1995) *Paternalism or Partnership: Family Involvement in the Child Protection Process*, London: HMSO.

Thompson, N. (1995) *Theory and Practice in Health and Social Welfare*, Buckingham: Open University Press.

Thompson, N. (1996) *People Skills*, Basingstoke: Macmillan.

Thorpe, D. (1994) *Evaluating Child Protection*, Buckingham: Open University Press.

Timms, N. (1983) *Social Work Values: An Enquiry*, London: Routledge.

Townsend, P. (1962) The *Last Refuge: A Survey of Residential Institutions and Homes for the Aged in England and Wales*, London: Routledge.

Tunnard, J. (ed.) (1994) *Family Group Conferences*, report commissioned by the Department of Health: London, Family Rights Group.

Utting, W. (1991) *Children in the Public Care: A Review of Residential Child Care*, London: HMSO.

Utting, W. (1997) *People Like Us: The Report of the Review of the Safeguards for Children Living Away from Home*, London: TSO.

Van de Ven, A.H., Angle, H.L. and Poole, M.S. (eds) *Research on the Management of Innovation: The Minnesota Studies*, Grand Rapids, MI: Ballinger/Harper and Row for the University of Minnesota.

Wade, B., Sawyer, L. and Bell, J. (1983) *Dependency with Dignity: Different Care Provision for the Elderly*, London: Bedford Square Press.

Watzlawick, P. (1990) *Munchausen's Pigtail or Psychotherapy and 'Reality': Essays and Lectures*, New York: Norton.

Watzlawick, P. (1993) *The Language of Change: Elements of Therapeutic Communication*, New York: W.W. Norton.

Watzlawick, P., Beavin, J.H., and Jackson, D.D. (1967) *Pragmatics of Human Communications: A Study of Interactional Patterns, Pathologies and Paradoxes*, New York: W.W. Norton.

Watzlawick, P., Weakland, J. and Fisch, R. (1974) *Change: Principles of Problem Formation and Problem Resolution*, New York: W.W.Norton.

White, D. (1997) *How Others See Us*, London: Relatives Association.

Wilkins, W., (1977) 'Expectancies in applied settings', Ch. 13 in A.S. Gurman and A. R. Razin (eds) *Effective Psychotherapy: A Handbook of Research*, Oxford: Pergamon Press.

Williams, F. (1992) 'Women with learning difficulties', in M. Langan and M. Day (eds) (1992) *Women, Oppression and Social Work: Issues in Anti-Discriminatory Practice*, London: Routledge.

Willcocks, L. and Harrow, J. (eds) (1992) *Rediscovering Public Services Management*, Maidenhead: McGraw-Hill.

Index of Names

Adams, P. and Nelson, K.   24, 222
Ahmad, B.   18, 32, 77, 95, 136, 181, 197, 203, 209, 215
Aiers, A.   73
Alinsky, S.   172
Amphlett, S., Katz, I. and Worthing, D.   77, 164
Angle, H.L. and Van de Ven, A.H.   112, 118
Audit Commission and Social Services Inspectorate   21, 62, 175

Barber, T.X.   156
BASW   50
Bateson, G.   162, 166
Becker, H.S.   157, 171
Beckhard, R. and Pritchard, W.   112, 120
Beresford, P. and Croft, S.   95, 138, 139
Beresford, P. and Turner, M.   32, 38, 45, 47, 140, 174, 175, 199
Bergin, A.E. and Garfield, S.L.   173
Bernard, C.   60
Brown, J.   37, 218
Butler, I., Davies, M. and Noyes, P.   73
Butt, J. and Box, L.   19, 32, 77, 142, 143
Butt, J. and Mirza, K.   18, 32, 77, 95, 142, 143
Bynoe, I.   124

Cabinet Office: Social Exclusion Unit   154

Caldock, K. and Nolan, M.   20
Cambell, J. and Oliver, M.   18, 19, 32, 77, 95, 124, 197
Cambell, P. and Lindow, V.   32, 47, 77
Cannan, C., Berry, L. and Lyons, K.   23
Capra, F.   95
Carers National Association   85
Carkhuff, R.   173, 197
Central Council for Education and Training in Social Work (CCETSW)   41, 195
Cheetham, J., Fuller, R., McIvor, G and Petch, A.   47
Children's Society   60
Clarke, J.   179
Clyde, J.   186
Connelly, N. and Stubbs, P.   23
Cosis Brown, H.   18
Coulshed, V.   154
Crosbie, D. and Vickery, A.   61
Cross, M., Brar, H. and McLeod, M.   18
Crowley, A.   59

Darvill, G.   67, 161, 190
Davies, M.   7, 154, 195
Department of Health (DoH)   14, 20, 42, 47, 60, 73, 74, 79, 80, 83, 85, 94, 134, 139, 164, 185, 186, 188, 199, 202, 221, 222
Dobson, B., Beardsworth, A. and Walker, R.   40
Dominelli, L. and McLeod, E.   18, 181

250

Eastham, D. 62
Egan, G. 33, 197
Eraut, M. 25, 27, 189, 191
Evans, C. 22, 45

Falshaw, L. and Browne, K. 59
Freud, S. 148

Glendinning, C. and Millar, J. 33
Goldstein, A.P. 62, 174
Goldstein, H. 4, 88, 146, 154
Graham, H. 33
Griffiths, R. 20, 22
Gulbenkian Foundation 94
Gurman, A.S., Kniskern, D.P. and
    Pinsal, W.M. 197

Handy, C. 67, 219
Hanmer, J. and Statham, D. 18,
    181, 202, 206, 210
Hardiker, P., Exton, K. and
    Barker, M. 19, 205
Harding, T. and Beresford, P. 32,
    46, 47, 65, 77, 78, 95, 138, 174,
    182, 199, 205, 206
Hemmings, S. and Morris, J. 108,
    111
Hoffman, A. 42
hooks, b. 18, 39, 197
Hunter, S., Brace, S. and
    Buckley, G. 20

Illich, I. 163

Jones, A. and Butt, J. 173, 201

Kearney, P. 65, 182, 219
Keith, L. 203
Kempson, E. 40
Kent, R. 64
Kolb, D. 67

Law, J. 61
Levin, E., Moriarty, J., Pahl, J. and
    Webb, S. 23, 61, 83, 147
Levin, E., Sinclair, I. and
    Gorbach, P. 85
Levin, E., Webb, S. and
    Moriarty, J. 59, 176, 190

Levin, E., Sinclair, I. and
    Gorbach, P. 85
Lindow, V. 124, 197
Local Government Management
    Board and CCETSW 21
Lobstein, T. 40
Macdonald, S. 209
Macleod, M. 74
Marsh, P. and Fisher, M. 70, 109,
    141, 209, 219
Mencken, H.L. 129
Merton, R.K. 156, 200
Minuchin, S. and Fishman, C.H.
    97
Morris, J. 18, 32, 38, 47, 77, 95,
    124, 139, 181, 197, 202, 206
Morris, J. and Lois, K. 18
Morris, K. and Tunnard, J. 199

National Commission of Inquiry
    into the Prevention of Child
    Abuse 60, 74, 75, 175
Neill, J. and Williams, J. 78, 209
Newburn, T. 37, 111, 182, 205
Nord, W.R. and Tucker, S. 112

Occupational Standards
    Council 195
Oliver, M. 32, 147

Parker, R. 16, 21, 61, 180
Payne, M. 49
People First 18, 32, 77, 142
Perlman, H.H. 6
Pincus, A. and Minahan, A. 4, 83,
    88, 146, 154, 195
Pitkeathley, J. 92
Platt, D. 20, 65
Platt, D. and Shemmings, D. 14,
    74, 77, 164, 186, 206, 208
Pottage, D. and Evans, M. 78,
    162, 190

Rogers, C. 197
Rogers, E. 113, 117, 119, 123, 125,
    173, 197
Rogers, E. and Kincaid, D. 125,
    197

Rosenhan, D.L.   157
Rosenthal, R.   156
Rosenthal, R. and Jacobsen, E.
    156
Rowlands, O.   18
Rowlings, C.   65

Schon, D.   25, 27, 67
Schorr, A.   47, 189
Seligman, M.E.P.   162
Shapiro, A.K.   157
Shotter, J.   191
Sinclair, I., Parker, R., Leat, D. and
    Williams, J.   85, 93
Smale, G.   26, 60, 64, 113, 114,
    119, 121, 124, 125, 162, 163,
    174, 205, 209, 217, 218
Smale, G. and Bennett, W.   220
Smale, G., Tuson, G., Ahmad, B.,
    Darvill, G., Domoney, L. and
    Sainsbury, E.   148
Smale, G. and Tuson, G. with
    Brehal, N. and Marsh, P.   200
Smale, G., Tuson, G., Cooper, M.,
    Wardle, M. and Crosbi, D.   88
Social Care Association (SCA)   50

Specht, H. and Vickery, A.   4, 83,
    88
Spender, D.   202
Statham, D.   20, 60
Sternfeld, S.L.   181
Stevenson, O.   226
Stocking, B.   123

Thoburn, J.J., Lewis, A. and
    Shemmings, D.   201, 206
Thompson, N.   25, 27, 195
Thorpe, D.   157
Timms, N.   46

Utting, W.   64

Watzlawick, P.   59, 97
Watzlawick, P., Beavin, J. H. and
    Jackson, D.D.   95, 112, 161
Watzlawick, P., Weakland, J. and
    Fisch, R.   46, 96, 97, 98, 112,
    161, 162
White, D.   87
Wilkins, W.   157
Williams, F.   19

Index of Subjects

Italics indicate where terms appear in headings.

Advocacy 111, 229
Aid *18*, *32*, 33, 35
Ageism 3
  see also Prejudice
Analysing the innovation 114, 117, *123*
Assessment *10*, 15, 20, 45, 57, 74, *109*, *131*, *226*, 235
Authenticity *204*, *227*

Behaving 'as if' 59, 70, 95, 100, 101, 104. 110, 151, 161, 162, 165, 167, *169–70*, 171, 184, 202, 206, 209, 217, 131

Carers (Recognition and Services) Act (1996) 56
Care *21*, *147*
Challenging 226
Change *5*, *21*, 104, *106*, *110*, *111*, *154*, *206*
Change agents 27, 38, *55*, 58, 62, 87, 94, 101, 119, 154, 172, 178, 182, 235
Child protection 45, 47, *79*, 117, 164, 221
Citizens 38, 46, *91*, 152, 235
Close collaborators 120, 123
Collaboration 23, 29, 150, *219*
Community 15, *88*, *90*, 124
Community Care (Direct Payments) Act (1996) 22, 91

Competition *219*
Control 32, *36*, *49*, *82*, *92*
Customers 91–2

Development *18*, *31*, 69, 237
Deviance *92*, 94, 102, *186*
Direct intervention 54, 59, 71, 154
Disabled people's movement 22, 38
Discrimination 18, 30, *41*, 74
Division of labour 21, 61, 127, 150, *216*
Dominant actor *167*
Dominant perceiver *167*
Downstream *32*

Early adopters 119, 122
Education 35, 38, 50
Empathy *196*, 227
Empowerment 32, *38*, 108, 124, 145, 232
Exchange Model *135*, *138*, 152, 185, 199, 218
Expectations 38, 42, 87, 93, 172, *180*

Feedback 108, *128*
First-order change 105, *111*, 162
Fragmentation of services 22, *24*

Gatekeepers 119, 153, 200
Genuineness *204*

Holistic approach   16–17, *24*, 31,
    45, 47, 65, 233
Hope   88, 172, 232

Independence   139, *179*
Indirect intervention   *54*, 60, 71,
    154
Individualisation of social
    problems   *19*, 47, *88*, 91, 151
Information   60, 77, 152, *199*, 224
Innovation Trinity   114, *117*
Innovator   119, 122
Intervention   37, 43, 86, *109*, *131*,
    212

Joining skills   *194*, 227

Key players   50, *118*
Knowledge   27, *126*, *188*
Knowledge-based practice   *25*

Late adopters   119, 122
Legitimate initiators   119, 122
Loss   132, 152

Management   23, 26, 39, 63
Mapping   *52*, *65*, *106*, *113*, 118
Marginal worker   *44*, *176*
Marginalisation   *178*
Marginality   153, 177, *178*, *206*,
    233
Mediating role   45
Minders   119, 122
Modelling   *207*
Monitoring task achievement   71
Mutually defeating interaction
    156, 163, 208, 220

National Health Service and
    Community Care Act
    (1990)   20, 61, 85
Negotiation   *44*, *65*, *125*, *198*
Neighbourhood networks   42
Network entrepreneurs   64, 120

Opinion leaders   119, 122
Opponents   119, 123
Oppression   *41*, 74, 108
Organisation   *102*

Organisation development   72, *125*
Packages of care   20, 23, 85
Parenting   *42*, 80, *226*
Partnership   13, 20, 22, 23, 24, 46,
    71, *186*, *209*, *214*, *219*, *224*
Patterns of interaction   *82*, *95*, 153,
    157, 176
Patterns of relationships   28, 47,
    90, 112, 131, 152, 217, 225, 236
Perception   29, *44*, *61*, 137, *167*
Personal assistance   22, 93, 147
Poverty   18, 32, 40, 110
Power   28, *37*, 70, 91, 132
Practice   22, *24*, 27, *80*, *93*, *107*,
    148, *152*, *223*
Practice theory   16, 27, 221
Prejudice   42, 95, 99, 100, 136, 189,
    204, 209
Procedural Model   *133*, 200
Product champions   119
Promoting social well-being   80
Punctuation   95, *100*, *102*, 109

Questioning   *201*
Questioning Model   *133*, *138*, *199*

Racism   155, 173
Reflection   67, *220*
Reframing   15, 171, *229*
Reinvention   13, *25*, 51, 130
Respect   *189*, *210*

Second-order change   105, *111*, 162
Self-defeating strategy   152, *157*,
    208, 220, 235
Self-fulfilling prophecy   152, *156*,
    235
Self-help groups   25, 127
Service delivery   18, *55*, 64, *109*,
    235
Skills   *27*, *126*, *194*, *212*
Social control   19, 29, *36*, *49*, *82*,
    92
Social entrepreneurship   *212*
Social exclusion   *40*, 89
Social inclusion   *40*, 25, 107
Social networks   16, 27, *29*, *41*, 85,
    125, *147*

Social problems   52, 60, 68, *82*, *86*,
    155, *184*, *230*
Social work   *13*, *19*, *21*, *53*, *65*, *94*
Solutions as problems   *161*
Spiral of negotiations   *65*, *70*
Stakeholders   20, 83
Stigma   21, 30

Team building   79, *127*, 150
Team development needs   79
Teamwork   29, *150*

Tending   21, 22
Timing   188, 228
Transition   152, 159
Trust   44, *169*, *171*, *174*, *205*

Unintended consequences   17, 22,
    47, *71*, 114, 128
Upstream   *32*, *33*, 60, 114, 223

Values   *27*, 70, 93